To Mary & Sy
We come from good stock.

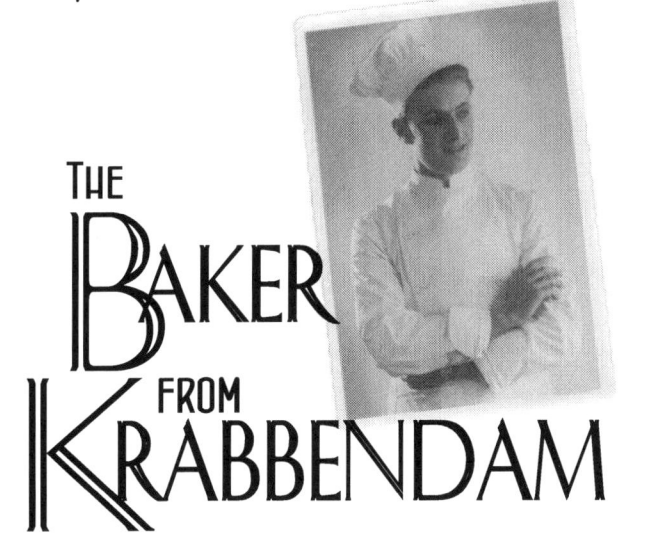

THE BAKER FROM KRABBENDAM

ELLY MOSSMAN
ASKEW CREEK PUBLISHING

Copyright © 2022 by Elly Mossman

All rights reserved. Printed in Canada. No part of this book may be used or reproduced in any manner whatsoever without written permission except in the case of reprints of reviews.

For written permission write to:
Askew Creek Publishing: publisher@askewcreek.com

The characters in this book are real, as are the events. Some names have been changed for privacy.

All photographs contained herein are the property of the author.

Cover photo: Johannes Grin, age 29 - August, 1947 - upon completion of his *banketbakker* (pastry baker) training.

Askew Creek Publishing

ISBN: 9781999148126

Oh Dad, I only wish I'd had you here with us longer.
Just a little longer. I miss you and I love you.
You're not forgotten.

Reviews for THE BAKER FROM KRABBENDAM

What Elly Mossman has written here is a story that - in some sense - will be familiar to virtually every first-generation post-war immigrant family moving to a new country. And as we move further away from that generation, these stories are no longer being told as often as they should.

Like her family, my parents also left the Netherlands shortly after the war, and eventually ended up in Canada. But I was surprised at how much her description of the struggles, the loneliness, and eventually the triumph of carving out a new life in a new country resonated with me.

Beyond the humorous anecdotes of typically "Dutch" childhood pranks, this narrative weaves personal struggles and family dynamics into a rich fabric that amounts to a first-hand account of the harsh realities that many of these immigrants faced - from cultural adjustments to financial deprivation and the difficulties of creating a "new home" - including what was essentially a "re-emigration" from Ontario to B.C. - all in a context of a completely foreign environment.

Highly recommended.

Al Siebring
Former Mayor, North Cowichan.

****

The Baker From Krabbendam is an amazing family memoir that starts out in the Netherlands and characterizes the courage, resilience and nationalism of the Grin and van der Molen family prior to and the beginning of the invasion of the Nazis into Holland on May 10, 1940.

The Grin family's immigration to Canada in 1950 and their eventual move to British Columbia is a heart warming epic, and a truly delightful read, depicting the struggles and challenges of these brave immigrants starting a new life in Canada.

Allan W. Waddy, Author
- Buckshot and Johnnycakes
Guilty Knowledge

The Baker from Krabbendam very likely began as a labour of love, intended to accurately record the lives and events of one immigrant family's history, to be passed down and enjoyed by current and future generations of the author's family. This incredible, well-written story evolved into much more than that.

Author Elly Mossman has carefully and skillfully researched historical data, significant world-wide events, and family records in chronological order, to create a riveting and often humourous story that undoubtedly holds global appeal. Upon reading this absolute delight, and from the beginning, the characters came alive. I could smell the farm fresh air, and I could envision the sun rising and setting on the horizon. I felt each and every hardship suffered as a direct result of Hitler's regime. I wept at the loss felt through a loved one's passing. I cheered at each and every triumph.

Mossman is to be commended for the passion and commitment evident on every single page. As a fellow author, it was an absolute honour and privilege to read *The Baker from Krabbendam*, and in my opinion, this museum-worthy book belongs in all homes and libraries.

Teresa Schapansky, Author
- the *Coinkeeper* series,
Along the Way series
Memoirs of a Pakhtun Immigrant
... and more

****

INDEX

The Early Years

Chap. 1	Krabbendam, Province of N. Holland, - 1920	1
Chap. 2	1926	8
Chap. 3	1931	11
Chap. 4	Feb. 10, 1934	17
	Photos	27-30

War

Chap. 5	1939-1940	33
Chap. 6	1942-43 - Alkmaar	41
Chap. 7	1943-1945	47
	Photos	56-58

Changing Times

Chap. 8	1945	61
Chap. 9	1947	66
Chap. 10	1949-1950	73
	Photos	85-90

Being Immigrants

Chap. 11	SS VOLENDAM - Atlantic Ocean, DAY 5, JUNE 17, 1950	93
Chap. 12	Québec City to Chatham	99
Chap. 13	Meaford to Barrie, Ontario	108
Chap. 14	Growth & Learning	119
Chap. 15	Dark Times	132
Chap. 16	1954-58	138
Chap. 17	A Visit Home	148
Chap. 18	Growing Children	151
	Photos	159-162

INDEX – continued

New Directions

Chap 19	Changes in the Wind 1961	165
Chap. 20	Another Place to Call Home	175
Chap. 21	A Home to Call His Own - 1961 - 1963	181
Chap. 22	1964 - 1966	189
Chap. 23	The Nest Empties	195
Chap. 24	Silver and Bells - 1968	209
Chap. 25	Separation - 1970 - 1975	217
Chap. 26	Family Growth - 1976 - 1980	228
Chap. 27	Breaking Down - 1980	240
	Photos	252-256

The Final Cake

Chap. 28	Going Forward - Looking Back - 1989	259
Chap. 29	Letting Go Again - 1990 - 1992	271
Chap 30	Fifty Years - 1993	279
Chap. 31	Incredible Journey - 1994	282
Chap. 32	Beginnings and Endings - 1995 - 1998	295
	Photos	308-315
	Glossary of Dutch words	316
	Resources	318
	The author	320

The Baker from Krabbendam

Elly Mossman

GENERATIONS

I've watched

as the next generation came into their own.

And now, again, I see,

as another approaches the threshold.

It evokes emotions

I can't even begin to describe.

Then, I think about all those

that came before.

We know a little of the one

immediately previous to us - our parents

- but not really.

Yet, they were watched by someone.

And I wonder,

did those same souls gazing,

feel the same indescribable emotions that I feel now?

So many from the past,

back,

and back ,

and back even further

than we can imagine,

forgotten now. Who were they, really?

May all the generations

in some small way,

always be remembered.

Elly Mossman

THE EARLY YEARS

The village of Krabbendam, 1930s

Left - The Grin Family - 1905
(Joh's paternal grandparents and their children) standing-L to R - Neeltje, Jacob (Johannes' father), Simon
Seated-parents, Pieter, Adriaantje, Willem

Above - The van der Molen Family - 1905
(Joh's maternal grandparents and their children) back row, standing L to R - Neeltje, Elisabeth (Johannes' mother), Johannes Jr.
Seated-parents, Elisabeth, Klaas, Johannes Sr.

NOTE: Three children not in this photo
Maartje (deceased 1904)
Klaas (1st boy named Klaas - deceased 1895)
Diewertje (deceased -before age of one 1895)

CHAPTER 1

Krabbendam,
Province of N. Holland - 1920

Elisabeth wearily climbed the stairs to the tiny attic, where her two-and-a-half-year-old second-born son slept. The bottle of brandy and a spoon were in her hands. *Doctor's instructions,* she reminded herself, still a little nervous that this might not keep little Johannes alive. She was willing to try anything. So many in their tiny one-street village of Krabbendam had already died, and her heart ached for each one of them. Typhus had swept through like a vicious beast, taking so many. They'd been her neighbours, her friends. Typhus. A dreaded name at the best of times, and this moment was not one of them.

The small blonde-haired boy was pale, weak, and lay in a sweaty stupor, barely able to respond to his mama's voice. She gently sat on the edge of his cot and propped the pillows up behind his head. Elisabeth unstoppered the brandy bottle and poured some of the golden liquid into the spoon.

"Here *schatje*, you need to swallow this," she urged him gently, lifting his head gently. The youngster complied, swallowed and made a face, but didn't complain. There was no strength. She gave him another spoonful and again, he swallowed weakly.

"Two or three spoonfuls every hour," the doctor had said. "that's the only thing I can suggest now. That, and pray. We've done everything we know to do, there's nothing more. The *Lieve Heer* must do the rest."

Elisabeth laid down the spoon and re-stoppered the bottle. She bent her head in fervent prayer. "Dear Lord," she prayed, "heal my son. Please, let him live."

---

schatje - literally, small treasure - a term of endearment
Lieve Heer - Dear Lord

The brandy feedings continued for what seemed like an interminable time. While young Johannes slept, Elisabeth washed all surfaces of his room, and she included even the few toys he possessed. The bedding was washed, and the floor, walls, and woodwork scrubbed. The rest of the house followed suit.

While she worked, her mind conjured up the germs, bugs and bacteria fleeing the house in terror to escape the invading cleanliness of the lye soap suds.

"Take that, you foul beasts! How dare you attack my son!" With every swipe of the sudsy rag, she sent the creatures, in her mind at least, fleeing or dying.

Johannes didn't remember much of the illness that almost killed him. He barely remembered drinking brandy. But he did remember the surprise he felt at picking up his toys, only to discover that they looked so clean!

Eventually, Johannes returned to play with whichever of his friends were left. Not much was said of the losses, and life carried on. More babies were born, children grew, and his small band of friends developed into a force to be reckoned with.

As time went on, some of the youngsters became a source of irritation to one Krabbendam resident in particular. The entire village of perhaps 100 people all knew each other, more or less, so it was not hard to understand why.

One such neighbour was a cantankerous old man named Joris, on whom eight-year-old Johannes and a few of his friends delighted in playing tricks. The houses were notoriously small, especially in the tiny villages that dot the countryside. In the tiny hamlet of Krabbendam, the front doors opened right onto a very narrow sidewalk, if they were lucky enough to have one. If not, they opened to the cobblestone road. Krabbendam was built along a *dijk* and there isn't much room on the top of one.

In the fall and winter months of the year, when daylight wanes early in the day, candles and lanterns were lit to illuminate the indoors. The old man was a bit stingy with the use of his candles and usually went up the steep and narrow staircase to sleep the dark night away. Typical of most Dutch staircases, should the home have a second floor, they were usually always situated right inside the tiny front hallway, with the bottom ending about a meter and a half from the front door.

The boys all knew the habits of old Joris. They soon came up with the perfect prank.

Young Johannes hung around after the supper hour had passed, with two other bored eight-year-olds. It was already dark, and an equally dark thought was running in loops in the head of one of them.

"Hey Kees, d'ja still have that old barrel out behind your dad's shed?" asked Thijs.

"I think so. Why'd you want to know?"

"Do you remember the last time old man Joris had his front hall and outside stoop scrubbed down?"

"Huh? Why would we remember a thing like that?" The other two looked a little puzzled at him.

Thijs stood his ground. Carefully, he laid out his plan. The boys were gleefully game and set to work. First, the barrel, which they'd managed to cart quietly away from the shed, and towards the deep, water-filled ditch on the other side of the road. The barrel was duly filled with *slootwater* and positioned near, but out of sight of Joris' front door.

dijk - *dike*
slootwater - *ditch water*

Thijs walked up to the old man's front door and pulled the doorbell lever. It rang shrilly inside, and they could all see, from the darkness through the tiny side window next to the door, that old Joris had gone to bed. The three waited for a moment, watching through that window, and when they could see the light from the candle come bobbing down the stairs, they ran.

The door slowly opened. With sleepy eyes, Joris peered around outside, shook his head, and slammed the door, after which the candle-light glow could be seen bobbing back upwards through the window and disappearing. The boys waited about 10 minutes and repeated the procedure. Again, the candlelight bobbed down the stairs, the boys ran, and the door opened. This time, however, after the door had slammed shut, they saw no candlelight bob back upwards. It was time.

The boys hefted the barrel between them, and very quietly set it down, tilting it to lean with the upper rim resting and balanced against the closed front door. When everything looked right, Joh gave the bell lever a good pull, and all three ran like the wind.

Joris, thinking he would outwit the boys at their own game, stood waiting inside the door, candle snuffed out, ready for the next ring of the bell. The door jerked open with a bang, and the entire barrel tipped forward into the front hallway, giving it, and much of what lay beyond, a good soaking.

Joris' curses could be heard up and down the quiet street, but the boys were long gone into the dark. After laughing uproariously at their success, they separated and made their way home through the secret back ways that only eight-year-old boys would know, avoiding Joris' house as they went.

It was the conversation at many a dinner table the next evening, including the one belonging to the Grin family.

"Did you hear what some rascals did to Joris?" Jacob announced in a stern voice. Joh tried to look as innocent as possible, but mother, with the week-old baby, Klasina at her breast, had a gleam in her eye. "No, tell us what happened."

Johannes' father recounted the tale as he'd heard it from Joris. He looked around the table sternly at his eight older children, daring them to confess to the misdeed. The children kept eating, but one or two tiny snickers bubbled up. Father harrumphed crossly, "It's not a laughing matter! Those hooligans ought to have a good whipping! If it were one of mine…" but he got no further.

The baby's head was bobbing strangely up and down on Elisabeth's breast, until Jacob, looking upwards, realized that Elisabeth was silently laughing, her face red, with tears streaming down her cheeks and her chest bouncing. When she saw that she'd been caught, she burst out laughing. Johannes snickered once and was just as lost as his mother. He too started to guffaw loudly. One by one, the rest of the large brood followed suit, until the entire family, except for Jacob, was laughing uproariously.

Jacob couldn't help himself. As hard as he tried to maintain the stern face, Johannes noticed the corner of Papa's mouth trembling, and his entire face reddened with the effort to hold it in.

Finally, mirth claimed the upper hand, and he too began laughing. He couldn't help himself any longer. "Blast you, anyway!" He scolded his wife, as he laughed. "How can I maintain discipline of my own children, when all you do is make me laugh over bad behaviour?"

"It was time for Joris to scrub down that filthy front stoop and hallway anyway!" Elisabeth laughed. "Now he's had a good head start. He should be thanking them!"

To be on the safe side though, Johannes thought it might be expedient to lay off the pranks for at least a little while. The air was still filled with days to do mischief, after all. He still remembered with relish a few weeks ago, when they'd gotten Joris good for accusing them of stealing a few eggs from his hen house. Stealing was one thing the boys would never have done, indeed, doors were never locked, nor guard dogs kept to keep out prowlers. Theirs was a simple, honest existence.

Johannes himself was the one who had thought up that prank. He'd somehow gotten hold of a large ball of thin twine. With it, they'd walked up to Joris' door one evening, and tied the end of it to the doorbell lever. Then they walked slowly away from the house, unwinding the twine as they went, making sure it didn't snag anywhere.

They got to the other side of the road down a way, where he had a long, sturdy pole ready on the bank of the wide ditch. After tossing the ball of twine, still unraveling, over to the other side, one by one they poled themselves over. That day the water level was rather high, they guessed about a meter deep, which was perfect for what they had in store for Joris.

The boys crouched down in the tall grass growing on the other side of the ditch. Normally it would have been be kept short by grazing sheep, but they hadn't been moved to the Krabbendam dike yet. Hiding from sight, the twine strung across the ditch, Johannes gave a mighty yank on his end of the twine, hard enough to move Joris' doorbell lever and make it ring.

Joris opened the door and noticed the string tied to the lever. Then he noticed the string leading away from the house and down the road. He could have just untied and left it, but no, Joris had to see where it led to.

He undid the twine from the lever and followed it down the road, winding it, as he usually did, around his hand as he walked. By the time he got to where it spanned the ditch, his hand was firmly encircled by twine. Joris hesitated, thinking how he could jump the ditch without actually landing in it, and getting his feet, or worse, wet. There was a nice sturdy pole lying on the opposite bank, but that was of little use to him, standing where he was.

Joris edged a little closer to the apex of the bank, judging whether or not he'd make the jump. At that moment, Johannes pulled the twine tight across the ditch and gave a mighty heave. Joris' captive hand was pulled violently forward and he flew straight into the water, helpless to divest himself of the twine quick enough to avoid being pulled forward into the water.

Johannes chuckled to himself every time he thought of the scene; Joris floundering in the mud water, bedraggled and cursing like a sailor, a lily pad and some long blades of soggy grass stuck to his shoulder, his hand still trapped by the meters and meters of twine. It served him right for calling any of them thieves.

He was pretty certain that along with everyone else, his Papa also knew who had done this to Joris, since the three of them had stood on the opposite bank for all to see, and laughed their fool heads off at him, standing up to his waist in water, with the twine still wrapped around his hand. But he knew even Papa took exception to Johannes being called a thief.

CHAPTER 2

1926

In October the wind already had a hint of the cold, damp winter to come, as it blew over the flatlands. Johannes was growing quickly now. He'd sprouted up a little and would be turning nine soon. He wished sometimes he lived like some of those rich city kids, who'd get fancy parties and expensive presents.

Vader was a *tuinbouwer*, a farmer, and they lived simple lives. Luxuries like parties and presents wrapped in fancy paper and ribbons were not part of their world. There would be felicitations from everyone, of course, and he would be made to feel a little special, perhaps even at school. There would even be a small present, like some pencils and maybe some nice drawing paper to go with them, from Papa, or perhaps a warm pair of knit gloves that Mama had made especially for him. He thought hard about what he could possibly get his Mama, whose birthday was close to his, excited to surprise her with something.

And while most birthdays were met with at least a little joyous welcome, Elisabeth's approaching fortieth, held a little trepidation for her. Dutch custom was, that when a woman turned forty, she was officially old, and needed to dress in black. Elisabeth hated black, and she didn't feel old. Not in the least. The few dresses she had were brown and a deep purple. She determined that on her fortieth birthday she would wear the deep purple, come hell or high water.

In the week before Elisabeth's fortieth birthday, her mother came calling in the afternoon, and sat with her daughter at the dining table, sipping her tea. "Do you have your dress ready yet, Betje?"

---

vader - father
tuinbouwer - horticultural farmer

"My dress? What do you mean?" Elisabeth knew exactly what her mother meant, but she decided to let her spell it out.

"You'll be turning forty next week. You should properly be wearing the black then. You know this!" Her mother looked at her sternly.

"Oh, *that* dress." Elisabeth picked up her tea and took a sip, looking at Johannes, sitting across from them at the other end of the table, working on a sketch. He looked up at her and smiled. She smiled back, curious to see what he'd been drawing, and proud of him that he could make a decent looking piece of art. Casually looking into her tea, she said, "Yes, well ... I don't plan on wearing black at forty. I don't feel old yet!"

Her mother put her cup down, clinking it heavily against the saucer as she set the tea down on the table in irritation. "So you say! But no proper woman dresses in colours after forty. It's not done, Elisabeth! What will people think?"

"Mother, I really don't care what people think! I don't feel old, and I refuse to wear something that makes me look as if I'm in perpetual mourning! I won't! I hate black!"

"Oh, Elisabeth! I raised you to be a proper and sober *huisvrouw*. Do you have to put me to shame like that?"

"I have a nice burgundy dress and a dark brown one. Those should be good enough! I think they're dark enough for me to look *fatsoenlijk!* "Don't worry Mother, I'll look proper," she sighed cynically, "I won't be putting you to shame, and wear flashy colours to be mistaken for a flighty eighteen-year-old!"

"Don't you sass me, Elisabeth!" her mother continued to harangue her daughter, but Elisabeth held fast. There would be no black after forty. Listening to all this, Johannes silently agreed. He'd seen enough sour old women at the markets and in church, looking for all the world as if they were part of some ritual mourning assembly at a funeral.

huisvrouw - house wife
fatsoenlijk - proper, decent

He would have been cuffed across the head by his grandmother if he'd voiced his opinion on the matter, but deep down, his heart swelled with pride at his mother's stand against the dubious practice, that turned women old before their time. He snorted inwardly. Even a *stomme kind* like him knew that much. He made a promise to himself, that his future wife would never have to wear black after forty. Even if she wanted to.

That evening, at dinner Elisabeth recounted the conversation to her husband, and reiterated, "I will not wear black when I turn forty! Do you hear me, Jacob? Do not try to make me. I'll fight you tooth and nail!" Jacob wisely held his tongue. He'd had enough of his dealings with people of different viewpoints and wasn't about to add any more unnecessarily.

The mindset of Johannes had turned to artistic dreams, once people began telling him he had a talent, but his father, Jacob had more practical ideas. After all, he thought, no man could make a living drawing pretty pictures.

"An artist? How would you be able to support yourself, let alone a family by selling that?" Jacob exclaimed when the boy began expressing his dreams to his father. They were in the fields, working.

"I could do better pictures!" he declared. "In school, I learned about some of the famous artists, like Rembrandt and Van Gogh, and the kind of work they did with oil paint! I want to do that!" Joh countered.

His father only laughed, "Van Gogh died poor, and he committed suicide! Rembrandt? That was so long ago, and it was a whole different time back then. Besides, oil paint? Lessons? And for what? So you can make pretty pictures? *Nee, yongen*, you have to be a little more practical. Put the dreams away. Life is hard now and you'd best get used to it!"

Joh ended that day discouraged but determined. God, he felt, had given him this talent to use for something. Some way and some day he would make it work for him.

---

stomme kind - stupid child

Nee, yongen - no, boy

CHAPTER 3

1931

"Come on boys, finish your breakfast! It's time to get to work!" Jacob barked at his sons to get moving. "Those potatoes aren't going to dig themselves up!" There was always work to be done in the fields, and today was no different.

Piet, the oldest, and Simon, Johannes' next-younger brother got up from the table, hurriedly wiping their mouths on their sleeves as they stood. Fourteen-year-old Johannes stuffed the last of his bread into his mouth and followed suit. His father was not to be trifled with. A belt could appear in his hands for any of them, even at that age.

The day was hot and fluffed clouds scudded across the sky, as only clouds over a flat country could do. The wind seemed to blow all the time, either from the North Sea or from the mysterious lands to the east. By the time the group got to the first of the fields to begin work, Joh was already hungry again. There never seemed to be enough. Mother had delivered her eleventh child a short two years ago and there seemed to be even less than before, even though the girl ate very little.

Johannes sneezed again and dug morosely at the potatoes, plunking them into the sack that hung from his shoulders. He seemed to be congested and sneezing a lot as he worked on the land. Another annoyance to be tolerated.

Suddenly, along with a muddy clump of tubers that he'd just dug up, an odd flash of cream showed through the dirt at the end of his shovel. Curious, he reached over and picked up the lump and brushed off the soil. A small face stared back at him.

Johannes didn't own very much, and this small piece of art looked priceless to him. The face was perfectly formed, and looked almost life-like. As he stared at it, it stirred an oddly familiar feeling in his gut, but he didn't know why and set the feeling aside.

The piece was broken at the neck and looked to be part of a small statuette. Perhaps he'd find the rest of it, and be able to glue it back together. He'd never owned a statuette before. Maybe he'd give it to *Moeder* for her birthday in November. How pleased she'd be. He pocketed his find and began digging in earnest.

More potatoes were dug up, but nothing else surfaced. Finally, the long morning ended, and womenfolk came to the fields with water and lunch. Johannnes showed the piece of statuette to Jacob.

"Huh! Lucky you, you've got a piece of something there. Let me see it." Jacob rubbed more of the dirt off and he turned it over in his hands.

The head held a stumpy pipe in its mouth, and wore a floppy hat, much like the farmers wore nowadays. "There's some writing on the back of the hat!" Jacob exclaimed, "What does it say?" He spit on the head and rubbed, trying to clean more of the dirt off. Both man and boy stared closely at it, reading the inscription crudely carved into the clay.

Anno

1577

17 Sept

"By gosh, this is really old!" gasped Jacob.

"That's... that's..." Johannes did a quick calculation in his head. "..that's over 350 years old!", he said incredulously. "Has it been there all that time?"

---

moeder - mother

anno - year

"I doubt it," answered his father, "it probably got broken and was thrown away at some point between then and now. But it's still 350 years old. That's when the artist made it. You've got yourself a little treasure there, boy!"

"If I could find the rest of it, I would have a birthday present for Mama!" Johannes sighed. Jacob laughed, "Well, just keep digging, boy! You just might find it, and a lot more potatoes for me too, while you're at it!"

Johannes spent the rest of the day digging as large an area as he could, piling the potatoes into his sack as he went. But nothing else showed up.

At the end of that long Saturday, father and sons trooped wearily back to the small brick home they all shared, bringing along a good portion of potatoes with them for the evening meal.

Elisabeth met them at the door with tears in her eyes. Jacob frowned and looked at his wife. "What's happened now?" he exclaimed in annoyance. He walked past his wife through the narrow doorway, to unburden himself of the potatoes, and saw his sister-in-law and an aunt sitting at the table, both looking rather sour-faced.

"What's going on? We weren't expecting you for company!" Jacob testily exclaimed. He had an inkling why they were there though, but said nothing. He waited for their visitors to reveal their mission. The two boys came in right behind their father and stood wide-eyed staring at the scene. Family drama was awkward and exciting all at the same time.

"You are going to Hell!" The aunt spat out at Jacob. "How dare you change your church membership! You've now joined these ... these ... " the aunt didn't even have a word for what she thought of the Christian church in the neighbouring village, so different in practice from the traditional church that the entire family had always belonged to.

The sister-in-law was in tears. "When you die, I won't see you in Heaven! We'll never see you again! How could you do this, Jacob?"

Jacob looked back stony-faced at his relatives. "What nonsense are you spouting now? Of course, we're still going to Heaven! And we're all still Christians!" he thundered. "How can you say we're not? Do you think we've stopped worshipping God? Do you think we've stopped believing in Jesus?" Jacob looked with disgust at the religious ignorance of his relatives.

"Just because they're a slightly different denomination shouldn't make a difference!"

Jacob's reasoning made no difference to the women. The argument raged on, with aunt and sister-in-law making their religious points over and over, to an unrelenting and, in their view, an unrepentant sinner who had basically "left the church".

After much arguing and many recriminations, the pair left with the parting words, "When you've come to your senses and admitted your sin to God, you'll be welcomed back into the family and the church!"

That night young Johannes crawled into bed beside his younger brother and thought about God and heaven and churches. He didn't understand what all the fuss was about, and he made a promise to himself. He'd never let a church affiliation determine whether or not he was a Christian. He believed. That's all that mattered.

The next day he remembered the little pottery head in his pocket and dug it out. Dried soil still stuck to the grooves and indents on the face, so he took it outside to the pump and cranked some water up from the well into a small enamel pot. Carefully he washed his find, picked at the dried mud and got it clean. He could see that it had had colour applied to it at one time, but most of it had worn off. Still, it was beautiful. Strangely enough, the odd sensations of familiarity that it evoked, stirred something in him, and still, he didn't know why.

It was enough though, that he had something of value, at least to him. It gave him an incentive to dig in the potato fields. Maybe someday he'd find the other part to fit the head. If he didn't find it, he'd give Mama the part he'd found for her birthday anyway. It was better than nothing. And she'd love it!

At the approach of fall, his father pulled Johannes by the shoulder nearer to the outbuilding. "Joh, I need to talk to you about something."

"What is it, *Vader*?" he asked.

Jacob sighed. "Money is tight, and I need you to go to work, to help with household expenses." Johannes looked at his father with narrowed eyes. "Work. You mean a job? Outside of working for you in the fields? What about school?"

"You're more useful working, *jongen*," Jacob told him, "your income will help a great deal." Johannes thought about it for a moment. Piet was already working and contributing. Why shouldn't he do it too? School didn't hold his interest much these days. In a way, he was sad to quit school, but on the other hand, he was anxious to get out into the world and prove his worth. Besides, he thought with pride, his father needed him to contribute to the household.

That fall Johannes began working for a merchant in town, who needed a *knecht* for all the odd jobs that came with running a store. Biking into town each day, He would run errands, repair small items that were easy to fix, sweep the floors, make some deliveries, and do anything else that the merchant needed.

At the end of the week, he came home, whistling cheerfully on his bicycle, with a pocket full of cash, payment for his work. Johannes handed the money over to his father and began to go to his attic room to rest. "Wait a moment, Joh," his father stopped him as he turned to go, "here's twenty-five cents; you need some spending money too."

Johannes felt suddenly grown-up, like the richest man in the world with his own money. That twenty-five cents would last him until the next payday. He already planned on how to spend it, but he'd do it carefully, being quite familiar with the frugal ways of his parents.

knecht - helper or aide
yongen - boy

Poor was all he knew. It was normal as far as he was concerned. He'd heard about all these rich men committing suicide over losing all their money because of something called a "Great Depression" going on in parts of the world - America, for instance, and he had to laugh. There were always ways to get money - lots of ways. But if you made money, you should save some of it, somehow, *Vader* always said, and he was good at that.

CHAPTER 4

Feb. 10, 1934

"You should not be having more children, *Mevrouw* Grin. You are not healthy enough and it could be very dangerous for you!"

The earlier words of her doctor a few years ago, echoed in her mind as Elisabeth lay in her bed in Alkmaar's hospital. Her thirteenth child was dead, still-born. She could still see the pale, tiny body in her mind's eye, before it was taken away, and wept both for the child and herself. If only she could have avoided getting pregnant. But how? Was she supposed to rebuff her husband? That would certainly create more problems than solve them. And what were birth control measures for people like her? Very few, if any. And now, she was ill from the result.

At home Joh knew he'd had another sibling, but that it had died. He knew his Mama was in the hospital this time, instead of giving birth at home the usual way. It filled him with a sense of foreboding.

He was 16 years old now, almost a man, and worked at a job, as well as helping in his father's muddy fields. It gave him a sense of purpose, although he hated the wooden shoes, heavy wool socks and leather inserts he needed to wear with them, in order to keep his feet warm and dry in the ice-cold winter fields. His Sunday shoes could only be worn on Sundays, so they wouldn't wear out so fast. They needed to last.

Joh had promised his father he'd visit Mama in the hospital that Saturday, and set out to do just that. Finally in Alkmaar, he approached the hospital, and his steps slowed. People around him stared at his wooden shoes as he clopped through the streets. He knew what city people thought of *boeren*. In many instances they were looked on as crass, lower class people.

Mevrouw - Mrs.
boeren - plural of boer - farmers

Suddenly overcome with shame at the shoes he was wearing, he turned around and walked away from the hospital. *I'll see Mama when she comes home in a few days.* It would be all right. He'd hug her tightly then, and show her another picture he'd drawn of her. It was pinned on the wall above his bed, along with all the others he'd done. Someday he'd be an artist. He loved to draw, and everyone kept saying that he had an "artistic" bent.

Feb. 13, 1934

That Tuesday, Jacob was called to the hospital by a man on a bicycle. In the meantime Johannes filled in for his father in the fields. He hoped Mama would be coming back with him on the return trip. The house was empty without her, in spite of him and ten other children that filled it. It seemed to Joh that a lot of them were already adults, and quiet enough, but the younger ones more than made up for that, filling the house with noise and bedlam.

The baby, Nelly, had only just turned five. The older girls, Elisabeth, twenty, and Arijaantje, eighteen, were capable of supervising and caring for the younger kids, but they weren't full-time mothers either, and all of the older ones had jobs to keep the income flowing into the household. Even Joh, who worked at odd jobs when he wasn't in the fields.

That evening Jacob came home, his face lined and pale. He sat down heavily at the table. Something was very wrong, and a sudden sick sense of dread hit Johannes like a loaded cart of cobblestones. The other siblings gathered round. They too felt the apprehension spreading from their father's demeanour.

"*Vader?* What's wrong? Can't Mama come home yet?" The oldest queried, hesitant to ask questions, but needing to know.

"No, boy. She's not coming home. She's never coming home again." As the words slammed home, they fell as great, lead weights on top of him, grinding him into the floor and crushing his heart. She was never coming home again. Gone. She was dead.

Joh fled the house, running blindly over the snow covered *Westfriesendijk*. If only he'd gone to see Mama on Saturday! If only he'd not been ashamed of his shoes! He screamed into the evening dark, and fell on his knees, slamming his fists into the frozen ground until they were numb. Filled with self-loathing, he grovelled, weeping on his knees on the road, his tears and snot mingling and freezing with the road dirt. He wished the earth would swallow him whole. Cover him up so no one would have to look at him. He had no idea how long he lay there, collapsed on the dike.

Hours later he returned to a silent house, rinsing his face the best he could at the pump outside the door. The house was dark, and he shivered as he crept up to his bed in the attic. His thirteen-year-old brother was still awake.

"Joh? You okay?" Simon's voice trembled in the dark. Johannes said nothing. The words stuck in his throat.

"I can't believe it!" Mama's not here anymore. I can't believe it." Simon's tear-filled voice scratched at the air around them.

"Can't either," Joh mumbled.

"Remember when she called us "her twins"? We don't look anything alike, but she thought we did. Isn't that funny?"

"Yeah. Funny..."

"We were always dressed alike. Did you notice that."

"Yeah."

"At least you got to see her one last time. "

"Yeah, lucky.... "

Westfriesendijk - A dike, with the name of West Friesian, with a road built on top, situated close to Alkmaar and runs along the village of Krabbendam.

Joh wished that Simon would stop talking. It was on the tip of his tongue to tell Sim of his stupidity from Saturday, but somehow the words wouldn't leave his mouth. Fresh shame filled him.

He rolled over in the dark and then rolled back again to face Simon, who continued to talk. "What are we gonna do without Mama now? We'll be alright, but what about the younger ones? Maybe Lies and Janny can take care of them. I dunno. Papa will figure something out."

"Sure. Pap will figure something out." Joh sighed, but he dreaded facing tomorrow, with the fresh sadness and grief they all had yet to face.

Simon added, "We'll get through it, I'm sure we will. Remember when *Opa* Grin died two years ago? How sad we all were? We got over it, didn't we? We felt better after a while, didn't we?"

"This is Mama you're talking about!" Joh hissed into the dark. "I'm *never* gonna get over it! I'm never gonna feel better, ever again!" His guilt tore at him.

Fresh tears wet the thin pillow then, and Simon held his brother while they both cried. They were still clinging to each other when Lies came to wake them the next morning.

A week later eleven children and their father stood at the grave site, a fresh mound of dirt was all that was visible of the life that had been; a mother so loved that each felt a raw wound raked down the insides of their being from some unnamed horror. Other family members stood further off, and as Jacob turned to go, they came to him, one by one, to offer their condolences.

"It's God's will."

"Take heart, Jacob, you will see her again."

"We cannot know the will of the Lord, Jacob. We can only accept it. Draw strength from that."

Opa - *grandfather*

The words, well meaning though they were, fell on an empty heart. It was also a heart torn on what to do with his children, especially the younger ones. Should he rely on his older girls to finish raising them? What of their own lives? He didn't know.

March 12, 1936

Eleven siblings sat in the front pew of the *Gereformeerde Kerk* in Alkmaar, watching with sombre faces, as Jacob married the woman standing next to him. The *Dominee* read scripture, and intoned the rites of marriage over the middle-aged couple.

Joh felt a sour ache in his gut, as his father stood at the front of the church and exchanged vows with another woman. *It almost seems like sacrilege, marrying another.* He knew Father needed a woman to care for and nurture the youngsters still in his care. But, couldn't she have just stayed working as their caregiver and housekeeper, the way his father had already arranged it?

He didn't understand why he had to go and marry the creature. The prior arrangement of the woman coming daily to cook, and care for the younger ones seemed fine to him. They could put up with her during the day, and still have the evenings free of her biting personality. They'd enjoyed those quiet evening all together, just them.

This woman was not Mama. In the time she'd had acted as caregiver, Joh had not seen a coal's glow worth of warmth from her for any of them. Not once. Still a spinster at 37, the thin, stick figured woman that stood beside his father, with her austere face and stilted posture, looked more like a scarecrow than a mother to him.

He'd be turning nineteen in November and planned to move away from home to work. He wanted to get as far away from her as he could, but not so far that he wouldn't know what was happening with his younger siblings.

<u>Gereformeerde Kerk</u> *- in N. America, the Christian Reformed Church*
<u>Dominee</u> *- minister, pastor*

He'd met a girl too. She'd caught his eye at a church youth gathering in Schoorl, the town a few kilometres away. He'd had a nice conversation going for a while. She seemed a little shy, and was a bit hard of hearing, but not so bad that he couldn't talk to her. He had a bit of a loud voice too, so maybe that was a good match? There was a lot of laughter involved, and God knows, he needed that. Time would tell. First things first.

There was a small gathering at the rectory afterwards for the newlyweds, but the entire event seemed a little off, and everyone soon departed. The next few weeks were a mixture of new routines, snapped remarks, and awkward silences. Soon enough, the few photos of Elisabeth standing about, disappeared one by one.

Arriving home from work, Joh made his way up to his attic room, and stared in shock at the top of the staircase. All the drawings of Mama were no longer on his walls. Who had come up here to do this? There was only one person he could think of.

White-hot with rage, he raced down the stairs to confront the stepmother. In the kitchen, she sat at the table shelling peas into a pan in her lap. Liesbeth and Janny were at the sink. All three heads turned and looked up, startled at the thundering coming from the stairs, and his sudden appearance and outburst. "Where are my drawings?" he demanded.

The stepmother continued to shell peas. "Those childish scribbles? They made your room look messy and I threw them out! You're a grown man now. What grown man has silly children's trash stuck to his walls?"

Liesbeth and Janny ducked their heads low, and turned back to the sink, fearful of the tirade they knew would come.

"Those were drawings of *Moeder!* You had no right to throw them away!" he bellowed at her. Livid with rage and grief he stared at the woman, and wondered, what kind of a person was she? Who would do that to someone, destroying a child's drawings of a dead mother?

"I'll thank you to speak to me with some *godverdomme* respect, young man! I am still your elder and I demand that you treat me respectfully! Your father should have you horsewhipped, as old as you are, for speaking to me like that!"

"If there was a horsewhip around I'd use it on you, you witch! You had no right to destroy my things!"

The woman began to scream obscenities at him. "You *godverdomme reetkever!* I'd have Jacob whip you right now if he was here! You *schijt! Hondelul!* Get out of my sight!"

Joh's youngest sister Nelly came and stood in the doorway just then. With large eyes, Nelly, at the tender age of six, could only stare as she listened to ugly words she'd never have heard from her mother. He strode over to where the girl was standing and pulled her to him, intending to leave the house, with her in tow.

"Leave that little *godverdomme trut* here! She's my responsibility now!" the woman ordered, her voice shrill now. Nelly pressed closer to Johannes as she screamed at them, and Joh wondered if she'd already been treating his little sister this way when he wasn't around. As he stormed out of the house, pushing Nelly ahead of him, he planned on having a talk with his older sisters when they were alone.

Away from the house, when he stopped shaking, he turned to Nelly. "Listen to me, Nelly. Those words! Never speak like that! Never use horrible words like that. Do you hear me, *meisje?* Stepmother should never have spoken like that. It's wrong!"

Nelly spoke in a whisper, as though the woman would somehow still be able to hear. "She's a bad lady, Joh. Really bad. She don't like me very much, and I don't like her at all."

---

godverdomme - goddamned	*trut* - bitch - derogatory term
reetkever - beetle's anus (slang)	*schijt* - shit (slang)
hondelul - dog's penis	*meisje* - little girl

"We all love you, Nelly. And Mama loved you. That witch doesn't really count at all."

Nelly hung her head. Joh realized it was the same way he'd noticed Liesbeth and Janny hanging their heads at the kitchen sink. The full import of what that meant, hit him like freight train. The woman had been bullying the girls since she'd moved permanently into the house months ago.

That night he got the two older girls alone, and began to question them. What he heard sickened him. He'd spent most days away, working, but the girls had been at home around her, far more frequently.

Both girls pleaded with their bother, "What do we do, Joh? No matter how much we stand up to her, the worse she gets! And poor Nelly gets the brunt of it. The bitch spends most of her time screaming at Nelly, and cursing her out every time she turns around. The poor girl gets it, no matter who does what!"

"We've all tried to be as nice as possible, and do things as carefully and precisely as she wants it..." Lies began.

Janny finished, "...but nothing seems to make her happy enough to stop mistreating Nelly ... she's horrible to all of us!"

"Have you tried talking to *Vader*?" Joh asked

Both girls gaped at him in shock at the suggestion. "You don't ask your parents something like that! That's way too personal, and I'm sure *Vader* would be very upset at us for even bringing it up!" Lies cried out.

"And insulted that we'd even broach a subject like that with him." added Janny.

Joh cursed the restrictive norms of the times. There seemed to be nothing he could do. There was nothing worse than feeling helpless.

"Try your best, please, girls. Nelly deserves better than this." Joh implored.

"We are, believe us, we are, but the woman is unstoppable, once she gets into one of her moods! We saw her take all those drawings of *Moeder* and burn them! There was nothing we could do!" The girls cried.

It struck him then, that this was his punishment, the loss of all his drawings of Mama, for being too embarrassed over his shoes to visit her in the hospital. Johannes would never pick up a pencil to make a drawing again.

From that point on he began to look for ways to extricate himself from the stifling cloak that hung over the household. He realized he needed a life's plan and career that involved more than just being a labourer, working at odd jobs. He'd be stuck where he was for a lifetime, if he didn't have a clear set of goals. Being creative could mean more than just putting pencil to paper, couldn't it? He loved building things. Although he still needed to earn some income for the household, there were always the evenings. As a start, he registered for evening courses in furniture making.

As the days carried on, Jacob seemed to remove himself emotionally from the goings on between his new spouse and his household. His second wife held the children, both young and old, on a blade's edge of dread. Nelly suffered the worst, and became more and more withdrawn and sullen.

One morning they heard stepmother retching in the outhouse. "She's sick! Maybe she'll die!" Nelly burst out with a unbalanced laugh.

Two months later it was established that stepmother was pregnant. The older ones certainly knew where babies came from, and how. It did not sit well with any of them, at the thought of their father and that woman ... well ... but of course they were husband and wife so ...

No one wanted to dwell on the subject. Soon enough, there would be another mouth for poor Jacob to feed. They all wondered how she would treat her own flesh and blood. They would never have the question answered. The baby girl, Anne died after three weeks of life.

The pall of misery hung over the Grin household for another eight years after the death of that unfortunate baby. The stepmother continued to scream, curse and rage at any and all family members. All of them were affected in some way. The older ones swore they would never forgive her for the havoc unleashed on the family.

On an afternoon in March, 1945, the forty-six-year-old stepmother sat at the table, shelling peas into a pan in her lap. A few of the girls, including Nelly, were in the kitchen with her. Suddenly she leaned over sideways, her hands dropping to her side. Peas spilled every which way over the kitchen floor. Her heart had stopped.

Nelly was sixteen years old. When she realized that her stepmother was dead, the girl threw her hands in the air, overcome with joy. Out the door in an instant, she ran, dancing in abandon over the *Westfriesendijk,* screaming over and over for all the world to hear, *"Die kreng is dood! Die kreng is dood! Die kreng is dood!!"*

Nelly never fully recovered from the cruel treatment she'd endured. In spite of it, she became a nurse, but spent half of her solitary life, caring for her patients, and the other half, a psychiatric patient herself.

Years later, Elisabeth's last-born son, Adriaan, who was nine years old when the abuse began, would make his family promise not to bury him in the same graveyard where Jacob and his two wives rested, because he didn't want to be anywhere near *that woman.*

Die kreng is dood! - That witch is dead!

The Grin family - 1924
Standing - back row, L to R: Pieter, Elisabeth.
Front row: Simon, father Jacob, Jacob Jr. (on lap) Johannes, Arijaantje, mother Elisabeth, Willem (on lap), Maartje. Three more were yet to be born. Klasina, Adriaan and Nelly.

Elisabeth van der Molen (circa 1908

Elisabeth's "twins" Johannes (standing) & Simon

1933

Youngest sister, Nelly circa 1939

1910 - Elisabeth's mother, Elisabeth van der Molen (nee Kwak) wearing her traditional North Holland's regional headgear, called a *"zuiker schepje"* (sugar spoon) due to the unique up-turned brim

Clay head - dated Sep. 17, 1577 - dug out of the soil in his father's field by Johannes - approx. 1930

Elisabeth's father, Johannes van der Molen - Circa 1912, posing for an official photograph, in his professional uniform as postman.

Johannes Grin's parents, Jacob and Elisabeth - Circa 1912

Jacob and Elisabeth - *1935*   Note: this is a photographer's composite photo with Elisabeth's image, taken from the last known photo of her. (shown on p. 27)

Johannes - a dapper young man at age 20 - *1937*

Pencil drawing of a canal and windmills near Krabbendam. The only surviving piece of art by Johannes - undated

Dairy farming in the Province of North Holland near the provincial border of Friesland

Joh, circa 1935

Raising rabbits, quite possibly for their family's source of dietary protein

WAR

LIFE IN 1939-before occupation

Arijanntje (Janny) de Yong-Grin - second oldest sister, bringing refreshments to her husband, Ynze de Yong, while he was at work in the fields.

Johannnes - flirting with the ladies - in traditional dress of the province Friesland-1935

CHAPTER 5

1939-1940

As Joh transitioned into his adult life, the sparks of war swirling around them, finally burst into flame. Poland had been invaded by the Chancellor of Germany, who, from the Dutch perspective at least, seemed to crave power and domination. World War 2 was declared.

Joh was not the only one that worried these new *Nazis* from Germany wouldn't stop with just Poland. They'd already annexed Austria last year. What other country would they threaten? The Netherlands, along with some surrounding countries, was very tiny. They'd be overrun in no time. It was an unimaginable thought.

Joh lay awake at night, thinking about what he should do. He'd found steady work as a labourer, but maybe he should try and enlist. Lots of his friends were doing just that. Joh's friend Thijs had been drafted at nineteen, served his required time, and had re-enlisted just last week. He almost envied the guy. They'd been drafted around the same time a few years ago, but Joh had been turned away. He still remembered the surprise of learning why....

≈≈≈≈≈≈≈

"Good morning boys, I see you've got your conscription papers for me! Are you ready to do your duty?" The officer boomed at the small group who'd come into the office.

They were led one by one through the process, and everything was going as normal, until the medical portion. Each one in his turn, sat on the sheet-covered table in his *ondergoed,* while the doctor listened with

ondergoed - underwear

his stethoscope, poked and prodded, hammered on various joints and examined feet.

"Oh, this is not good!" The doctor exclaimed as he lowered Joh's feet after the examination. "Oh?" Joh looked sideways at him, "what's wrong with my feet?" The doctor pointed, "You have flat feet."

"So I do, and I've never had a moment's trouble with them." Joh wondered where this was going. The doctor explained that his flat feet could become a problem while spending hours on his feet in the military. So far, he'd already spent hours on his feet, and never felt any worse for wear beyond the norm. He'd been able to stand and work for long hours, in spite of their condition.

The doctor shook his head slowly, "No. If you are flat-footed, you will be considered medically unsound. I'm afraid I can't approve you for the military." And that was that.

≈≈≈≈≈≈≈

As Joh made his way to his job that morning, he almost swung into the enlistment office to see if they'd want him anyway, but reconsidered, and continued on to work. The question had already been answered. If it came to war, keep working, and do whatever he needed to do to help the war effort at home.

As the days passed, Joh anxiously watched the newspapers and listened to the radio broadcasts, on the progress of the Nazis. It did not sound good.

France and Britain declared war on Germany two days after the invasion of Poland. Czechoslovakia fell.

Strangely, large amounts of people began disappearing, according to some reports, and no one knew where they'd been taken. Some said, to work camps. Others, just a re-location of sorts. But nobody really knew anything for sure. What was telling though, was that most of them were Jewish.

By April of 1940, the Germans had taken control of Denmark and Norway. Everyone was on edge, and they all knew it was just a matter of time.

A month later, on May 10, 1940, in spite of the Netherlands' neutrality, and Hitler's guarantee of non-aggression towards them, the Nazis invaded. It didn't surprise anyone that Hitler's promises were as empty as a devil's heart.

It took five days of fighting. When it was apparent that Rotterdam would fall, Dutch General Henri Winkelman ordered the destruction of the Dutch Shell oil reserves stored in Pernis, a municipality of Rotterdam, to prevent the Germans from using it to aid their war machine.

The noxious billows of black smoke could be seen for kilometers when the reserves were lit on fire. People talked about it for days. The centre of Rotterdam was bombed to rubble, and the Dutch capitulated. When the reality of the occupation finally sunk in, the resistance was launched. The Germans would discover just how stubborn those Dutchmen - and women could be. On May 17, 1940, Germany's occupation of the Netherlands officially began.

In June of 1940, Crown Princess Julianna and her two daughters were sent to Ottawa, Canada for safety, while her husband, Prince Bernhard escaped to England with Queen Wilhelmina. The queen established a government-in-exile in Britain, and from London, via radio broadcasts, she became the symbol of that Dutch stubborn resistance. She was 59 years old. In Canada, Princess Juliana gave birth to a third daughter, and the Canadian government temporarily turned the hospital room into Dutch territory, so the princess would be born a citizen of her own country.

No one trusted the Nazis or the Germans. Juliana's husband, Bernhard was a German himself, and many criticized the Prince, and questioned his loyalty, fearful that he would betray them.

In other countries, there were reports of too many people, even the elite, such as doctors and professors, stripped of their profession, status, and jobs in the public sector, or disappearing mysteriously. The Jewish population in each city was being sequestered into ghettos.

Joh continued to court the girl he'd met a few years ago at a church youth function. Her name was Nel, and he was falling in love. But their courtship would look a little different with curfews and blackouts in place.

By 1941, the Germans were running everything, including where Joh currently worked, in a German-commandeered railway depot, loading and unloading freight trains bound for other destinations in Europe. Those destinations included Germany, and the trains carried supplies stolen from Holland for Germany's war effort.

So, it was the unspoken policy of every Dutch worker to do whatever they could get away with. Large or small, anything that could be used by the Germans was sabotaged. Joh included himself in that company. Every day he would happily report to the German in charge, do his work, and just coincidentally, keep a careful eye out for an opportunity. He considered it his patriotic duty. Things would be stolen, broken, jimmied or trashed. Joh knew the risk he was taking because those who were caught were severely punished or outright executed.

He kept a constant watch for sabotage opportunities, and at work one day, Joh spotted a large wooden industrial spool in a storage area at the rear of the building. It had half of its one-centimeter thick wire cable still on it and looked like it was left over from last month, on a job involving a crane. It looked potentially like something the Germans would gather up periodically, and send back to Germany, and he decided then and there, that they would never have it. The proverbial light bulb went on in his head, but it needed to rain for his idea to materialize. Luckily it was April so there would be plenty of opportunity.

Sure enough, two days later it rained. Joh wore his loose, rubber poncho to work that day, and no one thought it odd. Very near the end of his shift he entered the rear warehouse, after looking around carefully to make sure there was no one about. The poncho came off. Joh wondered if his idea would work. He hoped so, and, nothing ventured, nothing gained, he tucked the end of the cable firmly into his belt. Next, he took hold of the rest and began turning himself around and around, winding the entire coil of cable tightly around his body.

Joh began to sweat, a little nervous that it was taking so long. There was more to the length than he'd first assumed. Anyone could walk in on him at any time, and if it was one of the supervisors or even a countryman who'd become a German sympathizer - they were around, unfortunately - it would not go well for him.

Finally, with a sense of relief when it was done, the poncho was slipped back on over top of everything, and he was ready to end the shift and go home. It was awkward trying to move with the weight of the cable on his body, and he tried to walk as normally as he could. He had to get past the guard at the entrance to the depot.

Joh caught a glimpse of himself in a pane of glass as he passed the offices. He almost burst out laughing. In the reflection, he saw a very fat man with a teeny tiny head! The guards posted on duty were usually so bored, that they never looked at the men exiting the building. They were more intent on who came into it. Joh hoped that tonight's guard would be doubly bored.

Sure enough, the German stood leaning against the wall, examining his fingernails. He only saw another worker out of the corner of his eye, a fat one apparently, going home from his shift. The wire was ditched somewhere safe, and its location was reported to the underground resistance, to use as they saw fit. His self-imposed assignment was complete.

Chuckling to himself, he made his way to Nel's house and joined her for a meager meal. Afterwards, they planned on taking a walk through a local park. It was dark by the time they got to where they were going. It was also after curfew, but he was in love and didn't give a fat fig about what the Germans demanded.

Joh knew of a certain bench near a pond, where the path split in two around the pond before it continued on. In the dark, they could sit and smooch in the pitch dark, no one the wiser. The two got to the bench in good time and sat down. Joh encircled his girl in his arms and the world fell away. Blackouts were good for something after all.

As they sat and murmured sweet things to each other between kisses, Nel noticed a pinprick of light coming towards them in the distance.

"I think someone's coming!" Nel whispered, "It looks like a bicycle light and it's coming straight toward us."

Joh looked over at what Nel had indicated. "I hope he knows there's a pond right in front of him. He probably can't see very much with only the illumination from the pinhole." It was black-out, and lights, even on a bicycle, were not allowed. Consequently, the bike lights were covered with a black cloth, leaving a tiny hole in the middle, so whatever light came from the bike could not be seen from the air by bombers.

"Humph, they might as well disable the light entirely, for all the good the tiny hole in the light cover does," Nel grumbled. "I sure can't see anything with it."

Joh thought for a second. "Well, we can do one of two things. Stop the guy and warn him of the pond, or let him run into it and get soaked. On the other hand, if we stop them, and it's a German, we're in trouble! We're out past curfew! What do you think?" Joh posed the choice, as they considered the implications for them if it was a German soldier.

"We really can't take that chance. Come on, get behind the bench and hide in the brush. If he knows there's a pond he'll go around, and if he comes around to our side, he'll see us for sure!"

Both of them hid, waiting in the darkness and tall growth behind the bench. The pinprick of light kept coming. Being very familiar with the area, they knew at a certain point, whoever was on that bicycle knew nothing of the pond in the way, nor the split path that led around both sides of it. They watched as the pinpoint of light carried on straight into the pond. From the cursing and swearing that followed, it was clear the rider was a German, probably an officer going to some meeting or a soldier on patrol.

Both lovers jammed their fists into their mouths, afraid the mirth from the two of them at the sounds of misery coming from the pond, would reveal their presence. The unhappy noises continued, accompanied by splashing and the metallic scraping of the bike in the dark. When the cursing finally faded away into the night, they both released a burst of pent-up laughter. Then, considering that they used up their luck for the night, they hurried home and called it a night.

The Soviet Union had, so far, allied themselves with Germany, and supplied them with raw materials for their conquest of Europe. With Russia on their side, Hitler had easy access to the Far East, which everyone believed he also had his eye on. Hitler, however, was intent on destroying Jews, Communists and anyone else who was considered to be dangerous to German rule on Soviet territory. On June 22, 1941, he attacked the Soviet Union. It spelled the end of their non-aggression pact and Russia quickly joined forces with the Allies.

The war progressed all across northern Europe; Belgium, Luxemburg, France, and Sweden were trampled by Nazi troops, Luftwaffe bombers, and tanks. All were overrun. Britain was being bombed to within an inch of her life. Previously, with the Nazi/Russia pact, the Soviet Union had fought the war in Finland, along with occupying three other northern countries.

As Joh read the newspaper and heard whatever reports came over the radio broadcasts, he couldn't follow the complications of who and when and why. There were stories of Japan also vying for power in southeast Asia, something to do with oil, the U.S., and the freezing of Japanese assets in the States. He didn't understand any of it.

On the other side of the globe, because of the U.S.'s economic sanctions and trade embargoes, Japan, long in conflict with China, bombed

Hawaii's Pearl Harbour. Joh couldn't believe it. It seemed the whole world, governments and leaders had gone crazy with power hunger. Everyone waited to see if another country would join the madness.

On December the seventh, 1941 the headlines finally screamed that the Americans had declared war on Japan. Three days later, Germany and Italy declared war on the United States, effectively thrusting the U.S. into the European war theatre. The U.S. would not only be engaging in a war in the Pacific, but also joining the Allied forces in Europe.

Australia and Canada had been in Europe almost from the beginning, sending thousands of troops across to fight alongside the Allies. Everyone hoped that the U.S.'s entry into the war would help change the direction for the better.

Joh sometimes still wished he could have enlisted. He felt as if he wasn't doing enough. But, what else could he do, besides what he was doing already?

CHAPTER 6

1942-43 - Alkmaar

"If you want to get married, you need to have a good profession to build a family life!" That advice was offered to him by more than one person when he started broaching the subject of marriage with his family. He wasn't sure what he could do, that would become a reliable source of income.

The war dragged on, but at some point, it would end, he knew, and whatever he did, it had to last after these days had faded into memory. The creative urge was still strong, but he still couldn't bring himself to draw. Instead, he spent hours taking broken things and finding novel ways either to repair or re-use them in some way. Once in a while, he'd try his hand at creative woodworking, but a lack of proper tools hampered his efforts.

It was while he was watching his sister try and fancy up a small cake somehow for someone, that Joh realized that pastry making and cake decorating appealed to him. The Dutch loved their pastries. He'd often stopped to admire the exquisitely decorated *gebak* in the window of the local bakery. If he could learn to do that, he'd always have a job. Maybe he could even start his own business. He was sure there were courses he could take and began making inquiries. Sure enough, there was a small school he could go to from where he lived, as soon as he had the payment for the course.

Bicycling to work each day, Joh somehow put enough aside each week for his tuition. Not a cent was spent that didn't need to be spent. His brother Piet pulled him aside one day. "So, I hear you have a girl and a goal

gebak - fancy pastry

these days. Is she the same girl as the one we ran into in Schoorl a few years back? You were a little smitten with that one, as I recall."

Joh laughed, "Yep, that's the one."

"Hmm. I know a few ladies who know her. Nel? Is that her name?"

Joh nodded his head. He got the impression that he was going to hear some things that he'd rather not.

"I don't want to say anything bad about her," Piet continued, "but you might want to hold off with getting too serious with this one."

"Why? Did she grow a third leg?"

"She comes from a fairly well-off family, and she was a little spoiled from what I hear."

"People always talk when they're jealous of someone, you know that Piet!" Jacob answered his brother testily. He was going to defend his girl after all. "That's true," Piet agreed, "but a lot of people saying the same thing can't all be wrong. This girl can be pretty difficult, so the story goes. At least when she's determined to have something her own way."

Joh was ready to walk away from the conversation, and Piet softened a little. "I know you're in love, but be cautious. If you're going to ask her to marry you, go in with your eyes wide open!"

"I'll do that," Joh shot back. "Thanks for the advice!" He had mixed feelings about that advice, however, and it left him a bit confused. Piet never gave thoughtless advice. Piet wasn't the only one to come to him privately and express their reservation about the match. They all said the same thing. "She's a little difficult from all reports, although she is liked by most."

Over the next months, as Joh continued to put aside his money, he worked as many extra jobs as he could find. They were getting harder and harder to get, and sometimes it was more to barter things, rather than getting paid. He took whatever he could to realize his dream. On his days off he and Nel would go for long bike rides in the dunes and do a little day camping along the way.

It wasn't an easy task with Germans in control and taking whatever they could for themselves. They all knew that Hitler planned to turn Holland into a part of Germany. The Dutch had the "Aryan" look that Hitler wanted for his dream society. The Dutch had other ideas.

After careful thought and consideration, Joh finally made up his mind. From the money he'd put aside, he bought an inexpensive gold ring. That evening, he quietly broached the subject of an engagement to Nel.

After also asking her father, Hendrik if he had the man's permission, Nel happily said yes. She too went out and bought a ring. There wasn't much available, and the gold turned out to be of less quality than usual. All resources were either used for the war effort or were expropriated by Germany. But a ring was a ring. In a small, informal ceremony of sorts, in front of family and friends, they slipped their respective gold bands on each other's left hands and were officially engaged.

Nel found work as a housekeeper to earn some kind of living. Financial resources were being strangled for the more well-off population, and it wasn't as easy as she'd thought. She clashed with many of the women she worked for. Most of them had their own ideas of how they wanted their homes to be run. She was headstrong and had her own opinions, and she could hardly wait until the day when she'd have her own home in which to be boss.

As best they could, both of them began assembling the bits and pieces they'd need for a proper household. They knew that the value of their money would soon be nothing if Hitler had his way. Whatever money was disposable, they invested in a beautiful, if simple patterned silver, eight-person cutlery set. Pieces of furniture were found, some in good condition or refurbished and given to them by family members. A breadbox, kitchen canisters, linen, a bed, table and chairs, slowly all the essentials were put together for their future life.

Joh went through whatever clothes he had. He had one Sunday suit, but as he looked at it carefully, he could see that the sleeves and cuffs were getting a little threadbare. He also noticed, as he carefully examined the details, that the colour looked lighter on the outside than on the inside of the fabric. Sun had faded it over the years. He knew he'd look shabby beside his bride if he wore it.

He took another peek at the inside of the suit, and his creativity came buzzing forward. Bundling up the suit, he got himself to a tailor in town and presented it to the man, with his idea. He hoped it wouldn't sound too crazy, but this was wartime. Everything was on the table.

"I'm getting married in a few months, and this is the only suit I've got!" he explained to the tailor. "But, look at the inside of this fabric! Could you take the entire suit apart, turn it inside out and sew it back together with the inside on the outside?"

The tailor began laughing. Joh was afraid he'd be laughed right out of the store, but the man clapped him on the back and said, "*Yongen,* you're a true Dutchman! Squeeze a penny where you can, and look like a million guilders while you're doing it!"

On May nineteenth, 1943, in the required civil ceremony at the city hall in Alkmaar, Joh and Nel made promises and switched those gold bands from the left hand to the right hand. In the *Gereformeerde kerk*, the ceremony was repeated in front of God and man. His married life had begun, and he was planning a whole new career. He felt great, in spite of the inside-out suit.

The couple moved into a *gemeentehuis* in Alkmaar, and set up housekeeping, Nel was finally happy to have her own place to run, without interference from another woman.

Joh continued to work at various jobs, usually for Germans, and continued to sabotage anything he could lay his hands on, if it looked like the Germans were interested in it. He'd throw nails behind the tires of a

---

gemeentehuis - literally 'township house' -
a house owned by a township

parked German vehicle, a jug of water in a German gas tank, or simply hide supplies destined for German use, in a spot where they could be picked up by the resistance.

Food was getting scarcer as the war progressed, and many times Joh was out after curfew looking for food. On a night doing just that, he had cut through an alley that ran between the row housing that was prevalent in any Dutch town. The alley was no more than two and one half feet wide -almost one meter- with a tall gate at either end that swung out, and connected parallel streets at the middle of the block.

Joh came down the passageway and approached the gate to push it open and step through. He felt resistance, as if someone was pushing back and a man's voice quietly said, *"Wait!"*

Waiting behind the gate, he wondered what was happening, but wartime experience told him not to question the command. He had his answer as he heard the dreaded German boot steps coming down the street. Joh wondered what the foot patrol would say to the man on the other side of the gate, but the boots never hesitated as they passed by. When they faded into the distance, the pressure on the gate eased, and the voice spoke again, *"Come!"*

He stepped quickly out into the street, ready to thank the man, but no matter in which direction he looked, there was nobody to thank. Up and down the empty street, going both ways, the only things visible were the long brick facades of row housing.

Too stunned to think, Joh stood there. "How can this be?" he thought. "I know there was somebody there. I heard him, and I felt him pushing on the door! There was nowhere he could have gone so quickly! I'm not crazy .. am I?"

Over and over he thought about the sequence of events. It just didn't seem possible. The only explanation he could come up with, that would explain it was … he'd been saved by an angel! He ran it through his head a few more times, just to make sure that he wasn't making a fool of himself, but there was no other possible explanation.

He hurried down the street to his door and stood inside, shaken to the core. Nel came down the stairs and looked at him. "Something happened, didn't it? From the way you look, I can tell! You're as white as a sheet!"

"You're not going to believe this," he started. And Joh told his wife what he'd just experienced. "People will think I'm crazy if I tell them that story!" He finished, "But I can't deny it either!"

"The only thing you need to do is thank God that He's looking out for you! You're not finished here on Earth yet, by the looks of it!"

Joh spent the next few days processing the entire experience in his head. *Could it be,* he thought, *God is so interested in me that He'd actually send an angel to save me?* The idea was hard to fathom, but there could be no denying it either. If he could come up with a plausible earthly explanation, he would. There just wasn't any.

CHAPTER 7

1943-1945

As the war progressed, the Germans became more malicious in their treatment of the Dutch populace. The Jews had either fled or were in hiding somewhere if they'd not already been rounded up and sent away.

All men of working age were also corralled, if they could be found, and sent as free labour to work camps or factories in Germany. Many never returned. For this, people in every town and village had their early-warning systems in place if they knew the Germans were about to arrive. The tip-offs gave the men time to skip town or hide somewhere.

The wild knocking and voice on the other side of the front door signified an excited Dutchman rather than an impassive and dour pair of Germans. Nel came to the door and opened it carefully. One always opened doors carefully these days. "Jan!" She greeted the familiar face, "what's the news?"

"They're on the way again!" They've just caught four men in Heiloo and they'll be here next! Tell Joh!" And the man was gone. The Gestapo was coming.

Joh was currently doing a job for a Dutch carpenter. She hauled out her bicycle from the back with shaking hands, and pedaled as fast as she could to his job site. "Joh! You have to come home now! Where's your bike? They're coming!" Horrified, Joh knew who she meant by "they", and realized his bicycle was still at the carpenter's house. They'd come to the jobsite in the old man's horse-drawn cart.

"It's not here!" he choked out.

"Take my bike! I can walk back!" She shoved her bike into his hands. Joh knew what he needed to do. They'd planned carefully a week ago. He took his rushed leave from the old carpenter, who simply waved and said, "Good luck! I'll see you in a few days!", then mounted the bike and pedaled hard for home.

By the time Nel got back half an hour later, her husband was already tucked away in his space between the attic rafters and the roof of the house. It was just wide enough for him to fit. There was a thermos of water and some bread, buttered with a thin film of margarine. The covering over the hole he'd crawled through wasn't quite in place so she pushed it a little further over to close the gap.

"Thanks, dear," said a muffled voice from somewhere in between the beams. She smiled nervously. "I just hope I can hide my anxiety from the *moffen!* I hate them! "

"Just use your anger! It will cover the anxiety." Joh suggested. As he lay wedged between the beams, his heart pounding, he listened as faint sounds came floating up from the lower levels of the house. His nose was runny again, and he'd been sneezing a lot. He hoped whatever ailed him wouldn't betray his hiding place.

The pounding on the door came soon enough. Nel slowly walked to the door to open it, with a tea towel and dish in one hand. "What do you want?" She asked the pair brusquely, trying to convey her anger just enough without getting herself into trouble.

"There's no man here, you've already taken him!" She retorted when they asked to see the man of the house. Nel stood scowling at them with the plate and tea towel in her hand, gripping the items hard to stop them from shaking. The two Germans looked at her with narrowed eyes, while she stared back defiantly.

———————————————

moffen - *plural of mof , a pejorative term for a German soldier*

"You can only take him once you know, I can't conjure him up again for you!" She bit her tongue, afraid that she'd pushed it too far, but they walked wordlessly past her into the house to search.

After a fruitless look around, they left. Nel closed and locked the door behind them, then hurried up to the cramped attic on shaking legs, to report to her husband. Both of them had decided he'd stay there for at least four days, in case the Germans would double back if they were suspicious. It was easy enough to post a lookout to watch for men going in and out of houses, if they suspected someone had been lying to them.

While Joh wedged himself in between the rafters, he dreamed of a day when he could walk free in his own country, and do what he wished. He had assembled a small sum of money so far to finance his chosen career path, but the vocational schools were closed for now. The people normally at school were all otherwise occupied with war activities. No. The word "activities" sounded more to Joh like fun things. War was ugly, evil and destructive to him. There were no winners here. Money was almost useless now, there was nothing to buy. He wondered if he would have enough when the time came and if it would be worth anything by then. So many things could change.

After four days, the Germans were reported to be done and gone. Joh climbed down stiffly down from his hiding place. He'd only been out for moments at a time, doing his business in a "pee pot" set up in the attic and monitored by Nel. He stretched stiffly and looked forward to a real, sit-down, hot meal. Nel had brought him food on a plate, trying to keep it as warm as possible until he could eat it. But, it was awkward with the room he had, and the logistics of it all. They had to be constantly on the alert. At any moment, the Germans could barge in and catch them. It would be repeated a few times over in the next couple of years, and became another source of stress to the residents of occupied Holland.

The new home life begun by the newlyweds was settled as best it could, amidst the occupiers of their postage stamp-sized country. More and more, the Dutch were angered at the audacity of these *moffen* that dared invade their homeland. They eagerly listened to the radio broadcasts when, where, and if they could. Many radios were confiscated, the Germans not at all pleased, as their subjugated "Aryans" listened to negative reports, buoyed up by encouraging speeches sent from Britain by the Queen, who was adored by her subjects. Every loss the Germans suffered was cheered on, and from all indications, Germany suffered far too many of them that year of 1943.

By the end of it, they'd had to withdraw from Kursk, Kharkiv, Kyiv and Tripoli, among others. They'd surrendered at Stalingrad and in North Africa. Other losses included the island of Sicily, to the Allies, the bombing of Hamburg and its many factories, and in the very last month of the year 1943, the British *HMS Duke of York* sinking the battleship *Scharnhorst*, their pride and joy. Hitler was furious at it all, while the Dutch laughed! To Hitler's chagrin, in the middle of all this came the reports of Mussolini's arrest, the Italian's peace settlement with the Allies, and finally in November, the start of the Tehran conference attended by Stalin, Churchill and Roosevelt.

Christmas was upon them, and all hoped for a peaceful one, if only temporarily. Joh still worked at the railway depot, and the Germans had doubled the guard at the entrance, concerned with too many acts of sabotage.

"Do you have tomorrow off for Christmas?" queried Nel of her husband. The Germans were less and less kindly towards their workers these days. It wouldn't have surprised her at all if they forced Joh and many others to work right through Christmas Day.

"Don't you worry. I'll be taking tomorrow off whether they like it or not!" he promised.

He was a little nervous walking up to his supervisor to make his intentions known regarding tomorrow, and at the end of the day's shift, decided to approach the subject carefully. A few men stood at his back, also hoping for tomorrow off.

"It's Christmas tomorrow. What will the hours be on Second Christmas Day?" he questioned. The supervisor looked at him questioningly. "It will be business as usual First Christmas Day and Second Christmas Day," he replied tersely.

"Do you mean to tell me that we have to work through the entire Christmas holiday?" Joh asked in amazement. "It's Christmas for God's sake!"

"So? You work. End of story!"

By now, a few more men had gathered, eager to hear what the outcome of this conversation would be.

"Sorry, but I'm staying home tomorrow. Shoot me if you like, but I'll see you the day after tomorrow bright and early!"

Angry now, and unbending, he turned on his heel and walked out of the warehouse. His father always did say his temper would get the best of him one day. Fully expecting to be shot in the back, he headed towards his bicycle parked in the iron bike racks in front of the building. His backside crawled, and he wondered briefly if it was true; that he'd never feel the shot that killed him.

The couple enjoyed a simple Christmas, gathering with family at church to celebrate. "I wonder what they'll say when we get back to work tomorrow." one fellow worker asked him. Joh laughed. "There might be some repercussions from this. As far as I know, everybody decided to stay home. If the supervisor and the Germans showed up, they didn't have any workers to deal with!"

"We'll find out tomorrow, won't we?"

Tomorrow came, and not a word was said, but the hours they had to work were extended by an hour each day after that. It was a sacrifice worth making.

The clock towers and church steeples peeled out a welcome to 1944, but with everything dark, and shops with very little goods to offer for decent meals and other essentials, there was little to celebrate. Dutch people everywhere held on to the only things they had left; Dutch pride and stubbornness.

Joh and his wife felt no less, the prevailing mood of their countrymen. They dug in, while all around them, horrified, they heard about people that were dragged out of their homes simply because they were Jews. The pair didn't know any Jews themselves, but they knew there were many in the Netherlands who, at least it was rumoured, had taken Jews into their homes, where they'd constructed secret narrow spaces between walls to hide them if Gestapo were snooping around, fully aware they were putting their own lives in danger. Some had assimilated Jewish children into their households, while the parents were on the run.

Food was becoming scarce, and Joh was more and more desperate as sources dried up. It was a hard scrabble just to get even a few potato peelings to wash and cook for some kind of meal. Towards the end of summer, someone approached him to tell of a farmer just outside of town, that had just harvested a crop of beans. Joh knew the man from a previous contact, and hurried over on his bicycle, hoping to get some. He'd hoped for something different. They'd eaten nothing but beans of all kinds for months now.

"What do you mean, they're all gone already?" Joh exclaimed in frustration, "you couldn't have gotten rid of them that fast, could you?"

"A relative of yours came and got them. He told me he was going to distribute them to the rest of the family. It saves me the time it takes to get them out to others. Go see him, if he doesn't come around with them soon."

Joh thanked the farmer and returned home to give the news to his wife that beans were in the offing. A few days passed and still, no news surfaced of the food. The couple finally approached the errant family member, to discover the beans had only been shared with their immediate family. Furious, Nel let loose with a piece of her mind on what she thought.

Both of them returned home, disappointed in the unexpected actions of their family connections. They'd have to tighten belts again and eat a few more vegetable peelings and sugar beets.

Nel didn't have much appetite as the summer came to a close. Joh noticed she'd become thinner lately, and she was often ill. He began to worry about her. He had always been a little skinny himself, so he thought nothing of the way he looked, but his wife had always carried a fair amount of weight about her. Not overly so, but enough. Now, she looked pale and haggard.

"I think I'm pregnant," she told him on a day in November. He was overjoyed and worried sick all at the same time. He needed to find food more than ever. Even the rations allotted for pregnant and nursing mothers weren't enough.

Along with every Dutch citizen, Joh was encouraged by the reports swirling around them now. In September there were Allied liberations of French and Belgian places that had been held by Hitler's forces, places like Verdun and Dieppe, Antwerp and Brussels. U.S. troops had reached the Siegfried Line in Western Germany.

In mid-September, the Allied airborne assault began in the Netherlands to drive out the hated Germans. They called it *"Operation Market-Garden"*. When it was over it was considered a massive failure. All the while, people starved.

At Queen Wilhelmina's insistence, her Minister kept her apprised of her subjects. She asked each day what the people were eating, and refused to eat anything, but that which her people ate. At a certain point, the staff began to worry about the Queen's health, and decided one evening, to present her with steak for dinner. She was reported to have looked at the steak and inquired whether this was what her people were eating tonight. Tactfully, and with crossed fingers, her staff answered in the affirmative.

October brought more good news, as Athens joined the liberated ranks. That same day, Field Marshal Erwin Rommel committed suicide.

There was little sadness over the news, even though Rommel had been part of a failed plot to kill Adolf Hitler, which the Dutch would have cheerfully applauded. Rommel was given a choice of a court martial, which would have seen his entire family assassinated along with himself, or death by suicide. The Dutch were only disappointed that he couldn't have taken Hitler with him.

The massive German surrender at Aachen, Germany, was welcome news indeed, as it signified to Joh that the Nazi Forces were weakening. Joh was determined to hang on through the winter, and not lose hope.

With the failure of *Operation Market-Garden*, the sole purpose of which was to bring it all to an early end, the war would rage on through the winter. The transition from 1944 to 1945 came and went with no fanfare. People like Johannes and Nel were exhausted, focused solely on surviving until they too were liberated. It was just a matter of time. Afterwards, that winter in the Netherlands would go down in history as the "Hunger Winter", as thousands of men, women and children starved to death.

The official daily ration for every person in the Netherlands was 320 calories each. Many survived by eating tulip bulbs, vegetable peelings, sugar beets and other questionable edible growth, anything at all that would assuage their hunger. Fuel ran out. There was no transportation. Citizens hung on by a thread that could snap at any moment.

How Nel survived that last winter before she gave birth, Joh would never know. He only prayed that the madness would soon end, and every German, as far as he was concerned, could drop into the nearest entrance to Hell, never to be seen again.

Everywhere in Europe, the tide turned with the advance of the Allied forces. In February of 1945 Canadian troops began to drive the Nazis to the east, and in April cleared the northeast of Holland. They pushed westward very quickly after that, where the major cities were located; Amsterdam, Rotterdam, and The Hague. Arnhem and Apeldoorn followed rapidly.

Everyone was worried at this point that the German commanders would, in desperation and spite, breach the dikes, and flood that part of Holland. It was unthinkable, but no one trusted what the *moffen* would do. Joh sat on pins and needles. Alkmaar was not that far away from Amsterdam, and if that area was flooded, they would be as well. It would be certain death for thousands. The Canadians recognized this as well and called the western push to a temporary halt. Food drops began for the starving people, as well as other relief supplies.

Then on April 28, 1945, Mussolini was captured and hanged by Italian partisans. Two days later, Adolf Hitler committed suicide.

On May 5, 1945, the German forces in the Netherlands officially surrendered. The Canadians drove through the streets of The Hague, Amsterdam and other cities, while Dutch citizens looked on, including Joh and Nel, silently at first, as if they were sleepwalking, unable to wake up. Then, as a single, waking person, realizing that they were awake and free, began to scream in joy, dancing and singing in the streets.

As Joh walked his streets afterwards, the air itself felt lighter, unfettered. The war had not yet been declared officially over, but he could feel it in the wind. Nel was gaunt, but doing well in her pregnancy. The war was over. The declaration came the day after the May 7 unconditional surrender of all German forces to the Allies. May 8, 1945, became VE Day, Victory in Europe. War, at least for Europe, was over.

Johannes and Nel's son was born a week later in the free Holland Joh had hoped for.

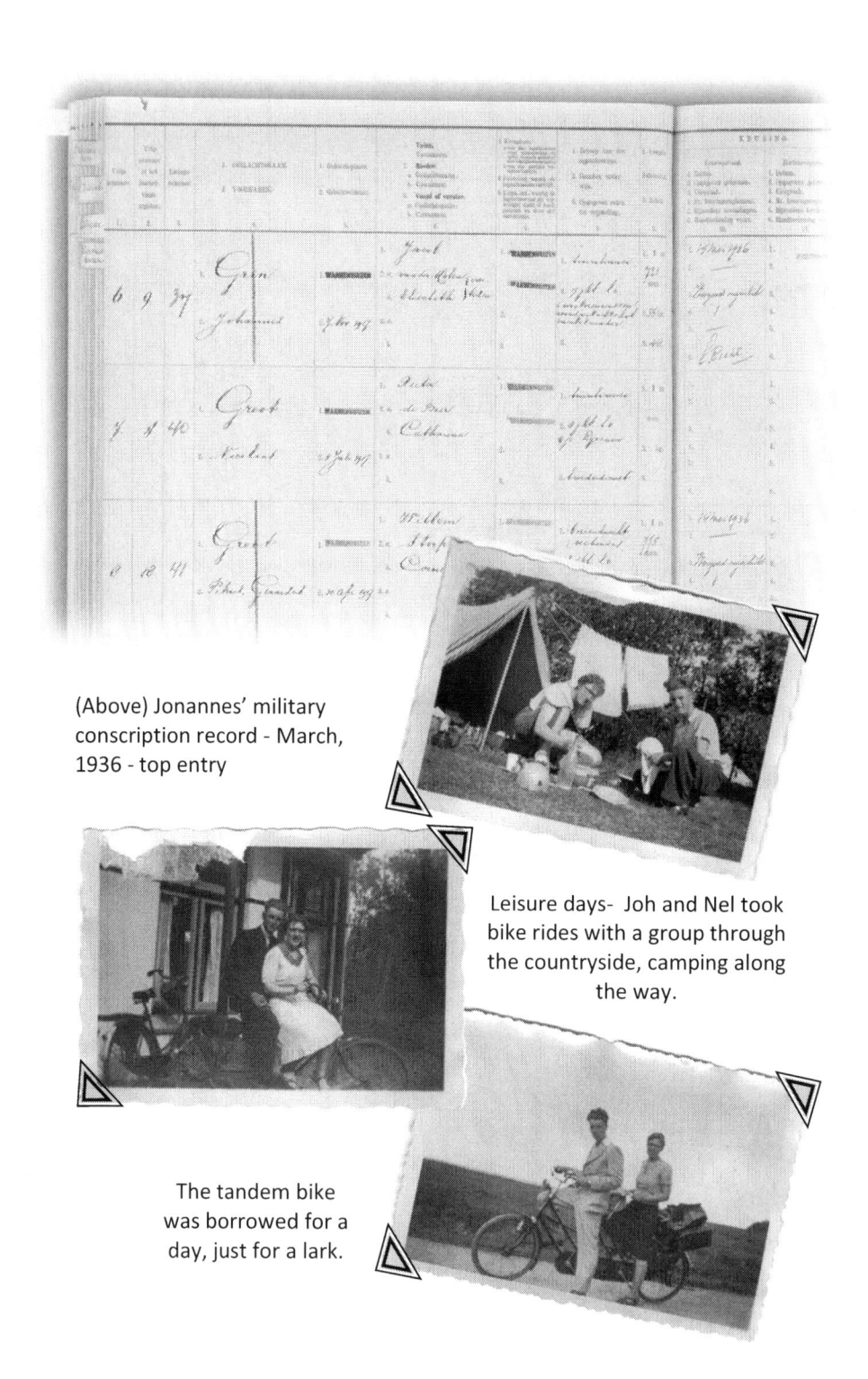

(Above) Jonannes' military conscription record - March, 1936 - top entry

Leisure days- Joh and Nel took bike rides with a group through the countryside, camping along the way.

The tandem bike was borrowed for a day, just for a lark.

May 12, 1940 - The burning of the Royal Dutch Shell oil reserves in Pernis (area of Rotterdam) (See pg. 35)

(Left)
Engagement photo
Oct. 1942.

(Right)
Wedding photo
May, 1943.

NOTE: *The striking difference in Joh's aged appearance in the interim between their engagement and wedding, speaks to the devastating effects of the Nazi occupation of his country .*

57

❧The Wedding❧

Traditionally, the couple first attends City hall for the civil ceremony, to legalize the marriage ...

... and then transported to the church for the religious ceremony.

The newly married couple and parents, in front of the Gereformeerde Kerk in Alkmaar. L to R - Hendrik Kelder (Nel's father), Joh, Nel, flower girl, niece, Carla (in front), Jacob (Joh's father), Joh's stepmother.

Official wedding photo

CHANGING TIMES

Joh's two children, Elly (L) and Jacob "Jopie", born in the Netherlands

CHAPTER 8

1945

"I hate that name. It's an ugly name!" This vehement statement from Nel shocked Joh. "But it's my father's name." he protested. "I want to name my son after Father. Hendrik can be his second name. The whole thing has a nice ring to it don't you think?"

"Don't think throwing my father's name into it will change my mind. I do not want my son to carry the name, Jacob. I hate it. As a first name or a second name, it doesn't matter. I don't want the name 'Jacob' attached to him at all." Nel wailed.

The argument had been an ongoing sore point for the last month. Nel had given birth on Monday and he needed to get himself to City Hall to register the birth. Joh wanted the names of both his father and hers, but Nel was adamant about the issue

"I have to register the birth. Please, don't be difficult." pleaded Joh. He left the house with Nel shouting after him, "Don't you dare put that name on the birth certificate. You hear me? Don't you dare."

Joh bicycled to City Hall, turning the possibilities of what he could do to get around the conundrum, over and over in his mind as he pedaled. As he neared the building, he had it. Many children in his family had given *roepnaamen*. Often, ones that were variations of chosen names. He would give his son a nickname. He just wouldn't be able to include it on the birth certificate. But, he would find a suitable nickname to use for the boy. He'd let Nel choose. With a sigh of relief that he had, what he hoped was

roepnaamen - plural of roepnaam
literally - call name, a nickname

a viable solution to his wife's objection to the name Jacob, he walked into the office of statistics to register his son's birth.

"Goede morgen, Mijnheer, what can I do for you today?" The dapper little man behind the counter peered over his glasses at Joh, questioningly. "I have a baby's birth I need to register," he announced proudly.

"Your's I take it?"

"Yes, mine ... and my wife's of course!" Joh added quickly. The clerk laughed. "I would think so!"

When his son's particulars were entered and made official by the registrar, Joh biked slowly home, rehearsing in his mind, how he'd put the whole name solution to his wife. He would do his utmost to leave the choice of a *roepnaam* to her. Maybe that would mollify her enough to keep the friction down to a modest level. When she had her mind made up over something, and he was not in agreement, there was little he could do. He remembered he'd been warned years ago, by more than one person.

As Joh walked into the house, he was greeted with, "Well? You didn't name him Jacob did you?"

"His name is Jacob Hendrik." He said and held his breath. Joh stayed silent, and let the storm that followed burn itself out. When things had chilled somewhat, perhaps too chilly as far as he was concerned, Joh broached the subject of a nickname. They bandied a few back and forth, her suggestions having the frosting of anger clinging to it. But she participated in the conversation, and that was a plus to him. Finally, Nel suggested 'Jopie' which suited him just fine. Jopie it was. Nel vowed, her fists clenched, "I will never call him Jacob! Never!"

Right afterwards he got himself to the printer, who they'd earlier picked out, along with the card of choice, and put in his order for enough cards to send to one and all.

 Goede morgen, Mijnheer - *Good morning, Sir*

The baby was beautiful. His family and friends, and even strangers on the street, commented on how fair his infant son looked. It made his chest swell. What delighted him the most, was that the child hardly cried. It was one thing he'd steeled himself for, having heard from other new fathers that it was the least delightful aspect of being a new parent. But nights were mostly quiet, and days, at least when he was home, had been very peaceful so far.

On Sunday, Joh grew restless. He wasn't sure why, but the thought of walking up the street with his wife pushing a baby carriage in front of her filled him with a sort of pride. He pictured himself strolling like a family man up the street, while those who knew them would, in his imagination, stop and admire the baby. He liked the thought of that, and so he urged Nel to bundle up his son and put him in the carriage.

She was less than enthusiastic, still hurting from the birth. Finally, she relented and they went walking. He had to go slow because Nel could not walk very fast. At the first cross street they came to, the baby carriage thumped down off the curb a little roughly, and he looked at his wife a little perturbed. "Gently, gently," he cautioned her. They got to the other side of the street, and he was up on the sidewalk and ahead of her before he realized that Nel was still on the road, struggling to get the carriage up on the opposite sidewalk. She was a little short with him, as she demanded that he take over the carriage.

"I don't have the strength to lift this thing to get it on the sidewalk! Can't you push it for me?" Nel complained.

Joh looked shocked. A man pushing a baby carriage? He'd never before seen a man behind a baby carriage on the street, and he wasn't about to start doing a woman's job now.

"Men don't handle baby carriages! That's women's work. Other mothers do it all the time!"

He knew she'd been a little spoiled by her family, being the youngest, and thought it was about time she learned to do things for herself. He was the man of the family, after all. Nel complied but not gladly. Joh thought she looked a little angry at him, but, he thought, she would learn that a woman's job was hers to perform, not his.

Food was still being rationed, and Nel was grateful for the extra food stamps she was getting as a nursing mother, just as she did as an expectant mother. With food stamps and the earnings Joh made, they were beginning to slowly build up the life they'd started partway through the war, a lifetime ago, it felt like.

The Netherlands was still reeling from the shock of Nazi occupation, and a few people had trickled home. All carried with them horror-filled stories; concentration camps where people were reduced to walking skeletons, millions consigned to gas chambers, stripped of gold teeth, buried in mass graves, or left in great piles like so much used-up garbage. They came from work camps and factories, where men like Joh were used as slave labour. Joh had escaped that fate more than once and raised his eyes Heavenward to give thanks, each time he heard another story like it. It didn't diminish the sickness he felt for all those others that came back, broken, or never came back at all.

The war in the Pacific seemed far away now, even though it was still raging on. That war was brought to a sudden, violent end with something that the world had never seen. On August 6, 1945, the U.S. sent two planes over Japan's airspace, and a bomb was dropped on Hiroshima that literally flattened any material, and vaporized every living thing in its path. A second atomic bomb was dropped two days later on Nagasaki. Five days later Japan surrendered.

It was over. All of it. But the aftermath of World War II would continue for years, including the forever altered opinions and habits of Joh and his wife Nel, shaped by a war that would cling to them like burrs, for the rest of their lives.

It was time to push his dream toward the front of his life's priorities. Vocational schools had slowly opened up again, and he began looking in earnest at what there was. He'd run into an old friend, Thijs, just a week before, who had been working as a helper in a bakery. Thijs wasn't a baker himself, but the work looked like fun to him, especially the cake decorating and the specialty items, like fancy *gebak* or sugar and chocolate confections. In the conversation he'd had, Thijs told him they were crying for good bakers. Still, he needed money for all of it; his home, his small family, and his schooling. Nel was expecting again. His son was barely a year old. He had plenty of reasons to improve his lot in life. He'd start by learning to be a *banketbakker*.

By June of 1946, two sisters were expecting again, Nel's baby due in February of the following year, and Anna, her second due in November.

"Don't you dare have that baby on my birthday!" Nel warned her sister. Anna had to laugh, "Thanks! As if I have any control over that!" Anna hooted, thinking Nel was making a joke. Nel was serious. "That's my birthday. I don't want to have to share it with anyone!"

Anna said nothing more, but the accuracy of her siblings' opinion that their mother has spoiled their youngest sister somewhat, was cemented in a little deeper.

Anna gave birth that November, producing a healthy baby boy, precisely on November twentieth, Nel's birthday. She was not to be forgiven for a very long time, if truly ever.

banketbakker - pastry chef

CHAPTER 9

1947

The very early morning hours on a Thursday found Joh hurrying up the street on his bicycle towards the doctor's house. It was mid-February, dark and cold. As he rang the bell and waited anxiously, he hoped that Nel would be alright on her own for a while. They'd moved yet again recently, their third house in four years, this time near Nel's sister, who lived on the same street. Anna was a little too nosey for Joh's liking, and she'd inserted herself in his family life a few too many times. He didn't want her around while Nel was giving birth in their upstairs bedroom, giving her own brand of advice to his wife.

The doctor promised to come quickly and Joh peddled furiously home again. After parking the bike, and as he came through the back door, he stopped off in the living room to get his cigarettes. Just then he noticed Anna, passing by the front window, peering in as she went. Glad the front door was locked, he shook his head, and went upstairs. *Meddlesome fool,* he thought. *Why can't she mind her own business?*

Nel looked anxiously at her husband. "Is he coming?"

"He's right behind me. Just breathe. It's fine. You're doing fine." He tried to stay calm, but it seemed to be taking forever. This had been going on all night, and he was exhausted. He thought, somehow, that baby should have been here already. Maybe he was just impatient. He couldn't remember that the last birth had taken this long, although Nel had emphatically told him it had. He just couldn't remember it that way.

The doctor arrived, and as Joh let him in, Anna stood there as well. "Go home, Anna! There's nothing you can do right now. It's all under control!" Joh barked at her.

"Stupid woman," he commented on the way up, "she just can't mind her own business." The doctor laughed. "They're all the same, my friend, they're all the same."

An hour later an infant, a girl, hung upside down in the doctor's hand, refusing to take her first breath. When Joh looked carefully, there seemed to be something covering the baby's face.

"Ah!" the doctor exclaimed, "We have a caul birth here!" He laid the baby down on the bed and carefully peeled the transparent membrane back from below her chin, and up over the little face. Again, she was held upside down, but the newborn still had a red-faced pinched expression, as if angry and rebellious. With his thumb and second finger, the doctor flicked against her tiny bottom, and insisted, "Come on. Cry!" A wail finally pierced the quiet room.

Joh looked at his new daughter, wrinkled, and a little fierce-looking, if newborns could look fierce. Thinking of the caul, he said with a little premonition, "If the old wives' tale is true, she might grow up to be a *bijzonder kind!*"

At that moment he also realized, his daughter had been born on the thirteenth, the date of his mother's death and the thirteenth anniversary of it. Three times thirteen. He wondered what that meant.

Nel looked at her new daughter, "Oh, she's not as beautiful as Jopie was!" The doctor smiled. "Her looks will change very quickly. Don't worry, the way a baby looks right after birth means nothing."

As Nel began nursing, Joh walked downstairs with the doctor, to help clean up a little. "I suppose I should go over to Anna, and let her know if we have a boy or a girl," he sighed. The doctor smiled at the little family dramas that seemed to swirl around every birth he'd ever attended. This one was no different, but he also wondered if the father's comment at the old wives' meaning of a caul birth would have any truth to it. He'd seen too much to discount it entirely.

bijzonder kind - *unusual child*

"Just let Neeltje rest for a week," the doctor told Joh. Nel growled at the doctor's use of her full name, but he never noticed. "Have your sister-in-law come over and help. It will do your wife good," Joh was told. Joh sighed again at the thought, but at the same time, the doctor was probably right. He couldn't do any of it himself; changing diapers, cooking, what did he know about housework or caring for babies?

Creating pastries, cakes, sugar and chocolate confections. That, he knew how to do. He'd be finished with his *banketbakker's* courses in the fall and was already working as a helper in the bakery, ready to take his place as a full-fledged baker. He could hardly wait to start and felt that this is what he'd been born to do, and why he'd been given this talent he had.

Nightly, his imagination played with the techniques he'd learned already, thinking about what he could create with them. The instructors had been happy with his progress, and his boss was anxious for him to start his real job. They'd had problems getting competent help while the country got back on its feet. Many young men were still in training to fill the holes in the workforce. Joh was glad to have found a niche for himself within the framework. Someday he'd open his own bakery, he knew it!

With the addition of the infant girl, who they named Nelly Elisabeth, in honour of the grandmothers, the little family adjusted to life as a family of four. Nel had briefly toyed with the idea of using her mother's actual name, Neeltje, for the baby, the same one she'd also been saddled with, but she hated her name so badly that she opted for Nelly for her daughter, a version which sounded far more pleasant to her ears. Every one of Joh's brothers and sisters had called their own first-born daughters, Elisabeth, to honour the mother they'd lost so early. To avoid confusion, the nickname chosen for this Elisabeth was Elly.

After registering her birth, his worries about how to feed his family were assuaged by the assurances from the clerk behind the desk, that his family's daily rations and food stamps would be adjusted with the baby's addition. Joh continued enthusiastically studying and applying what he'd learned at school.

He graduated in August of that year and began working full-time as a *banketbakker*. He learned the practical side of the baking business while he worked. Interestingly, he discovered that he'd developed an inborn sense of timing, so that he never needed to set a clock to know when the goods were ready to come out of the ovens.

Creating all the fine baking and confections that he'd trained so hard for, delighted him, as did finding that the workplace was filled with camaraderie, long missing from the last five years. It wasn't unusual to find himself with three other bakers sitting on overturned lard pails, the other workers surrounding them, watching, playing a raucous card game of *klaverjassen* after the work was done.

He often talked of starting his own business someday, but there were many obstacles he'd have to overcome. Most of the men delighted in listing these obstacles for him, accompanied by a bit of teasing and laughter. Joh laughed along with them, but deep down he began to fear that those roadblocks would become insurmountable for him. So much bureaucracy. So many regulations. It ate at his confidence.

Nel looked at the doctor's card her husband handed to her. "This is the food you're not supposed to eat?" she questioned incredulously, "what am I supposed to cook for you?"

Just recently Joh discovered that his constant sinus problems coupled with the endless sneezing were due to allergies. He'd paid a visit to the doctor who sent him to an allergist. That specialist had ordered him to start a three-week trial separation of himself and the food he loved. Milk, cheese, yogurt, and butter, along with vegetables like beans; black, green, and navy, all of the ones he'd been eating so far, had been cut out of his diet. Certain kinds of meat and fish, the little he got on his ration card, were also curtailed for the most part.

klaverjassen - popular Dutch card game

"It's only for three weeks, just to see if my allergies get any better!" He pointed out.

"So, you're going to be one of these people who are so hard to cook for! You'll be on this restricted diet forever!" Nel complained as she made her way to the kitchen.

"This congestion and sneezing are really bothering me. You want me to live like that for the rest of my life, so I won't be a bother to you?" Joh shot back, his anger rising. "It's not that hard! Just don't cook what's on the list. Simple!"

He worried about his wife, sometimes, thinking her contrariness might be due to the life-long handicap of her poor hearing. Now, she had a bad ear infection. Joh wondered if the difficult past number of years had made it any worse. He'd never seen it as bad and finally urged her to see the doctor.

"I've just put some oil into it again. It will disappear soon enough," she assured him. Joh could see the wad of cotton still stuck in her ear. He left it at that, thinking, she'd been dealing with this for years, and he supposed she knew what she was talking about. That evening Nel was still in agony, and by morning, Joh was once more, pedaling in the direction of the doctor's home, before going to class. When the doctor came around to have a look at Nel's ear, he began scolding her.

"You should have had me look at this a week ago! This looks bad!" Nel tried to minimize the problem, "It's always gone away before. I don't understand why it hasn't this time!"

The doctor seemed to be of the same mind as her husband, as he told her, "Your body has been through a lot, and has probably been weakened. You have an infection, and if I can't get it under control, you'll be spending time in the hospital!"

Medication was prescribed, but it was too late. A week later, the doctor made arrangements for Nel to be admitted to the hospital. Her niece, Bep, daughter of her brother Jan, came to look after the household while Nel was away. Bep was more of a sister or cousin than a niece, because of the closeness in age. Her brother Jan was so much older than Nel, that his children seemed to belong more to Nel and Joh's generation.

"Mama!" Bep looked at the baby, startled at the word. Elly was just beginning to attempt words and this was the first one that sounded like a real word! Excited, she told Joh about it when he came home that evening. "She's growing up so fast! Her first word! She'll be talking your ear off soon enough."

Joh wondered at the differences in temperament between his son and daughter. Jopie was a quiet, calm little boy, looking for all the world like he was contemplating very serious matters as he went about his day. His daughter, on the other hand, was a bundle of emotions, screaming to be let out of the playpen because her brother was free in the yard, but not her. Always demanding, wound up, on the go, and never content with anything for very long. Her temperament seemed to go from up to down in a heartbeat.

Nel came home two weeks later, permanently deaf in her right ear. The ear infection was so severe that the only thing the surgeon could do was remove the entire inner ear before the infection could spread to the brain. It was a bitter blow.

She kissed her son, glad to be home, and then picked up the baby for a hug. She was thankful that at least she still had her other ear to hear with, but she had to turn her head to the right, with the left ear forward a little, to hear everyone properly. It was something to get used to.

Bep took the baby out of Nel's arms, "You should go lie down, have a rest. I can take care of everything while you recover." The niece wondered if she should tell her aunt about her daughter's first word now, or later. As Nel turned to go upstairs to her bed, the question was taken completely out of the young woman's hands.

"Mama!"

Surprised, Nel thought she heard her baby say something. She turned around again and, with her head to the right to pick up the sound, looked over at Elly in Bep's arms.

"Mama!" Elly's little voice piped up again. Nel was overjoyed that her daughter had just said her first word …. only … the child was looking straight at her niece, not at her!

"Bep? She's calling you mama? She's saying her first word to *you?*" Nel was indignant. The loss of her hearing, and now this! Her daughter saying her first word to someone else, calling her 'Mama'. It was all too much. She went up the stairs, in a huff. Bep wondered later, who would be forgiven first, her or the baby?

Like so much else in a family drama, all was soon forgotten, or so it seemed. The children grew. Nel settled back into domestic life, and Joh into his new life as a pastry chef.

CHAPTER 10

1949-1950

Joh often thought of how little he'd minded the small inconveniences and disturbances of his first child's arrival. Their second one, however, was a different story.

"Oh! AH! What's so cold on my back?" Joh awakened with a start at the ice-cold something he suddenly felt. He half sat in the dark and looked over in the direction of where his wife should be. Nel's voice came at him, sounding annoyed. "Elly has been up again. I can't get her to stay in her own bed! Now she's ice cold, and I need to warm her up before I take her back."

Joh sighed, rolled over, and burrowed down between the covers. It had been happening off and on, all week. The girl would feel cold, get out of bed, stand in her parent's doorway in the dark and sniffle with her runny nose until her mother noticed. By the time she did, the tyke felt like a block of ice. All of these houses lacked central heating and were poorly insulated, and there was nothing he could do about it. Again, children were women's work and unless the universe somehow did a shift, he wasn't starting with that. He found it admirable enough that he'd fed the baby her mashed food once in a while, but it ended there.

Mealtimes became a training ground of sorts for discipline, the establishing of who did what job and when, plus making sure that the children were getting enough nutrition. There was still a lot of talk and government preaching about this nutrition business, even two years after the war, and things were still being rationed. The newspapers had hinted at rations ending soon, as harvests and food supplies were improving. Joh was just happy he was getting a belly full, no matter what it was.

There were things that seemed to inexplicably confound Nel once in a while, and it became apparent one evening, as she served him their daily ration of vegetables.

"Enjoy your beans," she said as she heaped a serving of something on his plate. "These aren't beans," He replied, smiling.

"I mean cauliflower …" she sighed.

"Nope, it's not cauliflower either." *This was going to be interesting,* he thought, *and I'm not telling her.*

Nel looked at him, clearly frustrated at herself. "It's beets." she pronounced. He shook his head, smiling, "Not beets."

Nel began to look wildly around, thinking, and then stared at the offending vegetable. Joh began laughing, "Now, what is it ?"

She took a deep breath, stared at his plate again, and declared decisively, "Carrots!"

Joh was laughing in earnest now because it wasn't carrots either. The children followed suit, just because their Papa was laughing. Mama, however, just stood there with her face looking rather funny, but just for a moment. Then she too joined in the fun. Had they been able to, the turnips on everyone's plates would have laughed at the joke, but the joke was on them.

Joh attributed his wife's odd lapses to her compromised sight and hearing. He knew she'd had some sort of tumours growing on her eyes when still very young, and her eyes had been permanently scarred. She'd also been partly deaf as a child, and now, of course, that had been damaged further. He could almost understand her mother coddling her in her youth, but sometimes he wondered at Nel's powers of perception.

He'd discovered that his wife also had very vivid, nightly dreams, dreams that had her sitting up in bed in her sleep, wailing in the dark, or just carrying on mumbled conversations. He still remembered the night when she'd shaken him awake, asking what the tea leaf strainer was doing in bed.

"What?!"

Nel had something in her hand. "The tea leaf strainer! What is it doing in bed?" she asked sleepily. He took it from her, puzzled at the absurdity of it. He found himself holding something bowl-shaped and familiar in his hand. Nel had picked up the loose item in her sleep while dreaming, and the dream had turned his upper dentures into the strainer.

"For heaven's sake woman! Those are my teeth!" He threw the dentures on the night table and rolled over. Ever after, Joh got into the habit of taking them out at night to place in a glass of water. Her ordinary dreams were bizarre enough.

From all the bureaucracy, and hoops that one had to jump through, by the time 1949 was partway through, Joh came away with the impression that the country was not ready for a freshly minted baker to open up a new business. He was not known for his patience either. And so, a scarce two years after graduating, the small family found themselves considering a journey across the Atlantic, looking for the perfect place to build a dream.

"Klasina has gone to Australia. Maybe we should go there," Joh suggested. "Or to Canada, where Simon and Willem have gone!"

So many had already left, not seeing any possibilities, and, not having any faith that the country would rebuild soon enough, left for parts unknown. For some, the memories of the places around them were filled with too much grief.

Both of them bounced the suggestion of one country after another during the quiet evenings together. "Or how about South Africa? The language there is very close to Dutch. It would be easy to assimilate, with not too much of a language barrier," Joh posed. "Or America? How about America? They're always boasting about how they're the land of the free."

"No! Not either of those. There's that ugly apartheid in South Africa, and the States have the draft. There's no way I'm allowing my son to be a soldier! What if he was killed in a war? And Australia? I don't know what got into Klasina and Max's heads to move to Australia. That country is a godless end away from us. We'll never see them again!"

"Canada looks to be about the best. It was the Canadians who drove the Nazis out of our towns. Besides, Willem and Simon are in the Eastern part of the country, closer to us than Jan will be when he goes!"

Nel's brother Jan, with his wife and all twelve children, some of them already adults, were pulling up roots very soon, bound for a place in Canada called British Columbia, to continue Jan's vocation as a dairy farmer somewhere in the Fraser Valley, on the west side of the Rocky Mountains.

"And Canada doesn't have the draft either!" said Nel enthusiastically. But all of those places seemed so very far away to the couple. Everything did. They mulled the choices over in their heads for weeks.

In the meantime, the family lived as they had been, working, congregating with friends, and family, and being parents to two small children. Finally, the decision was settled between the couple. They would emigrate to Canada and join Joh's two brothers in Ontario.

There was much to be done before emigrating, and Joh spent his time shuttling between work, and City Hall, filling in endless forms, writing letters to his brothers with requests for information, visiting friends and family to announce their departure, last visits and goodbyes.

First, the applications to emigrate, and make sure their passports were current. After that, since they rented from the township, there was the de-registration form to be filled out and delivered to the City Hall office. This enabled their townhouse to be re-entered on the wait lists for people looking for housing. And finally, nearer the time, the purchasing of tickets for the voyage across the Atlantic for the four of them. Then came the endless goodbyes. They started with the closest in Alkmaar.

They were settled in the front room of a cousin's home, happily chatting, when Nel suddenly looked around her and asked, "Where is Elly?" There was a momentary silence, as all the adults looked around, puzzled. The usual flurry of her noise and movement was conspicuously absent.

"She was here a few minutes ago. She probably wandered into the backyard," Marijke assured Nel, "but let's go look, just to be sure. The back is fully enclosed so she couldn't have gone far." Nel was well ahead of her cousin before the sentence was finished. The only small body in evidence was that of Jopie, playing alone in the grass to his heart's content, wearing his favourite captain's hat, slightly askew on his head.

"Have you seen your little sister?" Nel asked the boy. He replied, "No," and kept on playing. They checked upstairs and then out in the street, hoping she'd be in the tiny plot of grass and shrubbery that made up the front of the row house. The gate stood slightly ajar. They piled into the street, looking anxiously left and right, only to be met with a vista devoid of small blonde-haired bodies in any direction.

"We have to go to the police!" Joh decided. He wasn't taking any chances or wasting time looking any further. She could have gone in any direction, knowing his daughter and her insatiable curiosity. At the police station, they were met with an officer tending carefully to a familiar, teary-eyed toddler sitting in front of him on the station counter, a candy stuffed into a sticky, bulging and very wet cheek.

"Is this yours?" the smiling officer asked. "I found her wandering on the street, unable to find which house her parents were at!"

"They looked all same!" she wailed. The relief that mama and papa were suddenly standing in front of her was too much for the child, and she began to cry anew. Joh picked her up, mindful of the sticky fingers that greeted him. "Hey hey, you don't need to cry anymore! You've got your favourite thing in your mouth; candy!" Joh tried to soothe his daughter.

"It's not *Opa's* peppermint!" she retorted, and then continued venting her pent-up frustration, "I couldn't find house anymore! They all same! ALL!"

Nel had to laugh a little at the mention of her father's ubiquitous peppermints, and she thought back to last time he'd paid a visit and played his little game.

≈≈≈≈≈≈≈

The little girl stood eagerly before her *Opa*, seated at the table with his cup of tea, and looked up at him expectantly.

"Would you like a peppermint, *Schatje*?" the elderly gentleman asked, knowing full well what would follow. It was a routine he had started with his grandchildren, and they would continue to play the game as long as he allowed it. The child nodded, and the grandfather slowly, and with great deliberation and flourish, removed a roll of King Peppermints out of his vest pocket. With equal deliberation, he opened the foiled end, removed a single peppermint and held the thin, white disc up for her to see. Then, with a flick of his thumb and forefinger, he sent it rolling across the floor.

Elly chased after it eagerly and, instead of popping it in her mouth, brought it obediently back to her grandfather. Hendrik took the disc, broke off a small sliver and put it into her mouth. She wished silently for more than just a small sliver, the peppermint tasted so good! She hung around her grandpa while the peppermint melted in her mouth, in the hopes that more would follow. But, as before, the roll of peppermints disappeared back into the vest pocket, never to be seen again, at least during that particular visit.

Nel's father never gave a child any more than that one small sliver. She knew her father's reasoning for it. He was afraid that a child would choke on a whole peppermint. She also knew there was a second reason that he'd never admit to, He was a little stingy with things he'd give away. He called it being frugal.

≈≈≈≈≈≈≈

Money was very tight for Joh and Nel during those last few years in their home country. It had taken all their savings to buy the tickets from the *Holland-Amerika Lijn* for their passage on the *SS Volendam*.

Even while they were still saving, Joh brought something home that caused his wife to raise her eyebrows. One day he'd come with a balloon-tire scooter as a present to their son. It was a necessary extravagance as far as he was concerned. Jopie was growing fast, and he had very little in the way of toys and other child-friendly items to keep him occupied. Joh justified the purchase with the fact that it was second-hand, not new. He'd bought it from someone who no longer needed it. The little boy spent hours riding up and down the sidewalk, proud of his new skill in standing with one foot on the runner, while pushing off with his other foot.

Elly was also enamoured of the scooter, even though the handlebars were still much too high for her. She tried gamely to ride it the way she'd seen her brother do it. It led to a small disaster one day, while Jopie was in *kleuterschool*.

"Go home! I'm just going to see *Tante* Annie for a few minutes. I won't be gone long!" Nel stood on the sidewalk in front of their house, looking crossly at her stubborn little daughter. Elly was coming up behind her, pushing herself with difficulty on her brother's scooter, of all things. The child barely came up to the handlebars, and her hands were holding on awkwardly as she came.

"Elly! You bad girl! I told you, go HOME!" Nel scolded. Elly could be stubborn. Well, she could be just as stubborn and refused to let the girl come with her, out of principle now. Elly hesitated, afraid to disobey but desperately wanting to go see auntie. Her mother turned her back and continued on to the end of the block where Anna lived, angry at the child's obstinacy.

Holland-Amerika Lijn - *Dutch spelling of Holland America Line*
kleuterschool - *kindergarten*
tante - *aunt*

As she neared her sister's door, Nel stopped suddenly and turned once more, to make sure her daughter had obeyed. As she did, she felt something hard collide against her legs, and she cried out at the pain. Angrier than ever, at the prospect of another large ugly bruise, she looked down at the daughter-scooter combo that had run roughly into her. She was partway through her tirade but stopped when she saw blood streaming from Elly's mouth. It was the last straw.

"Oh, child! Look what you've done now! That's your punishment for not obeying me! You've cut your tongue on the handlebars! I've told you time and time again. You're too small to be riding Jopie's scooter! You're such a bad girl! Open your mouth and show me your tongue!" Nel scolded the little girl before looking at the tongue, now sticking out of a tearful face. It had a deep cut near the tip.

"Now the doctor will have to stitch up your tongue!" The angry mother hoped that the mental image of needle and thread violating that very sensitive part would frighten Elly enough to teach her obedience.

The visit to Anna postponed, Nel set her daughter into the front carrier on her bike, and pedaled to the doctor's office some streets over. Once again Elly was instructed to stick out her tongue. The frightened little girl complied obediently, tears and panic close to the surface of her suddenly docile demeanour.

She listened as mama talked of stitches with the doctor. 'Stitches' was an utterly surreal concept when that word was paired with 'tongue'. Fear struck like lightning, and the little girl wondered how she would eat. How would she talk? In the next instant, however, the dread was eased when she heard the doctor say to her mother, "Oh no, it's impossible to stitch up a cut like that on the tongue! That will heal on its own."

Nel was not happy with that news. She'd hoped that stitches would be a solid, sustained reminder of her daughter's disobedience. Upon arriving home, she set the two-year-old loose in the fenced and gated backyard and told her to play quietly with her doll and toy carriage. The next day, Elly was back on the scooter, pushing herself resolutely around and around the tiny backyard, her face pointed well away from those handlebars. Nel could only marvel at the dogged determination of the child.

The time to leave the Netherlands for good was drawing nearer, and both Nel and Joh were somewhat stressed at the prospect of the move; he, in excited anticipation, and she with second thoughts. She thought of her family. If her mother had still been alive, there would be no question of her leaving. Nel's father was getting on in years, and becoming senile. She knew he was in good hands with all her older brothers and sisters willing and able to look after him with love and care. Joh's father had died in July. Nel would follow her husband.

As she began making preparations for dinner, Nel heard the familiar cheerful strains of a *draaiorgel* in the distance. She groaned. If that thing was coming down her street, she knew what would happen next. Elly was fascinated with barrel organs. The music seemed to be the only thing that stopped the child in her tracks as she listened, but she knew that Elly would also wheedle her out of money to drop into the operator's copper cup, as he clacked it in time to the music. Money was so scarce, and she needed literally every penny for food and expenses. Sure enough. The music drew nearer, and Elly came running excitedly in from the yard and demanded a coin for the *draaiorgel.* "No! I don't have a lot of money to give away." Nel resolved to be stubborn.

"Please Mama, please! Please please please!"
"No, I told you!"

"Please Mama! I go outside and listen!" The girl's entire body seemed to dance with the deep thrumming and higher peals of the various musical notes produced by the large calliope-like instrument. Nel gave in, handing her a tiny *dupje*, and watched through the window as Elly ran out into the street, empty of all save the approaching barrel organ and its operator.

As Joh was turning into his street on the bike, he saw his daughter ahead of him, standing stock still, staring up at the massive barrel organ,

draaiorgel - *barrel organ*
dupje - *ten cents. (slang term for dime)*

her hand outstretched towards the operator's proffered copper cup. Joh stopped for a moment, got off his bike and savoured the scene. The man had ceased turning the large wheel that worked the bellows blowing air through the punched-out paper on the rollers. He waited for the tiny girl who held out a coin for him. He held out his cup, jingling it as he did, and she dropped the coin into it.

The man stood where he was with his barrel organ, and resumed turning the large wheel behind the ornate facade. As the rolling high notes and booming thunder of the drums washed over her, the little girl stood listening, spellbound.

To Joh, watching from the end of the street, who rarely saw his excitable little girl stand in one place for very long, it looked as if she was tied with an invisible cord to the source of the music. It wouldn't have surprised him to see the child follow the instrument down the street, and he hurried ahead on his bike to make sure that didn't happen. He needn't have worried. Elly went running back to her door with her face aglow.

He heard the youngster's high-pitched voice float through the still-open door. "I heard the *draaiorgel,* Mama! Wasn't it wonderful?" The child never realized it would be a long, long time before she would ever hear that sound again.

The voyage was imminent now. Joh had built the wooden crate that would hold all their worldly possessions, and it stood in a relative's barn, waiting for the contents to be loaded. There were still some last-minute decisions to be made such as; what was to be left behind? What was to be taken?

"You can't take that! It belongs to the township!"

Nel stood on a small step ladder as she argued with her husband. "I'm taking this, I don't care what you claim." she snapped at him.

The exchange came at the very end of yet another long-running argument. The object of her attention this time was the ceiling lamp hanging in the front hallway. Nel had grown attached to it and was bound and determined to take it with them.

"You can't take it, it belongs with the house! It's the property of the City of Alkmaar." was Joh's argument. It had already raged for days, to the point where even Jopie, barely five years old now, began to subtly drop hints that his father was right. Nel paid no attention.

Joh continued to assert; they'd moved into this house with the lamp already hanging in the hallway, the township owned the house, and what came with the house, stayed with the house. Those were the rules.

The rules fell on deaf ears. Nel took the lamp down, packed it with the rest of their belongings, and buried it deep in the wood crate. Joh fully expected someone from City Hall to come running after them on the way to Rotterdam with the booty. Perhaps he would find a letter addressed to him in care of his brother's address, demanding its return. If that happened he'd return it and bear the brunt of his wife's stubborn anger. Right now, he was weary of the arguing and gave up.

Suitcases stood in the hall, where the dangling electrical cord hung forlornly from the ceiling, minus its appendage. The house was empty, the crate had been shipped ahead of them, and the family stood ready to leave. At the last minute, Joh cut the cord away from the ceiling to make it less obvious that the lamp was missing. He hoped he'd be spared the embarrassment of being stopped on the way out of town, but Nel just laughed at him, "They're not going to come running after you for something so stupid." she fired back at him.

Family arranged to have them driven to Rotterdam, and the waiting ship, a good two and a half hours' drive away. Everyone was exhausted already from the upheaval, even the children, who promptly fell asleep in the car.

As they entered the harbour area, and finally stopped, the three-year-old child woke with a start. "Are we in Canada now?" she asked in a sleepy and querulous voice. The adults laughed, and Joh thought if only the Atlantic crossing would be that fast. It would be a ten-day journey and he knew there would be seasickness involved if there was any rough weather.

The family had gathered at the pier to say their final farewells. There had already been so many tears shed at exactly the same kind of parting, and this was just one more. It felt like a bell rang somewhere, tolling out its doom; an ending. Such were the distances that separated family members. Overseas letters became the last links between them.

On June 13, 1950, Joh climbed the gangplank with his family, never looking back. His dreams lay in the future in a new country, full of the hopes of young men just like him.

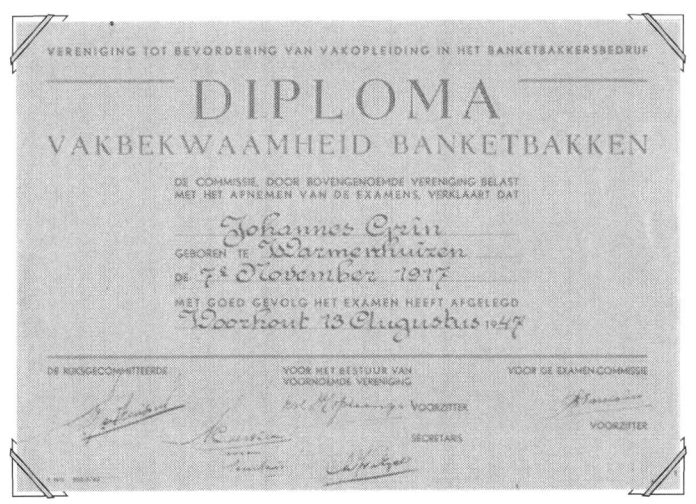

Alkmaar, Fall, 1947: Joh, and his young family in front of the last home they lived in

Summer, 1948: Jopie with his scooter on the sidewalk. Joh, watching through the living room window.

Joh's Pastry Baker's Diploma ; *(translation)* Association For the Promotion of Vocational Training in the Pastry Industry
DIPLOMA
PROFESSIONAL COMPETENCE
the committee referred to above, charged with conducting
the examinations, declares that
Johannes Grin (birthplace, birth date)
successfully passed the exam, dated Aug. 13, 1947

Joh (4th from left, in baker's cap) with his fellow employees at S. A. Muller Banketbakkerij, Alkmaar

Friendly game of *Klaverjassen*, after work. Joh w/baker's hat & cigarette in mouth, seen sitting behind racks of cookies.

(Above) Working the bakery machinery, mixing the large amounts of ingredients required.

(Above) Joh (back row in Baker's hat) and workmates, at another unidentified place of work.

Elly, father, and Jopie, enjoying a good story. Early 1950

Joh's ration booklet: post-war (both sides)

Various post-war ration stamps. These were issued at regular intervals to citizens and handed in as needed, when cashed for food and other necessities, such as fuel, clothing and even tobacco.

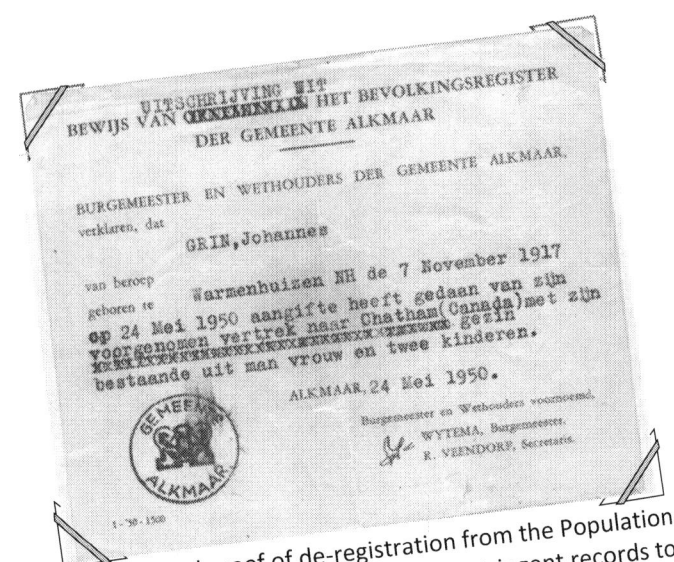

Official proof of de-registration from the Population Register. The township kept stringent records to ensure there were no squatters living in unoccupied homes.

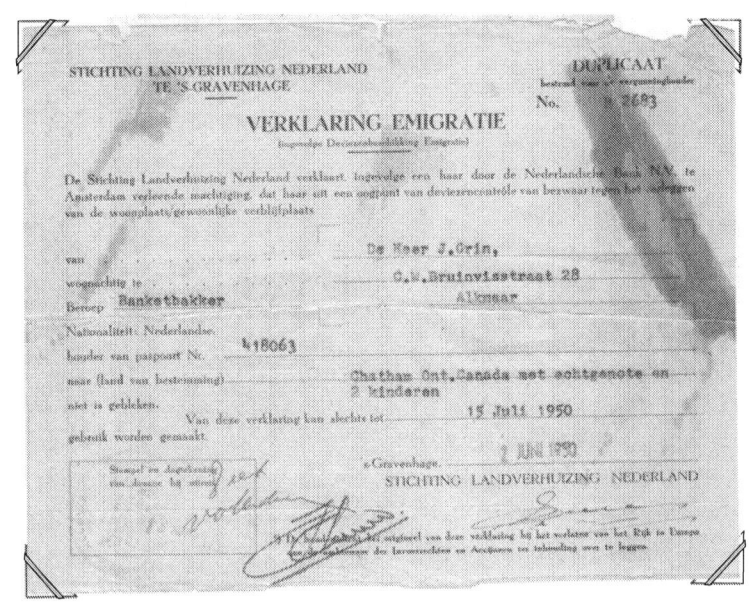

Declaration of Emigration. Issued June 2, 1950 and valid until July 15, 1950. Joh had a month and a half grace, to change his mind.

SAYING GOODBYE

Sitting with family at Rotterdam pier; from left, inside white frame - Joh, S.I.L Marie, Nel, Jopie, (in front of Nel) Elly, Lies (sister of Nel), Tinus & Jans (B.I.L & sister of Nel)

Joh's passport photo
- 1950

Holland America Line's SS *Volendam*

BECOMING IMMIGRANTS

Voyage to Canada

The Grin family on deck of the *SS Volendam*

CHAPTER 11

SS VOLENDAM,
Atlantic Ocean,
DAY 5, JUNE 17, 1950

Joh lay in his bunk, his young son in the one next to him. The cabin's floor pitched wildly under the bed, and he wanted to die, but couldn't. He'd never felt so sick in all his adult life and wondered how Jopie was faring. The boy looked white and an odiferous pile lay splattered on the floor beside his bed. He made a mental note to ask a porter for some cleaning supplies, but at the moment he just couldn't deal with it. Maybe the porter would clean it up. He could only hope, but for now, he didn't really care one way or the other. It briefly flitted through his mind, how it was even possible to care and not care, all at the same time, then, as another wave of nausea hit him, he stopped thinking altogether.

"Mama? Where's Papa and Jopie?" The question came over the howling wind as Nel and her daughter stood on the heaving deck, watching gigantic walls of water whip up around the ship. "They're seasick below deck, in their beds," her mother answered. "Oh." The child thought a minute, and then concluded proudly, "Only boys get seasick, don't they Mama! Us girls never get seasick!" Nel laughed, "No, we certainly don't! But we will freeze if we don't get inside!"

They stood a moment more watching the roiling water, then made their way inside to the comforts of the inside lounge areas. Nel doubted that the male contingent of her family would make an appearance for dinner.

The under-the-weather male members of the family seemed a bit better the next day, with the ship traveling in calmer weather. Jopie especially, ate ravenously, thanks to the lack of food intake the previous day. Joh's appetite still seemed a little dampened, and he picked at the plate in front of him.

"I wonder if there's much work for pastry chefs in Canada?" Joh mused aloud. Now that he was committed to his decision, self-doubt welled up in his gut. It felt a little uncomfortable, frightening even. What if he couldn't find work? His English was poor. He'd have to start learning all over again. All kinds of negative thoughts tumbled through his mind, as he sat staring at the food on his plate.

"If I can't work in a bakery, I'll have to find something elsewhere, until I get the job I want," he decided. Nel looked at him as she pushed her son forward so he'd eat above his plate. The children still tended to spill half the food into their laps. "I worry more about where we're going to live, and how. What are prices like for rent? Are people friendly? What about our crate?"

The spoonful of oatmeal she held, stopped halfway to her mouth. "What if they lose it? We'd have nothing!"

"It's on the boat with us, and clearly marked with my name and Wim's address. I wouldn't worry too much about that," Joh answered. Both adults continued to stress silently over their particular brand of worries, as they finished their breakfast. It seemed as if the ship was an island, with them captive on board in the middle of nowhere, almost, but not quite, isolating them from the doubts and insecurities that were bubbling to the surface. They could only bide their time and hope that the new world was kind in dispensing its favours.

Along with his private worries, Joh kept thinking about what they'd found when they boarded the *Volendam*. He hadn't thought about it much, but he'd had a distinct impression that cruise ships were supposed to be nothing but luxury. He'd discovered through various conversations with pursers and others that worked on board, that the tired old ship had served as more than just transport for happy-go-lucky vacation seekers. She'd been put into service by the Allies during the war and had served as a troop carrier, shuttling soldiers back and forth all over the world. After the war, Holland America loaned her out to the United Nations Refugee Association, to take German Mennonites to Argentina for resettlement. As well, the *Volendam* had carried emigrants looking for a new life, to the United States, Argentina, Australia and Canada.

Although the ship had been refitted in Glasgow, they found the amenities were sparse. There were no private accommodations. Instead, the cabins contained anywhere from four to eight berths, along with actual dorm-like spaces that slept around fifty. Men and boys slept separate from women and girls, so Joh and his son were assigned to a different non-private cabin from his wife and daughter.

Washing facilities were shared in each area, and Nel hoped they could give the children a much-needed bath in one of the bath areas. She waited with the chore until after breakfast when it was less crowded. There had been such a crowd in the facilities beforehand, and Nel could only hope that more people didn't come up with the same tactic as she did; waiting until the commotion died down.

Nel was more than a little put out that they had actually paid for this. Somehow, they'd missed out on a government resettlement scheme that would have seen their passage paid for. "I pay my own way! I don't take handouts!" had been Joh's response to her complaint.

She held on to that anger as she thrust her little girl into the shower stall, where water was already streaming from high above. Elly began to scream in terror, a reaction far removed from her usual bath time behaviour.

"Stand still while I wash you," Nel commanded. The child wailed and struggled to get out from under the stinging sluice of water. The mother had no patience left and forced her daughter to stay in the shower while she soaped her down. Nel fervently hoped that her husband was having an equal amount of grief in his own cabin, as she thought of all the money they'd paid for this travesty of a trip. To think it could have all been free.

Later that day, they sat in the lounging area. On deck earlier, the stiff wind had driven them back inside. Joh suddenly looked around him. "Where are the kids?" The alarm in his voice was noticeable. Nel looked up from her book and gazed around.

"They were here," she said. "They can't be too far away."

"I'll go look for them." Joh got up and made his way around the lounge and then out on deck. There were children on deck, but not his. He turned around and walked the other way. Inside, Nel was suddenly confronted by a purser with two children in tow.

"I found them on the upper decks, *Mevrouw*. They were having a bit of trouble with the strength of the wind." He handed the two back to their mother. "Your little girl especially, couldn't reach the door, the wind against her was too strong. I had to reach for her and pull her inside." Nel imagined, watching the purser's back as he walked away, *he probably thinks I'm an awful woman for not constantly sitting on my children.*

Joh came back, ready to tell his wife, the children were nowhere to be found. The relief he felt was palpable when he saw two familiar blonde heads accompanying Nel. "Where were they?" he asked as the worry dropped away.

"Oh … they were doing a little exploring, and just got back." Nel purposely neglected to tell him they'd been found by a purser, in a bit of trouble. There was no sense in upsetting him further. She'd mind them stringently from now on.

On the tenth day, the ship steamed up the St. Lawrence River towards Quebec City. A weary family stood at the rail watching as the city came into view. The day before, five-year-old Jopie had looked flushed, and seemed a little listless. Nel had wondered if he was simply overtired from the voyage or actually feverish. She had no thermometer to check, so she'd taken him to the ship's doctor. Jopie was diagnosed with a mild case of influenza and Nel had been told that before being allowed to go on to their final destination of Chatham, Ontario, the youngster would have to be admitted to hospital for more tests and a possible quarantine, depending on what they found.

Nel looked forward to disembarking with some trepidation. In her opinion, her son suffered nothing more than common flu and would be fine in a few days. These Canadians seemed to be a little overzealous in their reaction to a little bit of illness.

The ship's doctor had arranged for them to be taken to a hospital for check-in and she hoped someone there would be able to speak Dutch. Nel knew only a smattering of English and no French at all. Joh knew, or, in the case of French, didn't know, an equal amount, so, even between the two of them, their communication with the people at the hospital would be hampered.

Upon their arrival, the family was quickly whisked away to the waiting doctors and nurses and installed in a room overlooking a great expanse of lawn. What was noticeable immediately to the very Dutch Protestant couple, were the nuns that walked around in full imposing habit. Both of them felt immediately and completely out of their element.

Roman Catholicism was mysterious and eerie. There were strange rituals, incense burning and prayers in a language that nobody understood. Worst of all to them, was the worship of, and prayers to saints and other people who they felt could not answer them. That amounted to sacrilege to Joh and Nel. And now, here they were, in a Roman Catholic hospital, in the thick of them, unable to continue their journey.

Elly stuck close to her mother's side, overawed by the sight of her big brother in a bed, so high above her, and the stiffly starched, white clothed ladies that seemed to be bustling everywhere. One of those starched ladies came into the room shortly after Nel had undressed her brother and gotten him into the bed. She had a tray in her hand with something covered by a sterile white cloth. The tray was briskly set down on a side table. The cloth was whisked away to reveal a large glass and metal syringe.

After some unintelligible words in French, the nurse proceeded to take Jopie's arm and plunged the needle home. He began to scream. Nel's motherly instincts kicked in and her eyes blazed. The nurse uttered something in a soothing sympathetic voice, took the tray and walked out of the room. Nel tried her best to comfort the sobbing boy and rubbed his arm. Joh stood on the other side of the bed and did his best to look sympathetic, but he had other things on his mind as well.

"It was only a vaccination of some sort," he told Nel. "All kids cry when they get needles, you know that." He tried to reason. She was not so sure, her mother bear mode not yet tempered down to a pragmatic level.

"They bustled us off to the hospital so fast, I never got a chance to arrange for our crate to get shipped to the final address," he explained to his wife. "I've got to go and see about that. I have no idea what's happening with it. For all I know, someone could be walking off with it right now." Nel wished he hadn't told her that. Now, not only was she worried about her son, she was also worried about all their belongings.

"Are you going to be alright by yourself here?" he asked her. "I think so, as long as you're not too long. I can't understand a word of what they say!" she complained. "Try and find someone who can translate for you," Joh suggested. Nel promised she would and he gave her a peck goodbye and left the hospital.

CHAPTER 12

Québec City to Chatham

Joh thought he remembered the way back to the wharves and as he walked he looked for certain landmarks he'd noted on the way in. He'd only gone a few blocks when a police wagon showed up and stopped beside him. Curious, Joh stopped and looked at them inquisitively, thinking perhaps he could get them to verify that he was going in the right direction. They began speaking to him, first in French, then in English. He understood a few words, like "family", and "where", so he began to explain that his family was at the hospital. The officers shook their heads, they didn't seem to understand his Dutch. He showed them his paperwork and passport, which they took and stared at intently.

Before he realized what was happening, he was suddenly taken by the arm quite forcefully and pushed into the wagon. There was another man already sitting inside, who seemed equally nonplussed at being there. Joh tried speaking to the man, but he didn't understand Joh's Dutch either. The van continued on its way. Occasionally, it stopped, and a few more men were put into the van. When the van stopped moving altogether and both rear doors finally opened, the entire lot of men were escorted into a building. Joh read the words on the sign above the door perfectly: *Poste de Police*, and underneath, *Police Station*. But he simply had no idea why he'd been picked up.

In the cell with yet more men, Joh grew a little curious about why they'd all been rounded up. All of them appeared to be freshly arrived immigrants, and suddenly he began to have doubts about the country he'd chosen. For a moment it crossed his mind that this was some sort of a fascist regime they'd innocently walked into. Then common sense kicked in. Of course not. They'd done the research and heard the reports from his family already here. There was a reasonable explanation somewhere in this mess.

His ears picked up some Dutch in the rumbling of conversations around him and Joh button-holed the man who was the source. "Do you know why we're in here?" he asked as he sat down beside the Dutchman. "Damned if I know," he answered laconically. "So, I suppose we just wait it out until they tell us, right?" Joh answered back, hoping to start a half-friendly conversation with a fellow countryman. Another terse reply. "Yup."

"Where are you from?" "Schagerbrug."

"Ah. That's a little north of us."

The conversation petered out after that, and so they sat, each of them steeping in their own thoughts and fears. Some dozed. Throughout the rest of the day and into the evening, one by one, the men were taken out, Joh supposed, to be questioned. Then, just after sunrise the following day, someone called him. He was escorted to a sparsely furnished, windowless room, and faced two men.

"*Mijnheer* Grin," said one of the men. Joh felt a twinge of relief that he'd be able to understand at least one of the two.

"Yes, that's me," he responded politely. The man turned to his partner and said something in French. A translator, Joh thought, good.

"Do you know why you're here?" the translator asked him.

"Not really. It was going to be my first question to you." A bit of sarcasm crept into his voice. Now he was suddenly worried about what Nel and the kids were thinking, on top of the concern over all of their belongings. "I have a wife and two children stuck in a hospital with no idea where I am! There's no one to look after them, plus all our belongings are only God knows where, and I need to take care of all of it before we have bigger problems."

"We're sorry about that, but we have problems of our own with runaway family men, who are abandoning their families. We had to make sure you weren't one of them." Joh was a little shocked that there were men that would do such a thing and he assured the police that wasn't his intention at all. "Here are my references. I have two brothers waiting for me in Chatham." He pulled his brother Wim's address out of his pocket and handed it to them.

After some further questions, which Joh surmised he answered correctly, all his paperwork, and passport were handed back to him and he was free to go. Now he had to hustle to get things in order. He spotted a taxi and waved it down. In broken English, he tried the words for wharf and ship. To his delight, the driver responded with, "Ah, you're Dutch! Great, you want to go to the docks where the ships berth?"

Joh could have wept with relief at the sound of another Dutch voice. "Yes, please! I've been sitting in a police cell since yesterday morning. My wife has no idea where I am, and my crate with belongings could be halfway to hell by now." His relief, mingled with frustration came tumbling out, as he continued. "I've got to get down there and see if somebody can help me find out what happened to it."

"Hang on to your hat. I'll get you there and fix it up in no time," came back the enthusiastic reply. "Get in!" Joh climbed into the taxi and was flung back into the seat as the driver mashed down on the gas pedal. In no time they were at their destination. They stared in disbelief at an empty wharf, save for one, lone, familiar-looking crate, standing all by itself in the middle of the abandoned dock.

"There it is," Joh exclaimed. "I don't believe it!"

The driver got out of the taxi and began to laugh. "Somebody's looking out for you, my man! That crate could have been picked up by anybody by now."

It's unbelievable, but, all's well that ends well, Joh thought. Now, all he needed to do was explain it all to his wife and probably peel her down off the ceiling afterwards.

The cabby continued, "There's a shipping company nearby here. Come on, I'll take you over and get you sorted out." The men continued on to the shipper, and, with the cab man as a translator, arranged to have the crate shipped to Chatham. Next was the purchase of train tickets.

Joh and the cabby, who had introduced himself as Paulus from

Haarlem, made their way to the train station, the location of which was a familiar destination for Paulus. He parked and led Joh inside to the ticket booths, where the cab driver proceeded to request four train tickets, two adults and two children. Joh dug into his pocket for his wallet, paid the ticket agent and turned to thank Paulus for all his help.

"I'm so happy I met you," said Joh, as he shook Paulus' hand. "Oh, think nothing of it," the man returned. "I would have done the same for anyone. What else are we here for, if not to help? Come on, I'll take you back to the hospital. Your poor wife will be frantic."

It suddenly hit Joh, he had money left, but he wasn't at all sure that there would be enough left over after paying for the taxi, for what else he needed to do, like buy food and pay rent until he found a job.

"No, no! That's alright, I can walk from here. How much do I owe you for the fare?" Joh dug again into his pocket to pull out some bills. The cabby laughed. "You don't owe me a nickel! I'm just glad I was around at the right time for you. Use that money to help somebody else who needs it, somewhere down the road."

Joh stood for a moment, dumbfounded that after all the running around there would be no charge for the taxi. The cabby started laughing again. "Didn't you see that the meter was never turned on?" he said gleefully. Joh admitted he'd been too wound up over the overnight incarceration, worry about the crate, and his wife's expected reaction. "I should repay you with something," he insisted. "You can repay me by helping someone else," was the Cabby's answer. "Now, get back in the car. Your wife and children need you."

Joh didn't need to be asked twice and he slid into the seat, grateful he'd found some much-needed help.

At the hospital, the two men shook hands. And as he watched the taxi drive away, Joh could only marvel that there were still such human beings left in the world, after all the evil he'd seen in the past ten years. Then, still in awe, he ascended the hospital steps.

Coming down the hall where his son's ward was, he could hear loud voices and a child screaming. *Did that sound like Jopie?* And was that his wife's voice raised a decibel or two higher in sheer frustration? He entered the ward, only to collide with a nurse coming out. He narrowly missed knocking the cloth-covered tray out of her hand. Inside, he was greeted with a completely undone wife, a wide-eyed, frightened little girl by her side, and a red-faced boy with his mouth wide open in mid-shriek.

Nel flew into his arms. "Where were you?" The distraught woman stared at him, gripping his arms and giving him a shake. "You've been gone for a full twenty-four hours! Was the crate not there? Have we lost everything? I've been going crazy with worry! I've had an awful time here! Nobody would translate! We're not Roman Catholic, that's got to be the reason!"

"Stop, stop! Slow down. Let me tell you what happened!" Joh tried to calm his wife. "First of all, the crate will be on its way to Chatham today. No need to worry about that." Joh proceeded to tell her all that had happened while he was gone. "So now, tell me what's going on with Jopie, why is he so upset?"

"All they did was give him one injection after the other! It never seemed to stop and the poor boy screamed at the top of his lungs every single time, it hurt him so much!" The anger was palpable in her eyes.

"Just now, I finally stood between him and those needles and said no! No more!" Joh raised his eyebrows. "You told the hospital people, No?"

"Yes! And I think they got the message. There's nothing wrong with him!" Nel lifted her chin defiantly, pointing at Jopie. "Go talk to the doctors, I want to get out of here!"

They spent another day at the hospital, while Joh tried valiantly in his severely broken English, to get some answers. Finally, the doctor handed him a sheet of paper, which he looked over carefully. At the bottom, he saw a few words that he understood only as something negative. He shot the doctor a questioning look. "We can leave? Go? Goodbye?" He tried all the words that he knew might bring his question across. The doctor nodded his head, and made a shooing motion with his hands, but escorted him to a wicket before he left. There would be a small payment for the stay.

They couldn't wait to get out of there. Everyone was tired of sleeping in chairs. The food was sub-par as far as Nel was concerned, and the children were beyond tired. Joh splurged on a taxi, almost hoping he'd run into Paulus again so he could at least pay him for something. The taxi cab that he'd flagged down had a French-speaking driver, so there was no friendly conversation after the words train and station were uttered.

On the train, the family stared silently out the windows at the empty landscape that slid by. Joh marveled at the open spaces. So much land. So much room. It was a far cry from his own country, where every village, town and city seemed to butt up against one another, vying for space. There was farmland, to be sure, but what he saw now was space on a whole different level.

"It's not like Holland, is it?" Nel remarked. "Of course not. This is an entirely different country," Joh laughed. "You'd better get used to more space!" Nel was silent and he looked at her, asking, "What are you thinking?"

She lifted her shoulders in a small shrug but did not answer. Joh wondered if she would adapt. He hoped so for her own sake, as well as his. But he chalked up her reticence to fatigue.

Finally, the farmlands began slowly changing to include more buildings, homes, factories, and in the distance, higher buildings. His brothers were there, waiting for him to arrive. He'd sent a telegram ahead with their arrival time before they left. The ordeal was almost over but he wondered what other surprises awaited him.

As Joh stepped off the train behind his wife and children, he spotted his brother, Willem, and Grietjanne in the crowd on the platform. The reunion was joyous, with hugs, kisses, and back-clapping. The children barely remembered their *Oom* Wim and *Tante* Grietjanne, and held back behind their mother for a bit, until their aunt hugged them fiercely. It wasn't long before all were talking excitedly.

Wim and Grietjanne lived on a farm, growing vegetables for the

---

oom - uncle

tante - aunt

local markets. Again, the couple marveled at the spaces between as they drove to their destination. Joh had a sensation of excitement fluttering behind his breastbone, thinking, he'll be a part of something much bigger than the stifled milieu that he'd left behind. He couldn't wait to get started, but he'd had enough of farming. Digging in the dirt was something he'd done plenty of in his lifetime. No more.

Over coffee and homemade *boterkoek* and *zuikerkoekjes*, the adults discussed their plans for the future. The children played outside, exploring foreign soil. Grietjanne suddenly rose from her chair. "I have to feed the chickens!"

"Oh, why don't you let the children feed them? They'd probably love something like that," Nel said delightedly. "Are you sure about that? Those chickens can be awfully overwhelming when they see the feed pail coming. Especially for two small children," countered Wim.

"Chickens are harmless," declared Nel. Joh began to laugh. "To the kids, those chickens coming at them will look like monsters!" All the adults chuckled and agreed, Wim adding, "We have quite the flock, and they love their feed!"

Nel pulled out her old box camera. I have a few pictures left on the roll. It will make some great photographs."

"Are you sure about this?" Wim asked his sister-in-law.
"Sure, why not, the chickens won't kill them."

The four of them went outside, Nel, camera in hand, while Willem unhooked a pail from the side of the shed, filled it with feed, then called the two youngsters over. "How would you like to feed the chickens in that pen over there? It's a big job, can you do it?" Jopie nodded eagerly. He was a big boy, having traveled over a great big ocean, so he felt he could handle some chickens. Elly looked at her big brother. She could do anything her big brother could do. *Oom* Wim gave them instructions on taking the feed pail into the enclosed pen and spreading its contents around in a wide

---

<u>boterkoek</u> - butter cake - an almond flavoured square

<u>zuikerkoekjes</u> - sugar cookies

swath, so the hens would have some space to eat without being crowded with other chickens.

Both children nodded solemnly. They could do this. With the feed pail between them, they entered the chicken pen and walked toward the flock. As one, the chickens saw the pail coming and made a concerted scrabble towards them for the food. Both children stopped in their tracks, eyes saucer wide as they saw the beasts coming.

Joh began to laugh. "Throw the feed out to them! They want the food, not you," he shouted at them. Meanwhile, Nel took pictures, peering into the tiny top viewer, showing an upside-down image, trying to find the best view of the madly scrambling chickens and visibly intimidated children. She, along with all the adults, was shaking with laughter.

They began throwing the feed, but the chickens crowded them. Finally, in panic, both young chicken feeders turned and fled towards the safety of the fence, the now-forgotten pail still between them. They hadn't even emptied it yet. The hens scrambled after them, still determined to eat their fill of all they were entitled to. The four adults leaned over the fence holding their sides, but Grietjanne scolded the rest as she tried in vain to stop laughing. "Those poor kids! What were you thinking? They must be terrified!"

"Oh, they'll get over it, I'm sure," chortled Nel, wiping her eyes. "I just hope I got some good pictures."

Willem took the proffered pail from his nephew, who announced with bravado, "*Oom* Wim, I wasn't scared! They're just chickens!" *His eyes are a little too wide though,* Willem thought. He looked at Elly's white face. She stared wide-eyed back at the birds, now pecking frantically at the ground, saying nothing.

As the entire group made their way back to the house, Willem tried to distract the brother and sister from the all-too-recent monster encounter. "Listen, there's something else you two need to know. You're in Canada now, so, I'm no longer *Oom* Wim. You have to call me Uncle Bill from now on."

Jopie looked wide-eyed at his uncle and contorted his face in typical little boy mirth at something forbidden. The boy's Dutch was still in force. "Ung-kle-*Bill*," he snorted.

Willem's eyebrow rose, not only at his nephew's reaction but at the hoots that came from his brother and sister-in-law. Then he realized what his English name sounded like to freshly arrived Dutch-speaking folk. "Bill" was the Dutch name for a body part, namely the bum. Jopie was only too delighted to tag his uncle with that name.

Willem could only laugh at himself for not thinking this through. Of course. But he knew in the coming years that he'd be referred to as "Uncle Bill" after the children had become thoroughly familiar with the English language. Luckily, Grietjanne would have an easier time of it. Her name was Margaret in English.

CHAPTER 13

Meaford to Barrie, Ontario
1950 - 1952

Nel looked around the simple cabin her husband had rented as their temporary home. He'd found a job fairly fast in Meaford, at Wilcox Bakery, the local bakery in town. She wasn't all that impressed at the sparseness of the little house, but it was only temporary. At best, this was a summer cabin for people to spend their vacations in, not something permanent. She'd exercise a bit of patience until Joh could find a permanent home, hopefully before winter.

The crate had finally arrived with all their belongings, and the children were excited to finally see their few precious toys again. To them it had seemed like an age ago, when they'd watched as their Papa had packed everything in this huge box, to ship to a mysterious place far, far away. It stood now in the shadow of the sign "Hoppy's Cabins".

Looking at the large wooden sign posted on the highway, Nel thought at least she wouldn't get lost if ever she left the property. Not that she'd go very far. Everything was so removed from everything else. The immense spaces between one place and another, even going into town from where she was, made her feel small and helpless.

Joh had a borrowed crowbar in his hand and climbed to the top of the crate. He began prying the first of the planks off the top, while the children bounced up and down in excitement, waiting for the first glimpses of their treasures. Joh rooted around and finally brought two items up almost simultaneously: a doll's crib and a captain's hat. The children squealed with delight as their favourite things were lowered down to them. Joh thought children were so happy with such simple things, as he watched them walk off with their hands full.

He continued to unpack the rest of the crate slowly, handing things down to Nel as it came to his hand. By the end of the afternoon, it was half empty. The planks were nailed back, and each liberated item was carefully placed to help make the little cabin seem more like home.

They had no sooner settled in than Joh came home from work one day to discover Nel in a dark mood. He was greeted with "Jopie is sick again! He's full of spots, so I'm sure it's measles! I've been trying to keep him in bed, but he constantly wants to come out and be with me. Elly wants to stay in bed and play with him, instead of leaving him alone!"

Joh's reply was practical but didn't offer any foreseeable respite from sick children. "She's bound to get measles too, so why not let her stay in the same room and play if he wants the company? All kids get these childhood illnesses anyway, so the sooner she gets it too, the sooner it will all be over and done with."

For the next two weeks, both children were housebound, irritable, feverish in turn at the beginning, and finally bored with each other. When it had all passed, Nel was more than ready to divest herself of house-bound activities and get out more.

The Dutch lady in the neighbouring cabin took an interest in the young family and invited Nel over for tea one day. She took her daughter with her for a visit. Jopie had strict instructions to stay in the front yard to play if he didn't want to visit with the nice lady, which he happily agreed to. Tea didn't particularly interest him.

As mother and daughter sat on the sofa, and the lady served tea and biscuits, Nel noticed the large toy pandas that were displayed on the other side of the room.

"What large stuffed toys you have there! I have never seen such big ones before," she exclaimed.

The lady brought one down to show Nel, and as she brought it closer to the couch, Elly shrank back against her mother. "We won these over the years at the fair," the woman explained proudly. My late husband had an excellent aim at the bottle toss booths." She set the bear down beside the child, who buried her face into her mother's side. It was the same size as the little girl. "Oh no, you're not afraid of a toy are you?" Nel laughed. "Oh, come on. Be a big girl. Look, it's not going to hurt you!" She pushed the oversized bear closer to Elly, but the three-year-old wasn't having any of it.

The neighbour pulled the bear away a little, realizing it might be a little overwhelming. "Oh, don't force her. She's never seen one of these, has she?" Nel admitted that she never had, but at the same time insisted that her little girl not be afraid of something as harmless as a stuffed toy panda, no matter how large. Still, the tot could not be persuaded that, with its beady eyes, the unnerving thing beside her could be trusted. It was just a little too scary.

The ladies continued their visit while Elly kept a wary eye on the bears, all of them, as if they would suddenly awaken and lumber towards her with unknown horrors in mind. The one beside her on the couch was especially watched, but the bears kept their own counsel. However, she stayed alert for any possible attack. Cookies helped soothe the frayed nerves only a little.

Nel was practicing her school-taught English as much as she could, and her new friend coached her with more words to learn. When mother and daughter left, Elly was first out the door, a little too gladly as far as Nel was concerned.

That fall the family experienced their first ever Halloween. Nel knew that adults and children in costumes would be knocking on the door looking for candy. She hadn't give much thought to how her own children would react and when the expected knock came, the children were the first to reach the door. They opened it to a tall figure dressed all in black, with a wide-brimmed hat, hooked nose and green face. Both gave a shriek and ran for the bedroom, slamming the door behind them.

Nel could hear them whispering frantically to each other behind the door. "Will it kill Mama? What is it going to do? Maybe we should rescue her!" Nel was doubled over, laughing so hard she forgot all about the candy waiting to be dispensed.

Meaford was a tiny hamlet, with not much there to entice the family to stay. Joh began looking further afield. South of Meaford, the largest town that perhaps offered better opportunities and housing was

Barrie, itself a small town by Canadian standards, with a population of around 16,000.

It was there he found what he was looking for; a well-established bakery with a large staff, and a large older home, partitioned off to house at least three or four families. They could occupy the right side of the home, with neighbours on both sides. One family even had a girl, Elly's age, that he was sure would make a good playmate. A school was only one-half block further down the street. The downside was the tannery across the street from the school, which, if the wind was right, would provide a rather ripe aroma to his wife's oh-so-delicate nose. He wondered if he'd hear a barrage of complaints about it in the future.

It was mid-November when Joh and Nel packed everything up once more to make the move into Barrie. He'd started work at the Corner Cupboard Bakery, on Barrie's main street, Dunlop Street, and he was welcomed into the bakery's employee family.

The new residence on Bradford Street was equally welcoming and they became friends with the Clarks, who lived on the other side of the house. The Thomsons on the opposite side kept to themselves a little more, but Nel was busy with her children, and Joh with his work. They weren't into forcing themselves onto people who didn't show an interest in getting to know them. Elly did indeed make friends with the Clark's young daughter. Jopie made a few friends himself, and the family looked forward to registering him for school. Both children seemed to pick up the new language in leaps and bounds.

Joh's creative talent, and his training in sugar confections and candy making were eventually discovered. The boss gave Joh a special order to create in his off time, and it generated some extra pay. He spent the next two weeks, in his daytime off hours building an outdoor village scene, made entirely of sugar, built up on a two by three-foot wooden platform.

His work shift started at three in the morning and he was home a little after one p.m. So every day at home, Joh mixed, cooked, tinted and shaped the elements needed for the required scenery. The sugar shapes were carefully rolled and configured, then laid out on a borrowed bakery sheet to harden and dry. When all the pieces were done, he followed the plans he'd carefully drawn out, gluing it all together on the base with royal icing.

The children hung around watching, but they had strict instructions to stay well away from the work. A cuff across the arm, or even the head a few times, taught both of them to stay well outside the danger zone of their father's quick hands. Hanging around had its perks as well. Once in a while, a piece would break, punctuated by Joh's sharp, "ACH!" Hearing that meant a piece to taste was in the offing. It didn't happen often enough, according to the children.

When the sugar creation was finally finished, Joh summoned the bakery to arrange for a pickup. On the day, someone came with a delivery van. Neighbours, wife, and children all watched, not daring to breathe, as Joh and the bakery employee carried it out of the house and down the veranda steps. The masterpiece was carefully placed on the floor in the back of the van, braced so it wouldn't slide during transport. The children were sure someone would trip and drop the giant confection and held their breaths until it was safely inside the vehicle. Joh acted unperturbed, but he was happy that the nervousness he really felt, didn't show in his hands as he carried his end of it. When it was loaded, everyone else dared breathe again.

The family settled in slowly, learning English, simply by mixing with the Canadians as they could. Their close friends, however, were the Dutch people they connected with at church, a congregation made up of immigrants from the Netherlands.

Their English was still rudimentary. Joh had noticed that his wife was often inclined to assume she knew what words meant, simply by listening to them in context. But the Dutch context didn't necessarily mesh with Canadian context. "Are sure you know what that word means?" he asked on occasion. The Dutch/English dictionary would then come out.

She didn't have that dictionary with her when on the street one day, she found herself in a conversation with a woman to whom she'd been recently introduced. Somehow the conversation turned to ice, winter sports, and something called "curling". The woman asked Nel, "Do you curl?"

Nel had never heard of curling, but she thought for a moment, made some assumptions, and stated emphatically, "Oh ya! I loff to kur-el!" thinking of the hours of leisurely skating she'd done on the canals.

"Wonderful," the woman exclaimed. "Come to the curling rink on Monday nights and join us." Nel continued on her way, pleased with the friendly invitation, thinking, *I'd love to attach my skates to my boots again and do some ice "curling".*

Thinking of those days, Nel began to feel a little homesick. She missed her family in the Netherlands, despite all the letters that flew back and forth across the Atlantic. It couldn't take the place of flesh and blood family, paired with *gezellig* cups of tea and cookies.

Finally, Nel's sister Anna and her husband Maup, with their two children, after hearing about Canada in the letters that flew back and forth, decided that they too would immigrate to Canada. They arrived a little while after Joh had moved his family to Bradford Street and stayed there until Maup found a job and a place of their own to live. Nel was pleased that she had another sister close by.

A year after they'd moved into Barrie, Joh found it harder to meet his obligations. He still dreamed of running his own bakery and had been putting aside as much money as he could to finance start-up costs. But his rent was going up, the ever-growing children needed clothes, shoes and other items. He'd have to cut back somewhere, so he decided to look for a cheaper place to rent.

Just on the outskirts of town was a little area called Ferndale. There he found a two-storey house, with the lower level available for rent. The cost was substantially less than what he was paying. Joh immediately paid his deposit and gave notice to the landlord. They moved the following month, but it didn't take long to find out it wasn't ideal.

The upper-floor neighbours accessed their portion of the house via a set of stairs situated right alongside their own front door entrance. The

gezellig - cozy ambiance

floor layout above them mirrored their lower floor. Late one Saturday afternoon, the couple noticed quite a few visitors making their way upstairs, many loaded with cases of beer. Pretty soon the noise coming from above grew to uncomfortable levels.

As the evening wore on, it got louder and louder, until Nel remarked that, it didn't look like the party would wind down any time soon and she hoped she'd be able to sleep. Joh was grateful that the next day was Sunday, and he wouldn't have to start work at 3 a.m.

The party wore on after the couple went to bed. Even the children had trouble falling asleep due to the noise emanating from above them. That night, Elly asked her mother rather crankily if animals were living upstairs. Finally, Nel had enough, pulled a robe over her pajamas, marched upstairs and pounded on the door. A very drunk neighbour answered, only to be met with a very irate Dutch lady. There were many drunken apologies, and soon after, the noise, stomping and loud music died down, and people started drifting away.

For the entire week, the upstairs neighbours were especially polite. Nel hoped that there wouldn't be a repeat, but the following Saturday the bedlam started again. Another march up the stairs, and again an irate reprimand, followed by drunk apologies, this time accompanied by equally drunk lullaby songs in the background. The party took a little longer to wind down, while Nel and Joh fumed downstairs.

That week, the couple thought of ways to curtail the neighbours' wild Saturday night parties, which didn't involve anything illegal. Joh was working on some minor repairs under the kitchen sink, and at that moment realized they had the perfect solution to the noisy night parties.

Several weeks later, on a Friday night, after Joh had gone to work, there was a repeat performance above their heads. Nel gave them one warning to tone down the racket, or else. The neighbours didn't feel like apologies were in order this time around, and Nel supposed they weren't drunk enough yet. It didn't matter.

Back downstairs, Nel opened the cupboard door under her sink, reached in and calmly turned off the main water supply for upstairs. Then she went back to bed. Half an hour later there was a shout from above, accompanied by a commotion on the stairs with demands to turn the water on. Nel turned her good ear into the pillow and closed her eyes. What she couldn't hear, didn't bother her in the least. It took a few more parties and water shut-offs before the neighbours got the message. Parties, good. Racket, bad.

Anna heartily agreed that neighbours like that did no one any good. She was glad that they'd found a house that they didn't have to share with anyone else. Despite that advantage, Anna did not take to the Canadian way of life, even though her husband tried his best to help everyone adjust. Anna simply could not stand being so far from the rest of her family. Nel and Anna's father was still living as well but was declining rapidly. Anna wanted to go home. Canada was not for her.

Joh spent a lot of time biking between Ferndale and work in Barrie. The old bike frequently broke down so sometimes he'd hitchhike, but at 2 a.m. there weren't a lot of cars on the road. He began thinking about getting a car. He'd learned to drive vehicles back home but never owned one. Those things were for rich people. However, in Canada, everyone, rich and poor needed a car. It would cut into the money he'd been saving for the business, but necessary. Time was money too.

On his way home soon after, he spotted a car sitting in someone's yard with a "for sale" sign stuck to it. Out of curiosity, he decided to knock on the door to find out what price they were asking for it. He had no idea what a used car cost. The owner wanted one hundred fifty dollars because it was old, it was running poorly, and was at the point of going to the car wreckers.

"May I look under de hood?" Joh asked. "Certainly," the man replied. Are you a mechanic?" Joh wasn't but explained he'd had to work on a lot of engines and mechanical parts during the war in his home country and he might be able to get it running properly.

Joh took a good look at the old engine. It seemed pretty simple to him: carburetor, spark plugs, nothing he hadn't seen before. He offered the man one hundred dollars for it, with the promise that it would be driven out of the man's yard that day. Agreements were made with a handshake, and Joh turned around, walked back to Barrie, and withdrew the money from his bank account.

Joh came home that day a little later than usual, proudly driving a car, with the old bike stashed in the trunk. Nel could only shake her head. Over the next few weeks, a hoist was built behind the house, the engine unbolted, hauled out of the old car, and set on a few wooden planks up off the ground. Joh worked patiently and methodically, dismantling the entire engine, cleaning every part in a bucket of oil, and then carefully put back together again. Hoses were checked and replaced where necessary, new spark plugs were installed, and all wiring was gone over for breakage and fraying.

Even the seats were taken out of the car, and everything cleaned: floor, brake pedal, gas pedal, clutch, shift, glove compartment, and of course, the seats.

After the engine was re-bolted into the car, hoses and wiring all attached, Joh wanted to test it to see how it ran. Since the seats were out, he took an empty pail, turned it upside down to sit on, while he depressed the clutch and brake, and turned the key. At first, the engine just stuttered, trying to turn over. Joh tried again. At least there was something. On the third try, the engine roared to life. Joh shoved the engine into first, took his foot off the brake and onto the gas while letting the clutch up slowly. The car took an unexpected leap forward, throwing Joh onto his back on the floor of the car, the pail now under his legs and in the way of the brake pedal.

The momentum and the pail prevented him from getting up and taking control of the car. Nel could only watch and laugh hysterically as the car slowly aimed itself at their old wooden crate, the one that brought their belongings from the old country, and now in use as a coal bin at the side of the house. In slow motion the car bumped up against the bin and then kept going, pushing the bin along the side of the house, until it reached the corner. The crate decided it was happier around the corner where it parked itself and came to a stop. Car and crate parted company, the car continuing straight on until Joh managed to struggle upright to take the wheel and apply the brake.

He did not appreciate the humour in the situation at all. But the car ran. Joh had himself a 1939 Ford in working condition. He envisioned himself driving to work in style, come Monday, until someone reminded him that he needed a driver's license. In his excitement, he'd totally forgotten.

That fall Jopie started school. The children were learning English fast, and the parents were amazed at the language proficiency of their young son and daughter while they still grappled with pronunciation. Many times they had to repeat themselves to be understood. By and large, people were patient and polite as they mangled the language.

Unpalatable homecomings greeted the couple numerous times upon arrival when returning from somewhere. A sewer line which had backed up, or a small fire inside the house, from hot ash out of an unused and badly covered chimney flue outlet, onto a day bed placed directly below, were some of the more troublesome aspects of living there.

But the biggest bane of their existence continued to be the party-loving upstairs neighbours. One day the family arrived home from a week-end away, visiting close friends in another town. Nel immediately noticed that all the window coverings on the upper floor had been removed.

Nel cried out in joy, "The neighbours have moved out! Finally! Thank God!" The joy was short-lived, however, when they rounded the corner of the house and noticed all those window curtains hanging on the wash line at the rear of the house. The disappointment was acute.

They watched as the new highway 400 bypass south to Toronto was built behind the homes, and at the beginning of the project, the children spent hours playing on the great piles of gravel trucked in to build the overpass. When the heavy machinery moved in, it took many warnings to discourage them from entering the construction site, the dangerous mix of bulldozers, cranes and small children finally became too great.

Frosty treats of ice slivers to suck on, provided by the delivery man, who chipped them off the blocks of ice delivered to the families' iceboxes a few times a week, assuaged the children's disappointment at the loss of their latest favourite playground, as did feeding a carrot to the horse-drawn milk wagon's mode of power.

When the upstairs tenants proved to be too much for the family, Joh found another lovely little house to rent, on the other side of Kempenfelt Bay, across the water from Barrie's main business street. They could no longer tolerate regular interruptions to their sleep. They moved to Painswick in 1952.

An outhouse in the back yard of the new house instead of indoor plumbing was a new wrinkle for Nel. Joh was used to outhouses, having lived in the country, but Nel was a city girl. There was little choice but to go with it for the time being. A large tin tub was their bathtub for weekly baths in the small kitchen, and it also did double duty as the washtub for Nel's laundry, augmented with a ribbed washboard to scrub the clothes on. It would all have to do for now, until Joh fulfilled his dream of becoming a rich businessman with his own successful bakery.

CHAPTER 14

Growth & Learning - 1953

By the time Joh had moved his family to Painswick, Nel discovered that she was pregnant again. She'd suffered a miscarriage less than a year before without even realizing she was expecting and didn't think it would happen so soon again. The morning sickness alerted her this time around, and the washtub laundry sessions became a chore exacerbated by her condition. She needed one of those electric wringer-washer machines she'd seen advertised in the newspaper and began to drop not-so-subtle hints to her husband. The statement was direct. "I need a washing machine."

Joh was close to starting his business. He already had his eye on a location on Dunlop Street, a few blocks from the Corner Cupboard Bakery. It even had apartments above the storefront so he could be right there where he needed to be without having to travel any amount of distance to get to his work. Dunlop Street ran along the top of a raised berm that edged Kempenfelt Bay. This provided him with a storefront at street level in the front and a basement for storage below, and ground-level access in the back. He had back-lot parking along with access to the store above, straight from the basement. Just a few more months and he'd have it all in place.

But the cost of a washing machine would, again, like the car, eat into his savings. But he recognized the need as well, so he began inquiring about the cost of a new washing machine for his wife. The new ones he looked at in Eaton's Department Store cost anywhere from sixty to one hundred dollars, which was a lot of money. It would again take a large chunk out of his savings, so he shopped around for a used one in good condition. He was quite handy if any problems arose in the electrical portion of it.

Joh came home with a used machine in good working condition and Nel became the proud owner of her very first new-to-her GE wringer washer. After spending her entire adult life washing her household's laundry in a tub and washboard, she was delighted with the improvement in that particular chore. She felt like she was now truly part of the modern generation. Imagine, now all she had to do was put hot water from the kitchen tap into the tub, fill it to the line, add the soap and the clothes. The machine did the rest, agitating by itself and getting the clothes clean. Then it would even wring out the clothes as well! Where had this been all her life?

Some of the Canadian food was a little off-putting. "Pig's food? You eat pig's food?" she asked incredulously one day of a thoroughly Canadianized Dutch woman. The family had been invited to a corn boil. In the Netherlands, corn was fed to the pigs. They'd gagged in disgust at their first taste of butter, spread on a slice of bread. "Why is this so salty? It's horrible!" At home butter wasn't salted. The taste of cola was revolting, and dry cereal, completely tasteless and unappealing. Give them good old-fashioned *havermout* and *griesmeel* for breakfast.

For once, and in spite of the odd foods and tastes, the home seemed to be a happy place, in the absence of Nel's grumbling and complaints. Joh couldn't be happier for her, and himself of course. It was well worth the months of delay in getting his business off the ground. He only hoped that the location he'd chosen would still be available when he was ready.

Shortly after Joh and his family moved to Painswick, Anna visited her younger sister for the last time before taking her daughter and son back to the Netherlands. Maup would stay in Canada long enough to earn sufficient money to pay back the loan made to him for his wife and children's tickets. He would reluctantly follow his family when he could.

Christmas rolled around and the bakery owners, the Bloomfield family, once again planned their big Christmas party for their large staff and their families. Joh, his wife and two children had gone last year as well, and they'd enjoyed themselves immensely. Jopie, was especially delighted in the attention paid to him by a staff member who thought he was quite the

---

havermout - oatmeal
griesmeel - seminola

charming little boy. She insisted he sit with her during the photo session, and showered him with attention, preventing him from going off to "do his own thing" and making mischief. This suited Nel to a T, since she, six months pregnant, was not up to chasing her son around the large hall to make sure he wasn't making a nuisance of himself.

As all the parents did, Nel and Joh had brought small gifts for their children, to be given out at the party by Santa. There wasn't much to spend for Christmas that year, but Nel had managed to find a small doll in the Eaton's toy department, for which she'd knitted a pink dress and hat. It had come with a satin "undie" but not much else, so Nel, being quite a good knitter, had found some leftover wool in the perfect shade of pink, which was enough for the tiny outfit. Elly was thrilled with it, as was Jopie with his small beginner's Meccano set.

With the addition of the '39 Ford, they were now able to spend the three or four days that Joh had off from work, with their close friends Jan and Marie Klopper. The children called them aunt and uncle, and they'd met early on after arriving in Canada. Soon after, the Kloppers and their two boys, Gerald and Sam had moved to Bowmanville, as Jan had found steady work at the General Motors plant in Oshawa. Their boys were close in age to Jopie and Elly, and everyone had become more like a surrogate family. Both families missed their own, far away overseas and unreachable.

The two couples made a promise to each other when they found their circumstances taking them away to different areas of the province, preventing them from just dropping by for a quick chat and a cup of coffee, as they liked to do. Every Christmas they would take turns spending the holidays with each other. Christmas 1952 was a joyful time in Bowmanville that year.

The snow lay deep on the ground and the four children spent hours in the snow, staging raucous snowball fights, building forts and washing each other's faces with snow. Inevitably, one of them would come inside, red-faced, wet and crying. The adults would invariably respond with: "We told you so. When you play wild and rough, someone will be crying!" The scene would be played over and over until all children were finally ordered inside and commanded to go to their own corners and play quietly.

Christmas wasn't the only time they visited. Joh had a week's vacation time during the summer, and they'd gone to Bowmanville to visit Jan and Marie in their new home. But with the looming business plans, summer vacations in the future would have to take a back seat.

On January 30, 1953, they heard the news on the radio. On the night of January 29, their home country had been hit by a disastrous storm. The dikes had broken and water had poured in, flooding the lowlands in a surge of water. The news stated few details, but it was bad. Homes were destroyed, lives lost, possessions, cattle, and livestock, all gone. It was quite likely that they too would have been victims.

Shocked, Nel and Joh packed whatever they could find that they truly didn't need, as little as it was, to send back to the Netherlands for the relief effort. The children, hearing the news, were subdued, and even a little frightened. The parents tried to assure them that it wouldn't happen here. Canada was well above sea level.

As time went on, to save as much money as the couple could for the new business venture, Nel scrimped, saved and made do as much as possible. This she was already good at, having spent over five war years doing just that. She could make every penny squeak twice, and still make change. Joh would bring home brightly patterned cloth that the flour companies packaged their flour in. This trend started in the 1930s during the Great Depression to help housewives re-use and stretch their resources. The trend was petering out, but once in a while flour sacks still came packaged in reusable material. When Nel got hold of such material, she would sew clothing for her daughter.

Now, living in yet another place, thankfully with no rowdy neighbours sharing the same building, Nel found more ways to save their money. Why buy toilet paper, when they had newspapers that were only tossed away after being read or Sears Roebuck catalogues and magazines that were out of date and useless after a while? Those things worked just as well in the toilet stall or the outhouse.

Joh too, found it was cheaper to make a birthday cake himself for his daughter's upcoming sixth birthday, instead of buying one from the bakery. He had permission from his boss to create a cake using an idea he'd seen one day in a baking journal. He'd pay the boss a few cents for the ingredients he'd need but make it on his own time. The boss agreed.

Joh came home that February with a cake that enthralled his daughter to no end. It was baked in a half-bowl cake pan, turned upside down, with a doll stuck into the middle of it. The bowl cake turned into a skirt decorated with icing, royal icing roses and silver nonpareils. The upper half of the doll had an icing bodice for modesty's sake. Six candles were arranged around the bottom of the skirt; a present and a cake all at the same time. It was almost too pretty to eat. The cake concept became a popular item at the bakery and many little girls received a doll cake for their birthdays after that.

Nel looked forward to another baby in the family. The only twist in this new world was her doctor, who insisted that she deliver in the hospital. "I'm not sick," she protested. "I'm just having a baby! It's quite normal you know!"

Dr. Swann calmly tried to explain things to her. "This is Canada. In Canada, babies are born in hospitals! Besides, you have a geriatric pregnancy. If there are complications, you are better off in a hospital."

"I have what? What is gerry-ah-trik?" Nel looked at him with consternation. Was there something wrong with her pregnancy? Was there something he hadn't told her? "Geriatric means old. You are considered to be on the old side for pregnancy and are more susceptible to complications during birth" was his explanation. "What about my husband? Where will he be?" was the next question. Suspicious, she needed to know the exact ins and outs of this whole new way of having a baby.

Nel heard the other shoe drop. "Your husband can either stay in the waiting room until the child is delivered, or he can go home and wait for a call." They had no telephone. Nel thought it was all nonsense, her husband had seen it all with the birth of her other two children. But he was the doctor, and the doctor's words were law. She was duly booked into the hospital when labour began.

Joh brought her in, with the children in the back of the car, excited that their mother was going to bring home a baby. Both of them wondered whether it would be a brother or a sister. Since they had no phone, Joh's only alternative was to take the children home again, to get them out of his hair. He couldn't imagine spending hours in a hospital waiting room with active children underfoot.

Home again, he set about to find someone to watch them while he returned to the hospital. He did his best to feed them dinner and sent them to bed. They were still a little excited about the new brother or sister and refused to settle. The neighbour was due to arrive any minute and he was anxious to be gone. From the other side of the closed bedroom door, he could hear the two of them thumping around, and giggling about something.

A little out of patience, he snapped the door open again to find Elly bouncing up and down on the bed, and Jopie leaning out trying to hit her as she dodged back and forth. "Back in bed and quiet," he snarled at them in his best mad-daddy voice.

The two of them pleaded, "It's still light out, do we have to be in bed? Why can't we stay up? Please, Daddy, please?"

"No. It's little children's bedtime. You two need to be in bed!" He turned to leave the room, and as he began to close the door, he turned back to give them both the hard stare, to make sure his words were anchored home, just in time to catch his daughter sticking out her tongue at him behind his back. She dropped into bed with her hand clapped over her mouth in horror at being caught, fear of a spanking evident in her eyes.

He quietly closed the door, and as he stood there, he shook his head and began to laugh quietly. His daughter was a little firebrand. She'd prove to be a handful yet.

Three weeks after her daughter's birthday, Nel, at the age of 36 gave birth to her second daughter, whom she'd named Nancyann. Ann, for her closest sister, and Nancy, simply because she liked the name. For the first time in her life, she picked a name she wanted without having to argue with her husband or feel obligated to find a workaround for a name she hated. She was free of all complications in the New World.

Many hours later Joh came home with the news. They had a little sister. Elly bounced up and down. "I win, I win!" she crowed to her brother. "Haha, I got a girl!"

To Joh, it seemed she was always in some sort of competition with her brother. He let them be and arranged with the neighbour lady to watch his children when he went to work. Five days later they all trooped to the hospital to bring mother and baby home. Life went on as normal, along with one more tiny human being.

In the meantime, the Dunlop Street address had morphed into a bakery. The following month, Joh had bought bakery equipment, signed a lease, paid the rent for the first and last month, decided on a name, ordered supplies, hired staff for the front of store, and hired a baker helper. The Barrie Model Bakery opened on April 16, 1953. From the church he found another baker who agreed to work for him and the two of them spent the first night baking up a storm.

At home, Joh revealed the name of the bakery to his children, when they asked what the new store would be called. The question rather surprised him, because up to that point, both of them had shown very little interest in what he'd been so busy with.

"I'm calling it the The Barrie Model Bakery. How do you like that name?" Joh proudly asked them. Jopie walked away, satisfied, his question answered. Elly, on the other hand, kept looking at him, her nose wrinkled up a little. "Don't you like that name?" he asked.

She gave her shoulders a little shrug, too well trained by now to voice her opinion, but he knew she was not impressed. "The Barrie Model Bakery?" She repeated, wrapping the words around her tongue as if to taste them. She shrugged her shoulders, and walked away.

The newspaper was present at the grand opening and, to the family's delight, an article about the new immigrant and his baking career, along with a photo appeared in the next *Barrie Examiner*, Barrie's daily newspaper. "Daddy, you're famous!" The children beamed at him.

The next few weeks were grueling as routine and schedule was established for items to be baked, in what order, how much, and timing, so that the goods could be brought fresh to the front. The large room behind the store, where the baking was done, was hot. The ovens took up one third of the available space, with only one window and a lone fan above the opening to suck out the hot air.

His choice of the business name continued to bother him and he felt after the fact, that it was a little less than inspiring. Someone remarked earlier that it wasn't exactly the type of name that would catch anyone's interest. After a time, the idea came to him. He was Dutch. The bakery had food with a Dutch flavour. Where was food kept? The English word for it was pantry. He had it. He would call it, 'The Dutch Pantry'. When he broke the news to Elly, her face lit up in delight. "Yes, that's a much better name! I like it!" There was something warming about approval from a six-year-old.

Summer was just upon them and Ontario's summer months were sweltering hot. The counter staff felt the heat no less, and one by one they quit, unwilling to suffer that much. Joh was a hard task master, but not any less than he was on himself. He worked like a dog without complaint and he expected everyone else to do the same. He was wrong, they did complain, but the fans he brought in only pushed the hot air around. It did nothing to alleviate the heat and humidity. There was nothing he could do about that.

After the last clerk disappeared, in desperation and unable to find another one quickly enough, he told his wife, she would have to come in to fill the gap until he could hire more help. He knew full well, she would not be happy with that news, and he was right. From Painswick, she'd have to walk or hitchhike, two children in tow and a baby in a bassinet, to get into Barrie and the store. Nel made her displeasure known in no uncertain terms.

"I've got a brand new baby to look after. What do you expect me to do about her? What about the kids? School is out for the summer for Jopie, so there's those two to look after as well. I can't do it all."

"It's only temporary, I promise. As soon as I can find more help, you won't need to be here anymore," Joh pleaded with her. "Please! Just help me out for a bit!"

Nel reluctantly agreed, but only because it was very temporary. Depending on how long it lasted, she could perhaps get her neighbour to watch the two older ones, so they wouldn't have to hang around the store, or play in the parking lot behind the building. Thank goodness, she thought, there was a large grassy area around the small train station almost next door to the parking area. They'd at least have a somewhat clean place to play in, in the eventuality of having to take them along with her.

She worried about the lakeshore with the steep rocky breakwater one hundred feet away from the back of the building, and the train tracks that ran through. Nel tried to make sure she knew where the children were when she heard the train coming, but her anxiety level jangled at her constantly. Parking lot, train tracks and a body of water were no place for children to be playing. Joh agreed, but he was between a rock and a hard place.

The children discovered a small playground one half block away, so the two were sent to play there whenever possible. It would have to do for now. The playground was small, a set of swings, two teeter-totters, and a slide. The two soon got bored with it and went further afield to search for bigger and better adventures.

There were things to explore at the shoreline, interesting store windows to peer into, train tracks to balance on; who could balance-walk on top of the narrow steel ribbon the longest, or watching in awe as the menacing black locomotive went barreling past, with its stack belching cinder-filled smoke and its ear-shattering whistle, while they held their breaths and their ears. It was great fun. Jopie was old enough to recognize the dangers of the tracks and warned Elly to stay well back. He was a confident and cautious boy and took his role as big brother seriously.

Soon enough, another clerk was hired and Nel stayed gratefully home. But not for long. A few weeks later, she was called in again. The clerk had quit. Angry, Nel came in to help, both daughters in tow. Jopie had permission to stay the day with one of his young friends. There was now a definite dark vibe between the couple, as Nel juggled baby, children and store. Joh simply put his head down and worked, unable to do much else.

In the meantime, an added complication had arisen to further Nel and Joh's already hectic, upside-down lives. Their landlord had sold the house and they needed to move. The new owners wanted to live in the house themselves, but both apartments that were located above the store were still occupied. One would vacated at the end of September. They'd hoped to be able to stay in Painswick until then, but the home was sold sooner than expected. They would have to be out by the first of August.

Some of the church people had begun to come in every few days to buy the fresh bread, and support the new baker in town, seeing as he was one of them. The Groots lived a mile or so outside of Barrie, in a tiny hamlet called Shanty Bay. They'd come in one day to get bread, when they heard about the quandary Nel and Joh were in. They immediately offered to help. To young Elly's delight, Mr. And Mrs. Groot were ready to take her and her brother right then and there, in their fancy car, back to Shanty Bay.

Elly sat in the car, delighted to be riding in such an impressive vehicle, but Nel ordered her out. They would be going when Nel was ready to take them, not before. Later, after the few household furnishings had been put in storage, the Grin family had their temporary lodgings with the Groots in Shanty Bay.

The couple gave a sigh of relief. At least things were falling into place, sort of. Jopie and Elly were already booked into Barrie's Prince of Wales Public School, Elly would be starting Grade 1, and Jopie, Grade 3. But they'd have to begin the school year in the little two-room Shanty Bay School first, and transfer to Prince of Wales in October, as soon as they were able to move right into Barrie. They would thereafter, in effect, live in the bakery. It seemed to be the ideal solution.

Both children were delighted to spend their time playing with the four younger Groot children, some of whom were Jopie and Elly's ages. The two girls immediately became fast friends. The orchards that Mr. Groot owned, the barn that offered untold adventures in the maze of hayloft, unused animal pens and mystery rooms, and even the farm fields across the road, full of dried up cow patties that were thrown with gusto up against anything looking like a target, became another adventure land, with hours of sport.

Soon, the school year started. It was another new experience for the children to broaden their understanding of a new country and people. But a darker reality presented itself one Saturday, one that none of the children understood. Mrs. Groot, normally a kind but no-nonsense lady, suddenly left her busy kitchen and walked out of the house.

At first the younger ones paid no attention, but the two older boys called after their mother, "Ma, where are you going?" She gave no answer, but walked down the drive, rounded the corner onto the road and disappeared. Alarmed at the odd behaviour, the two oldest followed after, questioning her. There was no answer from the mother.

Alarmed now, one of them ran back and summoned the other children. "Something's wrong with Ma. We have to stop her!" All of them ran after her, catching up to the older boy and his mother, still walking resolutely down the road.

"Ma! Where are you going? Please answer us!" "This is scaring the younger kids!"

"Are you angry with us?"

"Did we do something wrong?"

Liz and Elly followed well behind, too afraid and mystified to say anything. The cries, at first, fell on deaf ears, and then, finally, she gave the cryptic answer, "I'm going away, far away, and never coming back."

This frightened them even more. "What did we do? What did we do?" They were a rambunctious group and they knew it, but even this was far from their mother's usual behaviour.

"Please Ma, come home, we'll promise to behave! Just come home, please Ma, please! Just come home!" they pleaded.

Abruptly, she stopped in her tracks, and just as suddenly turned her face to home. "Yes, you're right, I'll come home." For the rest of the day the children were subdued and behaved. Mrs. Groot gave no explanation for her odd behaviour, and the children could only sigh in relief that their mother was back, a familiar and comforting figure in the home. But it was a sign of sadder and darker things to come for the Groot family.

At the end of September, the rear facing flat above 107 Dunlop Street East was finally empty and ready for the new family. Joh and Nel had all their worldly goods set up in the new home and ready before the children were brought home from Shanty Bay. The view from any of the four windows was, to Nel at least, rather spectacular. Kempenfelt Bay glittered in the sunlight below them. Nel loved the view, even though it was marred by the gravel parking lot and the train tracks, but much preferable in her mind, to the other front-facing flat, occupied already by a French-Canadian family, whose own row of four windows overlooked the town's main street and the Queen's Hotel.

The flat was referred to as a "boxcar flat" because all the rooms were practically in a row, like a train's boxcars connected end to end: kitchen, a room, another room, then two tiny rooms side by side at the end. One simply went through one room to get to the next. The only deviation was a small bathroom off the kitchen at one end of the flat, and the two tiny rooms at the other end, both of which were more like walk-in closets. Of those two rooms, only one sported a window leading out to a rickety wooden stairs to the parking lot a few storeys below. This served a double purpose as the "backstairs" to exit the flat, and as a fire escape, fulfilling the fire regulation requirements. The other small room only had a transom above the door. Nel was a little leery with letting her daughters sleep in a room that anyone could climb up to from the ground, so that one was designated as Jopie's room.

Both girls, to be safer in Nel's fearful mind, were assigned the windowless room, much to Elly's unhappiness. She didn't particularly like not having a window to look out of, but complaints and protestations were not tolerated, and children didn't have opinions. The baby, Nancyann, didn't say much. She was still a babe in arms after all.

The family settled in to some semblance of order, the children off to school, Nel still worked behind the counter, her baby in a playpen, and Joh established a grueling work schedule for himself consisting of twenty hours work and four hours sleep.

He'd get up at four p.m., and spend the next nineteen hours, with a quick run upstairs at six p.m. to join his family for dinner. Hours were spent prepping pans and sheets, mixing the ingredients, into the oven, more mixing, pan prepping, over and over, load after load of breads, pies, cakes, cookies, cupcakes, tarts, bars, and buns made their way into the oven. Donuts went into the deep fryer, taken out, glazed or filled with jelly and sugared, huge sheets filled with rows and rows of aromatic donuts, all of which were laid out carefully in the showcases to present to the public. Special orders, such as wedding and birthday cakes took extra time.

His baker came in at eleven p.m. and by then enough pans and sheets were prepped again and ready to be loaded with dough and batters By seven a.m. the next morning, Nel's shift would start, readying things for the store's nine a.m. opening. The employee's eight-hour shift was up, the baking for the day done, except for the cleaning of the pans, baking sheets and other baking paraphernalia. By the time those chores were done, he had enough time for a fast lunch in the flat, then crash into bed for a few hours, only to have the entire schedule repeat itself at four p.m.

A year later, as requests for delivery service grew, he realized he needed another vehicle of some sort. The old Ford wouldn't do. It had no room, and he couldn't afford a second vehicle. Joh traded the old Ford in for a used 1951 Chevrolet delivery van. It was a step up from what he had, and he had the name *the Dutch Pantry* in its distinctive gold leaf logotype with Dutch boy and girl images, painted on the side panels. Now, everywhere he went, people would know who was delivering. He viewed it as free advertising.

This was the stuff of a baker's life but doing it with just himself and one other employee working, was a far cry from the large staff he'd previously worked with. It was a situation where perhaps he'd bitten off more than he could chew, but his stubbornness prevailed. He'd do it, make more money, hire more people and make a good living out of it. He just hoped he'd be able to do it soon. He needed more employees: bakers, clerks and helpers for the prep and cleanup work. He was dog tired. There weren't enough hours in the day to do what he needed to do, and four hours sleep wasn't enough. He needed to make more money, fast.

CHAPTER 15

Dark Times

It seemed to Joh that Nel was always angry; at the children, at the world, at him. Nothing suited. Couldn't she see that he was working his ass off? He was tired to the bone. It was always nagging, why didn't he do *whatever it was he was supposed to do*, nag and more nag. Every time he had an idea to drum up some more business, she'd veto it with an objection. *They didn't have enough money, it was a stupid idea*, on and on. Nothing he did was right. The promotional pens he wanted to order weren't worth the expense, the newspaper ads weren't bringing in more customers, why didn't he shave before going out to make deliveries? He'd look more presentable. He just wanted to get the job over with so he could sleep. Couldn't she understand?

To add to his woes, his allergies were getting worse, he'd sneeze constantly, especially in the spring when the ragweed was in bloom. He was in misery. And still, he stubbornly kept on.

Once in a while, when the coffers were a little more abundant, he'd hire a clerk to alleviate Nel's workload, but they were a hard bunch to keep for some reason. It seemed to him that no one wanted to work behind a bakery counter, or only wanted part-time.

He'd hired several different bakers, but a lot of men couldn't handle a night-time job. Jopie was nine by this time. Another few years, and he'd put the boy to work to help. Both older children were almost of an age where they be big enough to start taking up some of the workload. He knew there were laws in place against child labour but he'd done it to help support his own family growing up, and by God, it was only right that his children did the same. That was just the way it was. In a family business, family helped.

Employees came and went. He hired ladies for behind the counter, and a high school boy to come in after school to do the cleanup, which worked for a while, but somehow students and clerks always needed replacing. Church people that were frequent customers in the beginning were looking askance at a gaunt man, sleeping in the pew beside his family on Sundays, while his wife poked at him, trying to keep him awake. His baker watched as he stood in the bakery numbly adding ingredients to the bread mix kneading in the large mixers, looking for all the world like he'd be ready to fall asleep, and plummeting face first into the mixer. And yet he kept on, stubbornly refusing to quit the dream. He'd make it. He just needed to make more money to make it work.

More and more, bad news seemed to take the forefront. Nel's friend, Mrs. Groot, who, a year ago, had kindly provided them with a place to stay, was ill. Gravely ill. She complained privately to Nel that she'd been bleeding *down there* a lot, for a long time already. It wouldn't stop. Shocked and worried, Nel urged her to go to the doctor, but for some reason, Mrs. Groot wouldn't go.

"It's already too late," she said. "They won't be able to do anything." A month later, she died, a victim of uterine cancer. She'd known for the last year and a half already. Cancer was a killer. "Once you had it," she'd said, "you don't come back. It takes you." She'd had a premonition a year ago that she would be leaving her family soon. Elly's friend Liz, along with her siblings, were motherless.

"Mrs. Grin!" A former neighbour from Bradford Street, entered the store, as Nel finished refilling a tray of cookies in the showcase.

"Mrs. Clark! How are you? I have not seen you in a while," Nel greeted her old Bradford Street neighbour cheerfully. Mrs. Clark didn't look too happy, her voice full of indignation, "Do you know what your daughter is doing out there by herself? I saw her just a few minutes ago, talking to a man. I'm sure he is no one she knows!" Mrs. Clark looked displeased. "That little girl should not be roaming the streets by herself."

Nel said she'd seen her daughter come home just a short while ago and promised the woman she'd look into it. Later, when she had a moment, she walked upstairs to check on the girl. It bothered her that she'd been seen talking to strangers, something she'd been warned about on numerous occasions, and as she climbed the stairs, she entertained the possibility that *dirty things* had been tried or, god forbid, *done.* She quailed over needing to question the seven-year-old on such a taboo subject, but somehow, she'd have to broach it.

Elly was still upstairs working on something at the dining room table, and Nel started with the obvious, "Mrs. Clark came in today, and she said she saw you talking to a man. Who was it?" Elly looked a little sheepish, "I don't know."

"What did he want?"

"He had a question about something ... I don't remember, but I said something, and then ran away."

There was something about the answer that seemed evasive. Nel probed further. "Was he doing something *dirty?*" She couldn't bring herself to specify what, but the girl seemed to know what she meant.

"No." But Elly didn't look at her mother either.

"Look at me! Did he *do,* or ask you to *do* something *dirty*?

There was a pause, then "No."

Nel took a deep breath. "Has there been anybody else who had been *dirty* to you?"

Another pause, eyes downcast. "*Look* at me!"

The child couldn't look at her mother and lie. To Nel's utter horror, the eyes looked up, fearful, and she answered with a small, "yes."

In a strangled voice she asked, "Who? Tell me who! NOW!" Guilt was written all over the girl's face. Then, after a long pause, "Mr. Roy, down the street." Elly answered in a tiny, quavering voice.

"Stay there! Do not leave this house! Stay right there!" Nel angrily commanded her daughter. She rushed back down the stairs to the store. With shaking hands, she picked up the telephone and called the police.

As Nel listened to the ringing of the line at the other end, she shook, thinking, *Mr. Roy! The man had had the affront to stand in her store, speaking with her and her husband as though he'd done nothing sinful!* She almost missed hearing the voice on the other end of the line, as her drumming heart beat in her ears. "Barrie Police! How may I help you?"

Nel explained as best she could with shaking voice. Within ten minutes an officer stood in the bakery, and Nel escorted him upstairs to speak to her daughter. Elly still sat quietly at the table, whatever she'd been working on, forgotten in front of her. The officer sat down, asking the little girl some questions, then left again, with instructions to Nel, back at her post in the bakery, not to let the youngster play outside for the rest of the day, until they brought Roy in for questioning. She should also take her daughter to her doctor for examination, just to be on the safe side.

Nel went back up briefly, still shaking and angry, to tell Elly, under no circumstances was she to go and play outside. She was to remain in the house for the rest of the day. The girl was withdrawn and silent. Nel didn't care. It was too awful to even contemplate. The girl should have known better. Nel thought, she'd stressed enough times to Elly, *never to speak to strangers!* She should have known better! How was she going to break this awkward news to Joh? What would he say?

When he was told about it, Joh offered, "Maybe in time she'll forget about it. Take her to Dr. Swann and make sure she hasn't been harmed." It left Nel feeling as helplessly enraged as before. The next day they sat in the doctor's office, Elly silent and withdrawn, sitting next to her mother. She went meekly into the examination room alone when her turn came. Afterwards, with Elly sitting in the waiting room again, Nel and Dr. Swann talked.

"I don't think anything really serious has been done to her, Mrs. Grin," the doctor began. "There are no lesions or injury that I can detect. And there's no evidence of penetration."

"What do I do now, Doctor?" Nel was at a loss on how to go further or what to say and embarrassed at the whole conversation.

"If she's lucky, and bear in mind, most children are very resilient, her mind will, in time, simply forget. Children seem to forget many things at that age, especially if it was a bad experience," the doctor informed her, adding, "I don't think you need to be overly concerned, just keep an eye on her, and if there are after-effects from the experience, come and see me."

A few days later, a call came from the police station. Could Mrs. Grin please come in with her daughter to identify the man who had molested her. Nel duly brought seven-year-old Elly in, to be confronted with a line of men whom she'd never seen before, save one.

A man, not in uniform, explained to Elly that she was to go up to the line of men and touch the man who had harmed her. Elly hesitated, and Nel pushed her forward. "Go ahead, show us who it was."

Elly walked ahead slowly, and went straight to the man, Mr. Roy, who she had watched, fascinated, while he built boats with wood and steam at the old boathouses that lined the Kempenfelt Bay shore near their bakery; the man who had talked to her, given her bottles of 7 Up to drink, paid attention to her, and finally, done *bad things* to her. She, voiceless and powerless to say "no", acquiesced, because she had been taught over and over, to *mind your elders, obey adults, be polite*. It had been drilled into her, far more than the ambiguous, *don't speak to strangers*. He was no stranger. He had been her friend.

She touched his arm, and looked into his eyes, stricken that she had to do this. Roy smiled at her, and nodded his head, "It's okay," he said softly.

No one spoke a word more to the youngster. After the police had thanked Nel for coming in, her mother took her silently by the hand and marched out the door.

For the next while, Elly seemed more subdued than usual. Nel never found a good way, or an opportune time to talk to the girl about it all. She had no idea what words to even use, so she said nothing, hoping it would all go away. Roy was charged and his trial was held just before school began again in the fall. Young Elly was slated to be a witness, along with a number of other young girls, more victims, that the investigation had subsequently found.

Even during her testimony, the shame the little girl felt at the whole episode was palpable to everyone in the courtroom. She could barely speak of it, hanging her head in embarrassment. The prosecutor asked the court that she be deemed a reluctant witness, so that at least he could lead the child a bit with questions.

Were you touched? Yes. How? With his hand.

The more the questions asked, the more probing they became, the lower her head lowered, until almost disappearing behind the witness rail. The answers came with difficulty. Finally, it was over. Roy was found guilty.

Nel and her child left the courtroom in relief. On the way home, Nel knew she should say something to her daughter, that now was the time, but what? She just didn't know, couldn't get the words out that she really needed to say. It was awkward and embarrassing. How should she word something like *that?* One didn't speak of *dirty things.*

As they walked, she shook Elly's hand as she held it tight. In a strangled voice, and looking straight ahead of her, she threw out the words ahead of her, "I hope this will teach you *never* to speak to strangers!" It was the last thing she would ever say about it to her daughter.

The little girl was utterly silent in her guilty shame. Nel, lost in her own confused thoughts and social taboos, was unaware of it.

CHAPTER 16

1954-1958

Joh's oldest daughter continued to be withdrawn and difficult from time to time, much to Nel's frustration. School resumed in September, and the moods seemed to swing constantly. Nel fielded a call from the principal one day, wanting to talk about her daughter. Nel was afraid that the girl had been acting up in school and she cringed at the thought of Elly embarrassing her mother like that. Then, to her surprise, the principal began talking of some wonderful drawing she'd done that had truly impressed him.

"Your daughter has a gift!" he told her. "Really?" Nel answered. "Yes, I thought I would inform you so you could make some time to nurture it and encourage her to develop it to its full potential!" Nel didn't know what to think of that, she knew nothing about art, but decided to do whatever she could. Perhaps she'd buy a paint-by-number set to give her as a Christmas present.

Jopie, in his own quiet but determined way, was beginning to gravitate towards more a careful and independent reasoning. It began to grate a bit on Joh, that his son had his own way of doing things. He was all too anxious to instruct him on how to do things properly, as Joh's father had taught him. But the boy, more often than not, followed his own path. Joh was determined to train him in the bakery when he was older and the time was right. He imagined the near future, when all the children would have a hand in running the bakery. They were all growing up fast, and he remembered his father's cold and muddy fields, where he too had to work at an early age.

On Friday, October 15, 1954, after coming down from upstairs, and unlocking the door to the bakery, Nel had just finished setting the sample cakes in the window. The sky outside was darkly overcast and she wondered at the weather. They'd had an unprecedented amount of rain that week, and she knew that the southern states had had hurricane warnings, but she wasn't worried. Hurricanes never came this far north.

A customer entered and exclaimed in surprise, "Oh, you're open! I didn't think you would be …" and before Nel could ask why on earth she wouldn't be open, the client went on, "… they've forecast a hurricane you know."

"Hurricane? I hear we only getting bad storm. We do not close for de storm. De storm does not stop us."

The client laughed, "We don't either, but it will be worse this time. This is an actual category four hurricane, something we don't often see up here. It'll probably be the tail end of it, but it will be bad, I heard category one. Much worse than the usual summer storms we get here. Be prepared." She left hurriedly with three loaves of bread.

Nel turned on the little radio and waited for the news and weather reports. It didn't take long. She listened intently as the hurricane warnings were broadcast at half hour intervals. As she did, her daughter came through the door. She'd been sent home from school, and Nel presumed her son would follow shortly. Her one-year-old sat playing in the playpen at the rear of the shop, behind the partition that closed off the bakery work area. All her children were safe.

Joh was in the back, still baking the final products, cookies and cupcakes, the latter to be iced and sprinkled with coconut and a dollop of fruit compote, by Nel, after they'd cooled. The mood in the store kept pace with the darkness developing as the day progressed. The rain sheeted down now, and near noon they noticed water running down the main street outside. It lapped at the sidewalk, resembling a fast-flowing river. By lunchtime it was eerie, as dark as night outside, while the wind screamed overhead.

As mother and daughter stood in the store, staring helplessly through the plate glass window at the ominously black sky, Joh came running up from the basement below, where all the baking supplies were stored, shouting as he came. "The water is coming in under the door downstairs!" he exclaimed. "My supplies will be ruined if I don't get them up higher! Lock the door and help me raise everything up!"

There were no people left on the street; everyone had scurried home from the street or had never gone out. Nel did as instructed and in the basement as much as possible was set higher up on crates, pails, anything that could be used to raise the perishables above the rising water. No one could predict how high it would go.

The entire floor of the basement was concrete, and the rafters and supporting beams were old wood. The water rose to about two feet, and then stopped. Some things like boxes of raisins, dates, and sacks of flour could not be lifted quickly enough, although the family and whatever other help could be found, worked feverishly to find enough ways to lift the supplies higher.

The next day, Joh surveyed the damage. The water had, by that time, receded or drained out through the porous concrete, but the lingering damp due to the wood and bare concrete, turned much of the goods mouldy, ruining whatever had been initially saved from the encroaching water. Most of it had to be replaced.

Barrie itself suffered as much, if not more. The railway tracks behind the main street buildings were washed out completely, the craters under the rails so deep, a car could drive under them. Streets had turned into rivers, homes flooded out. When the storm finally dissipated by October 18, it was the deadliest and second costliest of the 1954 Atlantic hurricane season.

The couple continued to slog on, hours upon hours of exhausting work. Jopie was now in Grade 5, Elly in Grade 3. Nel, even with a two-year-old toddler underfoot, looked to be a permanent employee, with occasional hired help, and Joh, with a baker working alongside, followed the same punishing schedule of twenty hours work and four hours sleep.

He'd often come home in the mornings after making the deliveries, only to have Nel find him parked at the back of the store, sound asleep in the van. On any given Sunday or holiday off, with an outing to the beach as respite, found Joh laid out on a blanket on the ground, snoring. Any chance he found, any occasion he could take advantage of, he slept, exhausted.

On such a day, as Joh wearily entered the flat, ready to eat the sandwich Nel had prepared for his lunch, he noticed Elly staring at something on the old Dutch bookcase standing along one wall. The girl looked at him and back at a small clay head displayed on the top of the bookcase.

"Daddy? This face looks like you." She held up the old clay head he'd dug up years ago, out of his father's potato field.

Joh stopped and gently took the clay head out of her hand. It transported him back to a simpler time, one that, in his exhaustion he suddenly wished for. He remembered his mother, her birthdays when he had nothing to give her, and the feeling he'd had, when he finally found something that was worthy to give her as a birthday present. He remembered the strange feeling that face had evoked in him when he'd first found it. And now he realized why. He'd been looking at himself. He wondered then who it had been.

"Yes, it sort of does, doesn't it?" Smiling, he put it back on the bookcase, and added, "It's very old you know, hundreds of years." He told his daughter then of how he'd found it. Later he marvelled that only now, someone, his daughter no less, recognized the resemblance. He sat down to his lunch and ate, weary beyond description, and wondered what he'd chosen for himself. Had this been a wise decision? Should he stop? His father's words echoed in his head. "Whatever it is you find your hands to do, do it with all your might." He didn't have a lot of might left.

He didn't even have time to tend to the maintenance of his place of business. Somehow the back door entrance into the building's basement had been damaged. Jopie had come up into the rear of the store from below, white-faced in shock. "Mum," he'd said to his mother, "there's a man sitting in the basement. He looks scary." A tramp had gotten in and tucked himself in a corner under the open stair treads, and scared the poor boy half to death. From then on, both children negotiated the dark basement in fear and trembling.

Looking at the date on the calendar, Nel made an observation. "Our twelve and a half is coming up." In his home country, that halfway mark to the twenty fifth wedding anniversary was a big deal, and he knew she was hinting at a party.

It was the farthest thing from Joh's mind. He had other things occupying his head. But he made a promise to his wife that, "If I can get the new working section of the bakery finished by November the nineteenth, we can throw a party in there. Otherwise, where would we have one?"

What occupied Joh's mind were the plans for a new addition to the bakery, that would provide him with a bigger work area. A building permit from City Hall had already been obtained and work had started. When he wasn't baking or delivering, he was below on the parking lot at the back of the building, cementing in cinder blocks for the walls. A friend had been persuaded to come and help during the times when he was tied up with the business of baking or getting a few hours of needed sleep. It would be a simple structure, with access to the rest of the business via the original back door of the building.

The last thing on his mind was a wedding anniversary, but Nel wanted the Dutch custom of celebrating their halfway to silver, with a proper Dutch celebration. Joh comforted himself with the thought that he could probably use a good party to unwind and have some fun.

So, on Saturday, November 19, 1955, as another cold Ontario winter was about to set in, the new section was finished, and the couple celebrated twelve and a half years of marriage, with many of their Dutch friends in attendance, as per custom. The affair was full of singing, speeches, laughter, and reflection, but underneath, the undercurrent of exhaustion and discord could be felt, if one was looking.

In his new workspace, Joh continued to grind away at the twenty hour work schedule. One frigid winter night just after midnight, still working alone before his baker came in, Joh heard a knock on the door. He frowned. Who could be at the door this time of night? He opened the door cautiously. Two police in uniform stood there, cheeks and noses red with cold.

"Hey boys, what you doing here this time of night? There is trouble?" he asked, wondering what was happening.

"No, no trouble, it's pretty quiet tonight," declared one of them cheerfully. "Nobody in their right minds would be out in this cold except us poor cops out on patrol. Can we come in for a bit to warm up?"

"Sure, sure, come in, nice warm in here. You want a cup of coffee? And maybe a donut?" Joh offered. He thought perhaps he could butter his bread a bit. You never know how that might come in handy.

The cops gladly took him up on his offer. The hot coffee and still-hot-out-the-fryer donut was gratefully accepted and enjoyed. After fifteen or so minutes and a friendly chat, Joh sent two warmed up and eternally grateful cops on their way out into the cold night.

The next night saw the same two cops at his door, cold, needing a warm-up. The same the next night. The night after that, two new ones were at the door, with the explanation that this place came highly recommended. And so it went for the rest of the freezing winter. Joh didn't mind, he had no trouble with cops eating a donut and taking some of his coffee. It was the least he could do for the service they provided. Finding himself playing accommodating host to frozen cops, warming themselves on his coffee and goodies had its advantages.

One cold day, while making his deliveries, Joh came back to the van to find a parking ticket on his windshield. He picked it off, annoyed, and stuffed it into his pocket. That night, two patrolmen stood at his door again, seeking that warm cup of coffee and perhaps and donut or cookie to go along with it. Instead, they were greeted, not by that warm friendly smile, but a rather surly baker along with a crumpled piece of paper: a parking ticket, one that they were all familiar with, as all of them had filled out exactly the same thing numerous times over the years.

"Why you do this?" Joh questioned, a little insulted. "Every night you come, I give you hot coffee, donuts, cookies. You come here, get warm. Then I go through de cold snow to deliver, and I get a ticket?" One of the officers took the ticket out of his hand. "Let me see that." He read it through very carefully and noted the issuing officer's name at the bottom.

143

Then he stuffed it in his pocket, looked at Joh, eyebrows raised, and asked, "What ticket?"

Nel didn't enjoy winter at all. The deep snow made it hard to walk, the icy stuff would seep over the top of her galoshes, her legs got cold, everything was cold, it was just too much. Spring couldn't come fast enough. From November to almost May she was miserable, unable to freely go places. She simply couldn't and wouldn't abide the frigid, below freezing temperatures of Canadian winters. She could barely wrap her head around the Fahrenheit measurements that Canadians used. Celsius was so much simpler to understand, she didn't understand why, here, they would put up with the odd numbers their system had.

Her brother's letters, and those of her nieces living there, often described the British Columbia southern coastal area as mild. In some places it never snowed. She couldn't imagine it, but she started wondering if maybe they shouldn't have gone further on to British Columbia, instead of settling in Ontario, when they emigrated. She suddenly saw the downside of husbands making the final decisions.

Conversely, in the summers the heat made living almost unbearable, and there was no escaping the oppressive humidity. Where could she go, stuck in a hot store, with no air-conditioning, a luxury for people in their circumstances? Angry did not describe what she felt at times.

When it wasn't weather related, there were infuriating situations that she never in her life dreamed would be possible. They lived and worked right across the street from the Queens Hotel, including a pub whose entrance was in the side alley. She could smell the stink of beer, which she hated, wafting across the street. Some came out, more than a little tipsy, be it night or day.

One Saturday night, the one night of the week, when Joh and Nel had gone to bed at a normal time, proved to be too much. At two a.m. they'd been awakened by a rattling and banging on the door to their flat. It was, unfortunately, the first door at the top of the stairs from the street. On that night there was someone trying to get in.

Joh leapt out of bed, already upset at being rudely awakened. Whoever it was, they were up to no good. He jerked open the door and confronted a man clearly into his cups, mumbling something incomprehensible.

"What the hell you want?" Joh shouted at him. "Get out my house!"

The man continued to stare glassy eyed at Joh, uncomprehending and trying to fumble in his pockets for some unknown item, perhaps a key.

"Get out!" Joh roared again. Joh was not given to patience at the best of times, and this was definitely not the best of times. The man still didn't move back towards the stairs fast enough, if at all, and Joh was done dealing. He grasped the man by his shirt collar and the back of his belt, frog marched him to the top of the stairs and heaved. The drunk rolled loosely, end over end, down the stairs and stood up unsteadily at the bottom. He looked around briefly as though wondering where he was, and how he got there, then wandered out the door into the street.

Joh cursed the fact that the downstairs street door couldn't be locked. Anybody could walk up into the hall from the street. Anybody. The building was so old, that the street doors didn't possess locks, apartment bells, or any kind of privacy at all. Those kinds of doors were considered a sort of public access, even though only two families lived there. He could try and talk to the landlord, but the landlord was a cheap bastard, and wouldn't likely spring for anything as fancy as privacy measures.

They learned that even when privacy was obvious, it sometimes didn't mean much. Nel sat at the table mending during a rare half hour off, when she saw a movement through the open door of Jopie's bedroom. It was summer and the window leading out to the platform and fire escape was propped open. A stranger was in the process of climbing through into her apartment. Livid, she stood and ordered him back out.

"What are you doing in my house? she screamed at him. "This is my house! Leave! Now!" The stranger ignored her and kept coming. Nel kept at him and stood in his way, shouting as she did. He said nothing but pushed her aside. She turned and followed behind, pounding at his back as he ran through the row of rooms to the door at the end of the kitchen, where he exited, never looking back.

She ran back to the window to close and lock it, but before she could, she noticed a police cruiser slowly making its way through the parking lot. She deduced correctly that the man was on the run from the police and leaned out the window to shout to the police below, pointing to the alleyway leading up to the street. "He came up here through the apartment! He's on the street now!" The cruiser took off up the alley. It came to her that she'd just been confronted with a fugitive from justice, and it took a while for her to calm down. She'd been in harm's way and had been too riled up to even comprehend it.

On shaking legs she made her way down the stairs to the street. Joh was still in the bakery. She found him pouring over some of his old bakery-sized recipes for *Tom Pouzen* and *Jan Hagels,* among other delectable goodies. "I want to start making some of these Dutch recipes, to introduce our customers ..." Joh started to explain.

Nel never let him finish, instead demanding that something be done about the apparent easy access to their apartment, or danger pay for living where they did. Joh never found out if the fugitive was ever apprehended. It took a while after the knee-shaking occurrence was over, that they continued to discuss what should be offered as an introduction to "Dutch treats". *Jan Hagel* and *Bokkepootje* cookies were the first two to make the cut. They were simple to make and not too different for the palates of Canadian tastes.

Joh often thought of branching out into the exotic candies and chocolates he'd made in the Netherlands, but he'd have to manufacture more hours in the day first, in order to find the time to do it. He wasn't a miracle worker, so the idea was kept on hold.

In time, the two cookies became a regular and popular staple in the bakery's offerings, as well as a selection of Dutch deli items from a whole-

---

Tompoezen- *(Puss-In-Boots),vanilla slice, a cream filled pastry with pink icing on top*

Janhagel - *a cookie bar with roasted, shaved almonds on top*

Bokkepootjes - *(goat's feet) a cookie with both ends dipped in chocolate*

saler, such as , *ontbijtkoek, roggebrood,* Dutch chocolate bars, King peppermints, *hagelslag, muisjes* and *appelstroop,* all staples in a Dutch household. They were now proudly displayed on shelves attached to the wall opposite the display cases. Joh wondered if he should add a complete Dutch delicatessen to the business, but didn't dare bring it up to his wife until he could afford and find permanent staff for the front-of-store.

Nel continued to juggle the position she found herself in; being a store clerk and a mother. She had one skill that she'd somehow learned years ago, that of whistling loudly with her index and second finger stuck in her mouth. She used that skill almost every day now, calling her children home for lunch or supper. The whistle could be heard for a quarter mile echoing over the water to the Barrie dock, where they'd be playing, and they'd come running.

The cement pier was another source of worry for Nel. One day her fears came close to being realized, as Elly was brought home, soaking wet. She'd fallen off the dock and almost drowned, had it not been for a woman, who'd seen the plunge into the water and acted quickly. Swimming lessons, provided by the community were rapidly taken advantage of that summer for both children. Elly's consequent fear prevented her from entering any further than thigh-deep into the water, so she watched from shore to see how the others learned. She learned to swim just by watching. Ever after, her parents couldn't keep her away from water.

---

ontbijtkoek - *a sweet breakfast bread/cake cross*

roggebrood - *heavy dark rye bread*

hagelslag - *chocolate sprinkles. Used as a sweet topping for children's sandwiches*

muisjes - *a sweet, crunchy, almond flavoured children's sandwich topping*

appelstroop - *apple butter*

CHAPTER 17

A Visit Home

As the years slid by, the endless nights and days blurred, one into the other. Both baker and wife bent to the yoke of work. By this time, the old Chevy delivery van had broken down enough times to warrant the purchase of another car. He bought the next vehicle new, a 1958 Chevy Biscayne station wagon that served as both delivery and family transport.

There were times when Nel complained bitterly about everything, when she had her husband for an audience, but she stood behind the bakery counter dutifully at nine a.m. every morning. She'd be there from 7:00 a.m. on most days, icing cakes and cupcakes, among other small finishing touches to the baked goods.

Nel sat at the dining room table, reading the letter from home over and over. A sudden wave of homesickness overwhelmed her and she began to cry.

"I need to go home!" she said to the silent walls. There and then she made the promise to herself. She would go back to the Netherlands for a visit and take her youngest daughter with her to meet the rest of the family.

A long-ago argument with her brother Pete, suddenly surfaced in her mind. "A blue-eyed and green-eyed couple cannot have a brown eyed child," he'd declared vehemently one day, after an argument between them. Nel had claimed that it was possible, although it was pure conjecture on her part. Joh had green eyes. She had blue-grey eyes. The children had the same colour eyes, Jopie, blue-grey, and Elly, green. Now, to her great delight, the new addition to the family, Nancyann, whom Piet had never seen, had hazel green eyes, that took on a brown colour if the child was wearing yellow. She chuckled to herself when she pictured presenting her yellow clad, brown-eyed daughter to her brother and winning that very old argument.

Nel began talking about a trip to Holland to visit family. She'd been feeling more and more homesick, longing for the comfort and security of her older brothers and sisters. Finally, in late July of 1959, Joh acquiesced to Nel's requests to fly home for a visit. Tickets were purchased on a charter flight leaving Toronto. Nel and Nancyann would be gone for six weeks. School was beginning and Nancyann was scheduled to start kindergarten, so Nel had gotten permission to take her daughter out of school for the two-week absence in September.

It was six weeks of mixed emotions for Nel, after she'd had a tearful reunion with her family. Nel became highly sentimental of every ticket stub, flyer, label, or memento she managed to keep of her time in her own country. She saved them all and pasted them into a scrapbook. She took her husband's Kodak movie camera and filmed everything, wanting to take a piece of Holland with her back to Canada. And then she began to think of what waited for her there; more drudgery, heat, cold, virtual imprisonment in a store she'd never had any desire to be in.

She confided to her sister Anna all that troubled her about the circumstances she found herself in. The long hours in the bakery, a job she never wanted or expected, when her husband opened his own business. She found her country, as it was in 1959, a far cry from the war-torn country they left in 1950. It now looked and felt far more prosperous. She'd missed the Dutch ambiance and familial connections she'd been used to her entire life.

"I don't know if I can do it anymore, Anna," she tearfully confessed. "I hate it. I don't think I can look after my children properly, they're on their own so much."

Anna tried to comfort her younger sister as much as possible, and commiserated along with her until the week before the return to Canada. There were more tears that week and a realization of how much was lacking from her life. The misery came pouring out. "I don't even have a stove to cook on or bake," Nel cried. "I have a measly two burner hot plate that's been standing on my kitchen counter for eight years! Eight years! There's never enough money for a stove! I'm lucky I've got a refrigerator instead of an ice box now and an old wringer washer instead of a scrub board, but that's all!"

"I have no cool back yard to sit in, and maybe a nice flower garden. We freeze in the winter, with a big, ugly oil burning stove to sit around to keep warm. I hate it there! I *hate* it!"

Finally, in her agony, she made a decision. "I'm not going back," Nel declared to her three sisters. Jans, Anna and Lies stared in horror, shocked at the implications of that statement.

All three of them began to protest at such an idea. "What?"

"Not go back?"

"You would separate yourself from your husband?" "What about your other two children?"

Nel was desperate. The spectre of drudgery, of being a prisoner behind a store counter loomed dark and foreboding in her soon-to-be future. Surrounded by coziness and familiarity, the Dutch way of life sang its siren song to her heart.

"I can't! I can't! Dear God, I can't go back to that!" Nel wailed.

"Do you realize that you would be breaking your marriage vows? They were made before God!" All of her sisters cried.

They began in earnest to dissuade Nel of the idea. It took the rest of the week before departure, talking and counselling, all the while offering whatever support they could for their younger sister. It was a hard sell.

"I don't know if I can," Nel kept on, her head in her hands, and tears streaking down her face. Finally, Nel relented, but the preparations to return home were accompanied by reluctant feet and only half a heart.

CHAPTER 18

Growing Children

It was a Friday, the end of the work week. In the flat, Joh had just sat down to have dinner, the rest of the family already seated, when a knock sounded at the door. It was Dugan, the after-school helper Joh had hired a year or so ago, up to collect his pay. Joh went to get the envelope he had ready for him.

As he approached the boy with the pay in hand, Dugan began, "I've been working a year now and I believe I'm due for a raise."

Joh smiled at the cheek of the kid, and answered back, "No, I really can't afford to give you a raise right now, and just because you want one, doesn't mean you get one." I'm the one who makes those kinds of decisions. I'm the boss."

"In that case," Dugan answered back, "I quit, sorry."

Joh decided then and there that it was time for his son to start proving his worth to the family. At thirteen he was more than able, just like he himself at that age, to get up at four a.m. and start some kind of work day, as well as help to clean up after school.

But Jopie was not enamoured of that four a.m. start to his day. Every morning, Joh had to trounce the boy out of his bed, with angry words and recriminations.

"Get up! This is the *last* time I'm calling you," Joh pulled at his son's arm, as the boy stared up at him with half closed eyes and a scowl. He said nothing but growled in frustration. Joh shouted into his face, "Don't you growl at me, boy! You'll come when I call you! Be the man you claim you are and prove it!"

Slowly Jopie got up under his father's watchful eyes. Joh was going to make sure he didn't crawl back into bed. Determined to make the boy do as he was told, Joh stood there watching as Jopie slowly pulled on his clothes. He followed behind his father, sullen and silent, as the two of them climbed down the fire escape to the bakery below.

This routine repeated itself over and over each morning, neither one giving in to the other. Each time, as Joh put the boy to work, the silence between them became more oppressive with unsaid angry words. Joh wondered who would capitulate first. It wasn't going to be him. The boy would learn.

Finally, one dark morning, the routine escalated to the point of no return. Joh, in fury and frustration at his son's obstinacy, lashed out at him with a wild swing to the face. Jopie stumbled back, his nose running blood.

"You broke my nose!" he wailed.

"Man up, you ingrate! Carry your weight!" Joh roared back at him, and then added, "Your nose isn't broken, you baby!" Joh turned back toward the open window and the fire escape, calling over his shoulder as he went. "I want you down in five minutes, or I'll drag you down by the the hair!"

He shook as he entered the bakery below, the adrenalin still coursing through his veins. When was it going to end? If only the poor baker had known his son was sneaking out every night and roaming about town, doing whatever it was that young boys do at night during those stolen hours. He'd only have been back in his bed an hour or so before his father came to roust him out again, and it would have explained much of the difficulty.

Elly was less than thrilled with her new after school responsibilities. Her father had set her and her brother to scrubbing the mountains of dirty bake ware that the bakery generated. Both of them were more interested in playing or relaxing after a hard day at school. All too often John would catch them playing games in the bakery instead of bending to their work. One of those games involved a large serrated knife and an icing knife; swords in the hands of two youngsters duelling to the death. It ended with a slash to the bone across Elly's knuckle.

It wasn't the first time she'd presented herself, bleeding profusely. Elly had the habit of ditching her shoes, preferring bare feet to footwear. Nel had warned her on numerous occasions to wear her shoes, all to no avail. Early one evening, she came into the apartment, limping and bleeding from the bottom of her foot, just as Joh was set to go downstairs to begin work. There was a one and a half inch gash under her heel. She'd jumped down on an unseen broken glass bottle, hidden in the train station lawn, where she and a group of friends had been playing.

"I've told you over and over! Wear your shoes! Now look what you've done," she scolded. Then she turned to her husband, "I think you need to take her to the hospital!" Joh groaned. He'd be behind schedule for the rest of the night.

But he unhappily bundled Elly into the delivery van, her foot wound with an increasingly bloody towel, and presented her to the emergency department at the hospital. It seemed like hours before anyone came. Elly laid on the gurney with her foot propped up. Joh dozed in the chair. A doctor finally came; stitches were needed. Elly began to cry, frightened at the news, but one growl from her father silenced her. "It's your own doing," he snarled. "You'll wear your shoes next time!" Joh began his work much later than usual after taking a subdued daughter home to his wife. There were only a few hours sleep for him the next day.

The more worn out he grew, the more frequently the rod came out, but on some level he knew it had more to do with his exhaustion than their disobedience. And still, his son presented the same difficulty in waking up at four a.m., even with Joh stubbornly persisting in his efforts to get the boy to do so. He couldn't understand why he slept like the dead. The only one who never seemed to give him any grief was Nancyann, the youngest. He wondered, with a certain amount of trepidation, how much trouble he'd get from her as she got older.

Jopie had joined the Boy Scout movement a few years earlier, and relished going on the outings and camping trips that were organized each summer. Joh didn't want to deprive him of this, so that summer he reluctantly let him again attend the annual week-long camping trip. He would have to arrange for someone else to do his chores.

On Monday, he eagerly packed his bedroll and camp equipment in a duffel bag, kissed his parents goodbye, and set off to the meeting hall where his Scout Troop assembled. He was old enough to manage by himself, and, in their small town it wasn't too far of a walk.

"We'll see you in a week," his parents told him. "And we'll come to the campsite to pick you up next Sunday." A week went by, and on the following Sunday, two eager parents and two sisters drove to the Boy Scouts' official campsite on the shores of Georgian Bay to pick him up. The site was empty. At first Joh thought that they'd arrived too late or perhaps too early, but none of it made sense.

"I don't understand! Where are they all?" Joh puzzled. "Did he ride back with someone else?" After exploring a bit through the campsite, and finding no answers, the family drove home, only to find that Jopie had not arrived ahead of them. Joh phoned the Scout Master to find out how and if his son had made his way home. The answer enraged him.

"I'm sorry Mr. Grin. The camp was cancelled for this year. Didn't your son tell you?" He listened in disbelief at the answer. Where had the boy been for a week then?

Jopie came home rather sheepishly, later that evening, and Joh lit into him. "Where have you been all week?" The baker asked in a fury.

The story came out, and Jopie, showing not a shred of regret, made his confession. "The camp was cancelled, but I wanted to camp anyway, so I took the bus and camped by myself up there." He stated it as a matter of fact. He'd rented a canoe as well, using his saved-up allowance to pay for it. Unfortunately, a squall on the bay had slowed him down getting back to the campsite, and he'd arrived too late to meet his parents with the excuse of, *everyone left earlier than scheduled, so I'm the last one to leave.*

Joh couldn't get over the audacity of his fourteen-year-old son. Joh stared at him in disbelief that the kid would pull one over on him like that. Never mind, he'd work Jopie twice as hard as punishment. No kid of his was getting away with that kind of behaviour. His mother, on the other hand, secretly admired the boy for his spunk and resourcefulness in spending a week on his own camping. But she didn't dare share that opinion with her husband for fear of riling him up even further.

The teen years of both older children were becoming increasingly difficult for the baker and his wife to manage. Joh couldn't remember his own teenage years, nor those of his siblings, being so problematic to his own parents.

Sometimes he wondered what they were doing wrong, but neither parent had a clue. So, he continued on his present course, getting stricter with them to keep them in line. Come hell or high water, he'd teach his son his own work ethic; work 'til you drop.

There would be no boyfriends for Elly before the age of sixteen, she'd work as a clerk in the store on Saturdays to spell off her mother. There would be no makeup showing up on her face before she was an adult. Above all, both young teens would learn to listen and obey without question, even if Joh had to use the rod to teach them, and he did so on many occasions. The dam finally broke.

"Jopie has run away!" Nel stood, shaking in front of Joh, leaning over the bread mixer. "Find someone to mind the store, I'm going after him, if it's not too late!" She left without further explanation, and Joh made a few quick phone calls.

Nel ran as fast as she could to the bus station, where she suspected her boy would be. His behaviour had been strange that morning, before leaving for school. She knew his school schedule for the day did not include band practice, yet he'd carried his trumpet case out with him as he left. She'd checked his room, after puzzling over his almost secretive manner at breakfast, and found the trumpet tucked away behind his bed. It didn't take her long to put two and two together.

As she rounded the corner of the bus station, she saw him in line, waiting to board the bus, with his trumpet case doing duty as a suitcase. The bus sign read, 'Toronto'. Nel approached from behind, took the boy firmly by the arm, and pulled him out of line. "Where do you think you're going? You come with me!"

Jopie said nothing but hung his head and let himself be marched home by a furious mother. Again, Joh was pulled from his work to deal with an errant child, and again he struggled, as did Nel, with the rebelliousness of one of their teens.

Jopie's defiance, his insubordination, and the galling resistance against his parent's instructions, drove both of them to almost uncontrolled outrage. This time, his act of running away proved to be too much for one of them. Joh, praying for some guidance and patience, watched in horror as Nel let go of his son's arm, snatched a long piece of wood, used to prop open one of the windows, and began to bring it down on Jopie's head, screaming as she did.

"Miserable child! All we do for you! You ingrate, you snot-faced piece of work!! This is how you repay us?"

Without thinking, Joh lunged for the heavy stick before it could strike. He knew suddenly that extraordinary steps had to be taken before it all escalated completely out of control. They made an appointment with a child counsellor to try to find some guidance. Somehow, they muddled through it, not understanding if anything would work. They made a little headway here and there, and Jopie's behaviour showed small signs of improving.

Elly continued to be difficult, sneaking makeup onto her face, out of sight of her parents' watchful eyes, and having a secret boyfriend at the age of twelve, which Nel had to quash. Once again, a client had marched into the store, haughtily informing Nel, "I've seen your daughter cavorting with a boy at the fish and chips place down the street! An Oriental no less! You'd better put a stop to it before you find a little Oriental baby in your family!"

Nel coldly replied that her daughter wouldn't be presenting babies of any kind in the near future but confronted her daughter just the same when she came home.

"Someone tells me that you've been seen with a boy, an Oriental boy. Who is he, a boyfriend?"

Elly could still not lie to her mother's face, and when confronted with the question, answered yes. The earlier story Nancyann had confided to her suddenly made sense, when she'd told her that she'd seen her sister wearing a ring she didn't recognize. Suspecting, Nel asked her now, "Did he give you anything? A friendship ring maybe?" Again, yes.

"Give it to me." The offending ring was produced from where Elly had hidden it.

Nel marched down to the fish and chips restaurant at the end of the street, found him still sitting at the tables with friends, and held the ring out to a surprised boy. "Elly is not permitted to have a boyfriend yet," she told him sternly, as she pressed the silver friendship ring into his hand. "Leave her alone." She marched out of the restaurant, back to her own establishment and a broken-hearted girl. Thereafter, Nel kept a sharper eye on her daughter's comings and goings.

The relationship between the two did not improve after that incident, and Nel discovered that her daughter no longer wanted to be in her company with any degree of pleasure. Sunday outings became filled with excuses of why both their teenagers no longer wished to accompany their parents, but when parents went for a Sunday drive, the children, all of them, would go with them. There were long faces in the car more often than not.

Visits to the beach for the day were a little happier, but still, the teenagers always sat away from the parental beach blanket, unless sandwiches were doled out. This was chalked up to "children growing up and becoming more independent", until one day, on such a beach outing, when Elly was accompanied by her friend Liz. Joh followed them that day as the two wandered off, wondering what they were up to. He watched, dismayed as one of them produced a package of cigarettes and matches.

He angrily confronted both of them on the way home. Elly's sullen retort back left him a little chilled, "Well, you smoke too." He didn't know what to say to that. Nel coldly told her, "The deal we made with you, that if you don't smoke until you're eighteen, you'll receive $100 on your eighteenth birthday, is gone." They had no idea that Jopie had also begun smoking long before this, and his sister would not betray him.

More and more the relationship between Elly and her mother showed signs of disintegrating. Sometimes Joh caught her making snide remarks about Nel within earshot. At yet another one of those comments, Joh looked at his daughter with his old guilt showing in his eyes. Once again, it tore at his insides as he remembered his own mother. His stupidity still ate at him in the quiet of the night when he couldn't sleep, no matter how many times he tried to tamp it down.

He pulled his daughter close. "Oh girl," he began, "let me tell you something…"

And Joh, tears close to the surface, began to tell his daughter of his guilt, at not visiting his mother, how he never saw her again, all because of a pair of shoes and his pride. He hoped that his daughter would take away a somewhat different perspective when trying to deal with her mother. At the very least, he hoped that she would appreciate the fact that she still had a mother, and to have some understanding and compassion for a flawed individual, as all of them were.

He felt those flaws all too acutely in himself; how he seemed unable to connect with his son, how he and his wife always ended up clashing over things, and the heartbreaking realization that he had no idea how to change any of it.

Stepping off the train at Chatham, Ontario. Nel in front, carrying Elly, Jopie climbing down on his own steam just behind, and Joh inside the passenger car exit, carrying a suitcase.

The suitcase held by the porter, was donated to the Chemainus Theatre's props department in 1998.

Joh stands in the doorway of one of Meaford's, Hoppy's Cabins

Elly and Jopie, reach up excitedly as the first of their possessions is handed down

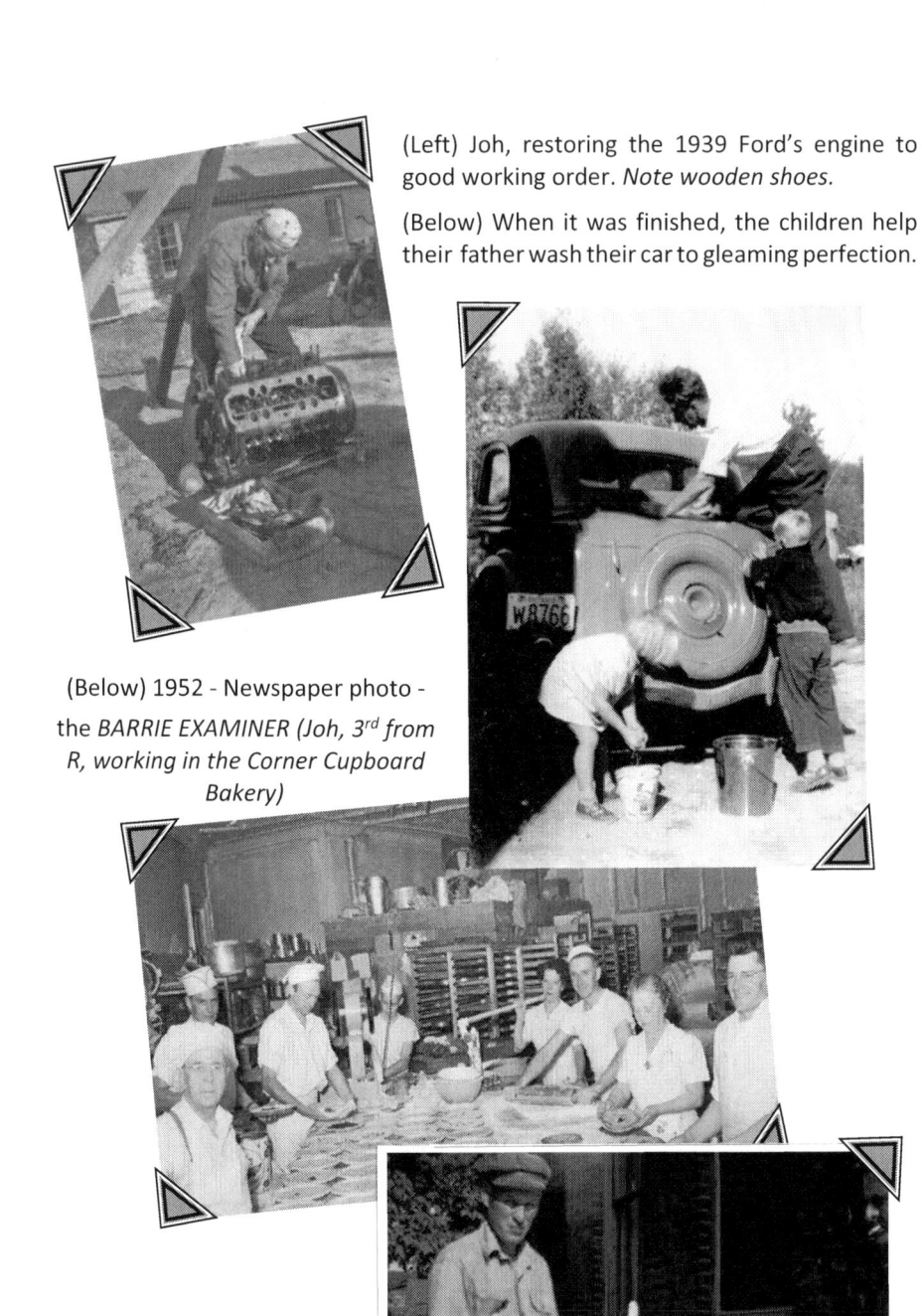

(Left) Joh, restoring the 1939 Ford's engine to good working order. *Note wooden shoes.*

(Below) When it was finished, the children help their father wash their car to gleaming perfection.

(Below) 1952 - Newspaper photo - the *BARRIE EXAMINER (Joh, 3rd from R, working in the Corner Cupboard Bakery)*

(Right) Joh -R, and another bakery worker load Joh's sugar creation into a delivery van. 1951

(L) Joh and Nel's little Canadian, Nancyann, making her debut.

Three Years Out of Holland, Opens Bakery

(Above) 1953 - from the BARRIE EXAMINER

(Left) 1950s: Joh's sense of humour making an appearance

Kempenfelt Bay in winter. Elly, skating on the ice, little sister, Nancyann, running in front. In the background to the left the 4 apartment windows, fire escape, and, lower down, the new addition to the bakery can be seen (marked).

(Above) The bakery store front at 107 Dunlop St. E.

Note: The three of the four windows of the front upper storey tenement. The Grin family resided in the rear apartment. Doorway (marked 105) with the stairs leading to the apartments, is on the right, (behind car).

TOP - Joh's 1951 Chevy delivery sedan.

Evidence of Joh's exhaustion on a Sunday afternoon at the beach.

NEW
DIRECTIONS
WEST

Joh tends to the station wagon and U-Haul trailer, during the long trek to British Columbia.

CHAPTER 19

Changes in the Wind
1961

Joh stuffed the very last of their household goods into the U-Haul and slammed the door. He sighed and looked around, wondering and saddened at the turn his life was taking. All his dreams, crumbled to dust, his failure like a palpable weight in his gut. How had it come to this?

He thought back to the moment it all changed.

≈≈≈≈≈≈≈

"I'm not helping you anymore!" This emphatic statement came from an angry and determined wife. "And the children are not helping anymore either! I won't have you using them like small slaves in your business!"

He'd confided to her earlier that, the lease being up, he had big plans to further his ambition. He'd rent another space, buy some fancier store furnishings…" Nel had stopped him in his tracks with her angry outburst.

She'd continued: "All we've been doing is working ourselves into the ground! You are literally killing yourself, we're constantly either in debt, or simply too poor to afford things, the children are rebellious with good reason, and we're done. I don't even have the time to raise my children properly. This is destroying us all."

Nel went on to give him three choices; they could return home to the Netherlands, they could move to Chatham to be closer to his family, or they could move to the West Coast, to British Columbia, to be closer to her brother Jan and his family. Seeing his wife with her heels dug firmly in this time, he mulled over those choices, but any one of them meant his failure to some degree. It was disconcerting to find himself seeing her point, realizing that she was right. He knew it, but he was still obsessively intent on forging ahead with his plans and ambitions, unwilling to give in.

Going back to the Netherlands was unthinkable. He still remembered one baker telling him that his plans were ill-thought out, that Holland would recover and do better than before. He should stick it out. From all Nel had told him of her trip home, that's exactly what had happened. The country had recovered and things were prosperous almost to a fault. If they went home now, he'd hear nothing but, *we told you so*. His pride mattered.

That abject feeling of failure didn't abate when he pictured himself facing his brothers in Chatham. Those two had been incredibly successful, his youngest brother, Wim especially, with his booming brick and stone business. Simon wasn't far behind, with a beautiful house on a large piece of property on the river, something he had yet to achieve after eleven years of toil. All he had to show for it was a run-down rented tenement that wasn't even his, and some miserable sticks of furniture.

In the parking lot behind the storefronts, he'd had to auction every possible thing off to drum up enough money for the move; bakery equipment that sold for pennies on the dollar, any furniture they couldn't fit into the U-Haul, the children's bikes. He could still see Elly, standing at the apartment window above him, as the auctioneer eliminated all of what he'd been able to part with. She'd watched, with a look of profound disappointment on her face, as her bike, the one she'd been so proud of, was being auctioned off to the highest bidder.

It seemed even good friends were affected by the apparitions of his failures. His good friend and employee had died of a massive heart attack one night just a few weeks before. Tinus Ott was a hard worker like he himself was, willing to do whatever it took to get ahead, no matter what. Joh almost felt he'd had a hand in his death. They were both heavy smokers. Ott's doctor had warned him to quit, otherwise he wouldn't last another month. He couldn't, even as Joh himself found it impossible to deny himself a cigarette.

There was nothing left in Barrie that didn't leave a foul taste in his mouth. The only choice left to him on where they could go was British

Columbia, far enough away that, if it were possible, he'd leave all the heartbreak, disasters, and disappointment behind. He made his decision.

The apartment was cleaned out, the store, a blank face with only the name "Dutch Pantry" above the window to indicate anything had ever been there. Young Jopie had successfully passed his driver's test, and he'd be able to spell his father off during the long drive. Joh hoped that the camping they'd do every night along the way would somehow bring the children closer to their parents. Jopie seemed to take to the camping life anyway.

He had to laugh to himself, when he remembered the boy's stunt from a few years ago, camping all by himself for an entire week, under the pretense of attending the Boy Scouts' annual camp. Then he remembered his oldest daughter's latest escapade not three weeks ago and he stopped laughing. It had scared him more than he cared to admit.

They'd come home a little early from a Saturday night social function. At fourteen and sixteen, two of the kids were old enough to be left at home by themselves and babysit their eight-year-old sister. But they found that Elly was gone. Jopie would only shrug, and say, "She said she was going to the arena to skate. I don't know why she isn't home."

Joh drove to the other end of town and walked into the arena lobby. He approached a man still behind the ticket counter. "The skating is over?" he asked, for lack of a better question. Of course, the skating was over, he thought. It was almost eleven p.m. He knew that Saturday night skating was usually over by ten. "Skating?" The man looked at him, puzzled. "There was no skating tonight, it was cancelled for the concert."

Joh returned home in dismay. It was now well after midnight. The thought of his teenage girl out at this time of night made him very uneasy. He informed Nel of what he'd found and watched as she started hyperventilating. "Don't panic, don't panic!" he told her, fearful he'd have to deal with an overly emotional female.

Up and down the stairs he went, from the apartment to the street, looking to see if he could spot her coming home. He didn't know what to do, where to look. When he wasn't on the street watching for her, Nel would go out, walking up and down the sidewalk, looking at cars, the few that went by, hoping someone was bringing Elly safely home. In the meantime, he'd gone out again, unable to sit still and wait. After a fruitless search he came home again and found Nel waiting for him at the door. "She's home! I found her! I've sent her to bed."

His relief left him weak in the knees. Then the rage set in. Where had she been? It wasn't to a skating session at the arena, that's for sure. He rushed into the bedroom and yanked the covers off the girl, lying in the top bunk of the girls' bunk bed. "Get up," he demanded. "You want to be an adult, act like an adult!" A small, tearful voice came from the bunk, "I'm not an adult." "Get up! I want an explanation! Where have you been?" Joh insisted.

Elly climbed down and stood in her pajamas in front of her father. He instructed her to sit at the table and began to grill her on her whereabouts during the evening, and with whom had she been.

Slowly, the story came out. She knew there had been no arena skate that Saturday night. Instead, she'd gone to the concert with her friends because they were going and she wanted to as well. Dugan was also there, yes, the same Dugan who'd worked for Joh. Afterwards, she'd joined him in his car. They'd driven around for a while. She'd had a huge crush on him for a long time, and well ... and after she realized how the time had suddenly gotten away from her, he'd driven her home, dropping her off at the end of the street, just in case she'd be seen.

As she was coming down the street towards her doorway, she'd seen her father step out of it, looking the other way down the street, and she'd ducked into a dark, recessed store entrance, terrified. She stood there, hidden in the shadows, not knowing what to do, unable to face her parents' wrath at being out so late, and without permission. She'd watched as her mother walked up and down the sidewalk, looking at the few cars passing by, adding to her fear and guilt, until she couldn't stand it anymore. She'd stepped out of the doorway as Nel passed by again. All Nel could do was hug her daughter in relief.

Joh couldn't believe it. "You went to a concert? You went with Dugan in his car? What were you thinking?" And then another thought came to him. "Why didn't you just *ask* if you could go to the concert?"

"You never let me go anywhere," she answered in a small voice. Again, her answer chilled him, and, at the same time Joh realized the implications of that answer. *Say no too many times, and they stop asking. they just do it, with or without your permission.* As before, he didn't know that he'd do it any differently. There was certainly no way he'd let his daughter run wild or give his permission to do any old thing she wanted.

"You're grounded until we move!" he finally informed her. "If Liz is over, you'll stray no more than ten feet from home and be within earshot at all times."

≈≈≈≈≈≈≈

The family left Barrie very early August, 1961. They took the opportunity to head south while they were still close, to say goodbye to friends and family. In Bowmanville, the Kloppers waited for their arrival, sad that they were moving to the other end of the country. The goodbyes were bittersweet. Jan and Marie knew that things were not going well in many aspects of their friends' lives and hoped that the move would bring better days. Wim, Simon and their wives wished the same. The brothers were well aware of the blow to Joh's pride, considering all the plans and ambitions he'd had.

When the visiting was done, Joh finally turned his face west and new opportunities, with a station wagon and U-Haul, fully loaded. Two adults, three children, a large dog, all silent in the car, and, except for Lassie the dog, that simply hung her head out the window sniffing the air, each of them seemed to be reflecting on what they were leaving behind and what lay ahead.

That whole first day they drove, following Highway 400 north, then Highway 69 towards Sudbury. As they approached Sudbury, the tops of the nickel mine stacks could be seen in the distance, belching out white billows of smoke, resembling nothing less than the fluffy cumulous clouds in their everyday sky. From the back seat, Nancyann suddenly piped up, awe and discovery in every word, "So *that's* where the clouds come from!"

The silence was dispelled with peals of laughter from everyone.

That innocent epiphany broke the oppressive mood of loss and failure that pervaded the interior of the vehicle. And everyone began to chat and make remarks about what they saw.

Only a few things marred that first day's drive. The mattresses, that Joh had tied to the roof of the U-Haul had come loose and flown off onto the highway. They were hastily retrieved and retied as tight as possible. They'd been lucky no one was driving close behind them. With the children all in urgent need of a washroom, Joh stopped at the next gas station. There, while everyone saw to their needs, Joh redid the hasty tie down and as a precaution used some extra rope to make a few more loops.

On the road again, one of the children had suddenly noticed an absence, and asked, "Where's Nancyann?" To Nel's consternation, they'd left the youngest behind at the gas station. They drove back and found her standing near the shoulder of the road, a little insulted at the glaring omission. Again, laughter and teasing followed.

As they passed Sudbury and turned onto Highway 17, Joh grew a little tired of driving, and suggested that Jopie should take a turn at the wheel. Jopie slid behind the wheel, his father sitting next to him on the seat. Joh gave him a few pointers and suggestions on handling a station wagon pulling a trailer, then sat back to relax.

Half an hour later, Joh could see that his son was having a hard time of it. The incessant weaving and drifting told him enough and Nel was increasingly worried they'd be driven off the road at any moment. Too late, he realized that a car pulling a heavy U-Haul, made driving a little different. Kicking himself for his over-confidence in a new driver's abilities, Joh took over the wheel, much to Nel's relief. Young Jopie never drove on the trip again.

By the time they reached Sault Ste. Marie it was nighttime. They hadn't spotted a good camping site yet but finally stopped out of necessity, somewhere in the pitch dark. The illumination from the headlights provided enough to see a clear, flat space beside the road to pitch the two small tents for the children. The girls stumbled around with the tents, finally erecting them under their brother's expert tutelage, unrolled the bedrolls and crawled into them for some much-needed sleep. Joh and Nel had their mattress laid out in the back of the Chevy station wagon, and gratefully crawled in, beyond exhausted from the long day.

The next morning, much to everyone's surprise, the youngsters found themselves camped out at the edge of a swamp. Jopie, in his pup tent, laughed. The girls, on the other hand, were not so impressed. Both tents were floor-less and offered easy access for ground crawling unknowns. The girls complained that they'd felt "things" making their slow way over their sleeping bags all night. They were a little squeamish, not knowing what kinds of creatures it might have been. Probably frogs, Jopie told them, or maybe snakes. Or both! The girls both squealed at the thought. It made their brother grin all the more. All of them were covered in itchy mosquito bites. Elly decided that wouldn't happen again and after a simple breakfast of toast and tea, she spent the rest of that day's travels, planning on how to barricade the bottom edge of their tent.

Due to the weight of the U-Haul, Joh could only drive fifty miles per hour or less. Anything faster would make the station wagon fishtail. He knew it would take more days to get across the country than he'd counted on. Following the Trans-Canada Highway, it took four days to cross the expanse of Ontario, two for Manitoba, a little over one for Saskatchewan and one for Alberta, at least as far as Calgary.

Somewhere in Alberta they discovered that Elly's glasses had broken in half. Joh groaned inwardly, *another expense I really can't afford right now.* The girl was severely myopic. It couldn't be helped at the moment. She'd have to do without them until he had enough for a replacement.

Joh had been warned that the shorter route through the Rogers Pass was not completed yet, so they would still have to take the old, long way around. He was to look for the turnoff at a little town called Golden. That route was called, appropriately, the Big Bend Highway. It wound, in a 305 kilometre loop, up and back through the Selkirks, one of the most mountainous areas in Canada. Joh considered what he'd seen coming into Golden plenty mountainous already, and he wondered how much higher those craggy reaches would get. Nel found them rather claustrophobic.

When they turned off at Golden, the farther they travelled through the silent forest, the more ominous it felt for Nel. Joh had never seen such limitless wilderness in his life. It left him feeling awed and small. The children simply stared, mesmerized by the endless rows of giant tree trunks marching by.

Joh's reverie was abruptly interrupted by a chorus of squeals from the back seat. *"Dad, Dad, stop the car!! Lassie jumped out!"* The dog had seen something no one else had and lunged straight out the window in her excitement to give chase. The car came to a stop, billowing dust around them, and everyone clambered out to begin calling, hoping the dog wouldn't lose herself in the maze of trees. It only took a few minutes, but she came back, happy and wagging her tail furiously. Whatever it was she'd seen, was forever a mystery in the minds of the family.

The Big Bend's designation of "highway" was a bit misleading. Rather than a smoothly paved road, it resembled more a narrow gravel logging road for a great deal of the way, with steep, hazardous grades, and chasms with simple timber crossings to get to the other side. At the sight of a crossing just like that, Nel clamped her jaw shut trying not to give in to the desire of begging to go back. The road led straight down towards an opening in the earth, a canyon, so deep that it seemed to reach straight into an abyss.

Joh stopped the car a small distance from the gorge. He could see, far below him, a narrow ribbon of water. The road on the other side was a steep grade straight back up, before curving left. He didn't like it all. Another one of those narrow wooden bridges, with little to no safety railing lay before him. Worse than that, there was no level spot on the opposite side so he could get up a good speed to make the grade. He knew he was heavy. He could feel that in the steering. He just didn't know how heavy. If he couldn't make the grade, and couldn't hold the brakes, the car and trailer might roll back and plunge into the chasm. He needed a plan.

After slowly crossing the wooden trestle, he stopped and ordered everyone out of the car.

"Okay, this is what we're going to do!" Joh looked at his family. "You two," he pointed at Jopie and Elly, "go find yourselves a good sized, heavy piece of log about eighteen inches long, or a big rock that won't roll."

Nel was instructed to keep the dog with her on a leash, and stand well off to the side, and Nancyann, to stay close to her mother.

The teenagers each found what they needed and came back to their father. "What I'm going to do," he said, "is to try my best to get up the hill."

Joh continued, looking at both teens with a dead serious expression. "You two, walk alongside the back tires of the car, each on a side. If I can't get up the hill, and I start to roll back, throw the logs right behind the back wheels. If that doesn't hold it, and I keep rolling back without being able to stop it, I'll jump out of the car and let it go into the canyon."

Both teens both nodded solemnly and took up their positions at the back tires of the station wagon. Joh slid behind the wheel again and started up the grade. The chunks of log were held at the ready for an eventual throw-down, if necessary. The car engine strained, as it slowly ground forward, creeping up the grade. Every inch forward seemed to take an eternity. Nel could feel a tension headache coming on. Nancyann walked beside her, wide-eyed. Both of them imagined the entire car, trailer, everything, plunging down into that bottomless pit. Nancyann only hoped her daddy could jump out in time if everything started rolling backwards.

With his heart pounding in his ears, Joh finally made it up to the top, stopped the car, legs weak and shaking from nerves, and let out a ragged breath. He'd made it. He closed his eyes for a moment while the family piled back into the car.

The day was getting late and with mountains looming overhead, the sky seemed to darken early. Were they ever going to get to the end of this 'Big Bend'? It seemed everlasting. Several times they met cars coming the other way, and they barely had room to pass each other. Each time one did, Joh was surprised that the two vehicles didn't scrape each other in passing. Once it was a logging truck, fully loaded, and Joh was half in the shallow ditch to give it enough room. An ambulance came by, racing as it went. He wondered who behind him wasn't as lucky as he'd been.

On and on, the road endlessly carried on. Finally well after dark, and below another steep grade, they saw lights twinkling in the distance. The final town with the odd name of Revelstoke marking the end of the Big Bend "highway" lay below them. The family was exhausted. Joh decided, just for one night, he would splurge and stop at a motel to rest. The rest of them welcomed the respite.

The next day, rested, clean from baths, they were ready to go on. Thankfully, the highway was paved again, the mountains seemed less ominous, but, looking at the map, they still had a long way to go. But at least they were in British Columbia. Joh wasn't stopping until they'd reached Langley and his brother-in-law.

Finally, at two a.m. the next morning, the lights of Langley made an appearance, a repeat of Revelstoke's welcome twinkle.

CHAPTER 20

Another Place to Call Home

It had taken them ten days to cross the country. Nel thought it was ironic that it was the same amount of time that the sailing across the Atlantic had taken eleven years ago. *Was it only eleven?* It felt like a lifetime ago.

"It's so late," Nel groaned. "I wonder if Jan would appreciate a telephone call?" Joh said, matter-of-factly, "You haven't seen them for eleven years. I would think he'd be happy to get a call to let him know we're here. Besides, we can't afford another motel and I refuse to sleep in the car again."

Joh drove around the streets of Langley until he spotted a telephone booth and Nel made the call. They waited where they'd parked and fifteen minutes later headlights approached slowly. The car stopped and a man got out. Joh and Nel stepped tentatively out.

"Jan?" Nel queried. The figure in the dark looked familiar and not familiar. She wasn't sure.

Then there were hugs and cries of welcome, *I'm so glad to see you safe, we were getting concerned!* Then, after a little more chatter, Jan told them, "Follow me, there's plenty of room in the big farmhouse!"

The relieved and tired couple climbed back in the car, and Nel turned to Joh, a little shock in her voice, "Jan has gotten so old looking!" Joh laughed inwardly, thinking, *yes, he's probably thinking the same thing of us.* They followed the red taillights and drove out of town. Surrounded by the beginnings of farmland, they turned off the road up a long driveway. A large house loomed in the dark, with one doorway lit up. In it stood a small round figure, a housecoat hastily thrown on, and her long, grey hair in a braid down her back. Marie stood waiting. The weary family piled out of the car and followed Jan into the house. There were more hugs, kisses and cries of *welcome!* The sleepy children stood off, a little shy, two of them overwhelmed by an aunt and uncle they could barely remember and one had never met.

Marie bustled the children off to bed upstairs. Much older than their mother, Jan and Marie would become surrogate grandparents, something none of the kids had ever had. In reality, they were 'Uncle John and Aunt Mary' and would become a stabilizing presence in the children's lives.

Downstairs, the adults continued to talk awhile, before crashing into bed themselves. In the morning, all of them looked around with curiosity. The kids were particularly interested in the barn, the milk cows, and the surrounding fields. They'd spent their entire lives in a city setting, with sidewalks and parking lots as front and back yards. This was new, this open grassland and wide spaces.

The next day was Saturday, and the older couple's youngest son Joe, who still lived at home, re-acquainted himself with his cousins. The rest of Jan and Marie's children, eleven more of them, began arriving to meet the newcomers, some with spouses and children in tow. The large farmhouse living room and country kitchen was suddenly filled to capacity. Joh's head was beginning to spin, listening to the clamour of exuberant nieces and nephews, many of them not much younger than himself and his wife. Added to the cacophony were the voices of great nieces and nephews, the grandchildren of Jan and Marie. The oldest of the twelve was close to Nel's age, and the youngest, Jopie's age.

Jopie and his cousin, Joe, who he still remembered from the Netherlands, had escaped the hoards of relatives and gone out to the fields. Elly sat by herself in the hayloft, contemplating her changing living arrangements, a little overwhelmed herself, and Nancyann either clung to her mother or was cuddled by female cousins, who were more like mothers or aunts.

Out of curiosity Joh had the U-Haul trailer weighed at a truck inspection station. To his shock it weighed 1500 pounds over its load limit. Considering the bumper hitch he'd used, and the roads he'd traveled over, it was a miracle they'd made it in one piece.

Labour Day was quickly approaching, and all the children were registered for school in Langley. In the meantime, Joh was actively looking for work and a place to rent. He started in Langley, then moved on towards the areas closer to Vancouver. Vancouver itself was a little too large and spread out, so he chose the North Shore, on the other side of Burrard Inlet. There, he found work in a small bakery run by another Dutchman.

While Joh looked for work Nel found ways to be helpful around the house for Marie. Her sister-in-law was in the middle of her canning and Nel lent a hand. Elly thought she'd help too, and stepped up beside her mother, about to pick up the next jar to begin filling it with peach slices. Marie stopped her with a cry of alarm. "No! You don't touch anything!" Elly looked shocked at her mother, and then at her aunt. "Why not?"

"You just started your period, didn't you?" the aunt said almost accusingly. "Well, yes. What does that have to do with anything?" Elly glanced at her mother again, questioning this oddity. Nel gave the girl a silent warning shake of her head.

"You'll ruin the peaches and the canning will go bad." Aunt Mary told her. The reaction was instant, despite another warning shake of her mother's head. *"What?* That's an old wives tale." and Elly began to laugh. Marie insisted that her niece not touch anything to do with the canning, and the teen, laughing, left the kitchen, not knowing whether to be glad she didn't have to work, or be insulted by the whole thing. Later Nel explained to her that with her aunt's much older generation, old wives tales still held true.

After a month, Joh had enough saved to move his family to a small rental home, high up near the top of a mountain road. That night, after Joh's family had finally moved in, they all stood in the living room in awe, gazing down at a blanket of glittering jewels spread out far below, the lights of Vancouver. They'd never seen anything like it. For a while it became a sort of evening ritual, to stand in the living room and take in the view. It almost felt as if the entire little house would slide down the mountainside and plunge into a treasure chest filled with sparkling diamonds and rubies.

For a while life seemed calm, happy and ordered, a far cry from the horrendous existence of even a few months ago. Somewhere during this time, Jopie, feeling like he was getting a little too old to be called something that sounded like a girl's name, decided that he'd re-name himself Joe. From then on the two cousins with the same name were referred to as "Our Joe" by their respective families.

Nel's niece, Bep - Betty, as she was now called, her husband Gerrit and children lived in North Vancouver as well, and she'd noticed something that her aunt and uncle might be interested in. Betty telephoned Nel the same day.

"*Tante* Nel, there's a beautiful house for rent right across from me. It would be perfect for you! Come and take a look at it as soon as you can," she called excitedly.

Nel buttonholed Joh the minute he came through the door from his shift in the bakery. "Let's take a look at it! Betty says it's perfect for us!" Joh sighed. He'd just finished an eight-hour night shift, and needed coffee, food and a bit of sleep, in that order. "We'll go, we'll go, but first ..." and he let his needs be known.

"Well, I didn't mean right now, did I?" she threw back at him. "I'll go make you coffee and a sandwich." Nel sat on pins and needles after she'd made her husband his meal and as she watched him eat she hoped upon hope that he'd agree to go and see the house right after he'd finished. It wasn't that far away, maybe ten or fifteen minutes tops. But Joh fell asleep in his easy chair afterwards and she waited impatiently until he woke up.

When he did, she'd dropped some not-so-subtle hints to go look, so he roused himself to acquiesce to the request. On the way he wondered how much the rent would be, hoping it wasn't too much. He'd already determined that from this point on, he'd be squirreling away as much money as he possibly could for a down payment on his very own house. If he could save enough money to start his own business, he could do it for a house too. At least he wouldn't feel like such a failure any longer. He felt sure that owning his own home would certainly remedy that.

"Are you sure you want to give up that glorious view?" Joh questioned. Nel thought a moment.

"The view is nice," she admitted. "But there's a lot of things wrong with the place." "Oh? Like what?" He couldn't believe she was already finding fault with it.

"I've had a rat run out from behind the toilet," she grumbled, "*while I was sitting on it!* "And the floor slopes down towards the window. I checked it with a marble!" Joh laughed, "Well, no wonder I always feel like I'm going to roll down the mountain!"

The two of them laughed over it, and then sobered up. "I want a stable, long-term place for the family, not something we may have to move from sooner rather than later," Nel continued. "If that place is shifting down the hill, it might need a lot of work to fix it, Or, it might even be condemned!" Joh had to admit to himself, despite the phenomenal view, there was a lot wrong with the little place, not the least of which was the small size.

All three children would agree, but on an entirely different matter. The road ran steep, straight up the mountain, and the walk home from school every afternoon was gruelling.

The following month the family moved into the new rental after giving notice. Betty had been right, the house across the street was perfect for them. Nel had fallen in love with it; a cozy, old fashioned two-storey, with three bedrooms on the upper floor, all of them with windows, a living room with a fireplace, a dining room, and a kitchen with a real stove. To Joh, the place appealed more due to the large backyard with a plum tree, and enough room to start a small garden, an enclosed back porch where he could keep gardening equipment and other "guy things", and a small front yard, hedged in with boxwood, with a giant cherry tree at the corner of the house. Perfect!

Nel caught Joh's ambition to save money for their own home, and she answered ads that she'd dug out of the *help wanted* columns in the newspapers; people looking for cleaning ladies. She could easily do that on top of her own home. The hours guaranteed she'd be home when her children came back from school, and they were a far cry from the ones she'd had to adhere to in the bakery. Before long, with both of them saving, money started to build up in the bank account.

At the same time, Nel knew she would need to learn to drive, to get her grocery shopping done. The stores weren't walking distance anymore. The bus system was handy here on the North Shore, but now, everything was more spread out. Barrie had been more compact, so, they had to make some adjustments. Joh was roped into making some of those adjustments by giving driving lessons to another family member.

Joh drove a standard vehicle; gearshift, clutch, gas pedal, and brakes. Nel had never driven in her life. Inwardly he rolled his eyes as he imagined himself teaching his middle-aged, uncoordinated wife to synchronize the shift, clutch, gas and brake all at the same time. And steer too.

In good time Nel successfully applied for and got her learner's license. Now came the hard part. The lessons began on the street in front of the house. Joh prayed for patience as Nel started the car for the first time, slid the car into first gear as instructed, and drove slowly forward. Inside the house, the three children, acting as audience at the front window, screamed in fits of laughter, as they watched their mother bunny-hopping down the street.

The next day presented a completely different problem in the form of a horse and rider on the road in front of them. "Go right," Joh instructed. Nel steered right.

The distance to the horse was growing shorter. "No, no. To the *right!*" Nel edged right again, as far as she could.

"To the RIGHT, to the *RIGHT!*" Joh shouted, fearful that they would run right into the back of the animal.

Nel had a problem. "I can't go anymore to the right, I'll be in the ditch!"

There was a pregnant pause, then Joh wiped his hand over his face, "*Ach* ... I mean to the *left* ... just go around the horse, to the left."

At long last, between equal portions of patience and stubbornness from both participants, Nel finally got her driver's license.

CHAPTER 21

A home to Call His Own
1961- 1963

For the first time Joe, Elly and Nancyann could remember, Christmas would be completely different. There would be no Sam, Gerald, Nelly, John or Jackie, no Aunt Mary and Uncle John. To them, the Kloppers were synonymous with Christmas. So, this first Christmas Eve in British Columbia, as they sat around the Christmas tree was quiet. Too quiet. The kids missed their cousin-friends, the camaraderie, and as much as they hated the extreme cold, they missed the snow. "It should snow only on Christmas," one of them grumbled.

Joh and Nel, tried to be as cheerful as possible, but even she admitted, "It isn't the same without Jan and Marie." Everyone agreed. But it was Christmas Eve after all, and they were, once again, following their version of *"pakjes avond"*. From the time they landed on Canadian shores, they'd tried to keep up the Dutch custom of separating *Sinter Klaas* from Christmas as unobtrusively as possible. Thus, the gifts were opened on Christmas Eve.

Joh still remembered the few times they'd try to revive the traditional Dutch *Sinter Klaas* celebration on December 5. He regretted that it never took off within the family, because they'd been so focused on work, and early December came and went so quickly, that the moment was over before they even had a chance to plan.

The children seemed to gravitate more to the Canadian custom of mixing the two versions of the holiday, anyway. *Of course, they would,* he thought to himself, *they were fully immersed in the Canadian way of life now. I made that decision for them by coming to Canada.*

<u>pakjes avond</u> - literally, gifts evening
<u>Sinter Klaas</u> - St. Nicolas, Santa Claus

For both parents, this was the one time of year they regretted leaving their home country. He'd still thought that the best solution had been their compromise of celebrating Santa Claus on Christmas Eve, and reserving Christmas Day exclusively for the birth of Jesus. It was still a separation of sorts.

They sat around the tree, its lights twinkling merrily, as though doing their best to lend some gaiety to the evening, while the family quietly opened their gifts. Joh and Nel tried to be as cheerful as possible, but they felt a certain flatness to the evening. It ended as quietly as it started.

Sometime during the week between Christmas and New Year, as Nel was finishing up the last of her dusting and about to pour some more coffee, the phone rang. She ran for the telephone hanging on the kitchen wall, thinking maybe one of her clients wanted her to come do some extra cleaning, or maybe it was her brother Jan.

It was Jan, but not the Jan she thought it was. "Merry Christmas!" A voice shouted at her over the line, and then other voices right behind, "Merry Christmas!" It was Jan and Marie Klopper from a life recently left behind.

"Jan? And 'Rie! How wonderful you called! Merry Christmas!" She shouted back at them. It was such a pleasure to hear those familiar voices, and it instantly felt like the Christmas feeling had seeped back into the holiday. Almost.

The Kloppers had news. Jan and Marie spoke of a visit to British Columbia this coming summer. Nel was ecstatic. "Of course! We would love to see you! Please come!"

"We also want to go to Seattle for the World's Fair!" Marie said, the eagerness in her voice palpable. Nel agreed. "Oh yes!" she said at once, remembering, "The kids have been begging us to go! We are so close here!"

They talked some more, and with long distance calls being so expensive, decided they would make further arrangements by letter. Joh came home shortly after, and Nel bombarded him with the happy news as he walked through the door.

"Jan and Marie are coming for a visit …" she began. Joh looked a little perplexed, "Weren't they just here the other day?"

"What? No, they want to come and also see the World's Fair…"

"Jan and Marie? Can't they just go from their place …"

"It's a little far. They want the kids to see a world's fair for the …"

"*All* of them?"

"*Stop* interrupting me! Of course, all of them." Nel looked at him sharply, wondering why he was acting so dense. Joh blinked his eyes, picturing it. Then, a little light went on.

"Wait, you're not talking about your brother, are you?"

They stared at each other for a moment, rapidly trying to shift the images in their heads. Having two couples both named Jan and Marie in their lives had its moments.

There were other occasions that first winter; one jarring event, to Nel at least, that shattered her pre-conceptions of British Columbia for good.

"You *lied* to me!" Nel shouted at her bother. Jan looked abashed. "Well, up to now, it was the truth! It hardly ever snows here. This? This is really not normal!" The "this" Jan was referring to was the three feet of snow that blanketed the Lower Mainland that year; three feet, that Nel was convinced fell for her benefit, because she'd tried so hard to get away from it. Nel was not impressed, and she needed someone to blame, as she once again struggled to wade through the icy stuff seeping into her boots.

Joh was just as excited as the children were to see his friends again. His summer holidays approached and they'd coincided the Klopper's visit with his vacation. The entire family waited eagerly as Joh retrieved the family from the airport. The station wagon was crammed with bodies, the smaller ones in the rear area, delighted to be able to look out the back window, making faces at the drivers behind them, while their older brothers and sister pretended to disapprove, adult-like.

Young Jackie, the curly-headed baby of the family wasn't quite the baby anymore and big enough to be enamoured of the giant Bing cherry tree in the front yard. He was also well able to climb it. The cherries were large, sweet, and ripe. All the adults watched in amusement, as the tree filled with children, trying to pick and eat at the same time.

"Be careful, all of you," Joh called up to them. "If you eat too much, you'll end up with stomach aches!"

The warning went as unheeded as all past warnings had. That evening Jackie groaned, his tummy distended and hurting. For a while the toilet upstairs became his best friend. In the meantime, with an eye on the trip to Seattle, and the planned excursion to the Fraser Canyon that Joh wanted the Kloppers to see, a rental car was arranged. There were just too many bodies for one car, even a large station wagon.

The few days spent at home were time for speaking of things to come and reminiscing about old times. In the evenings the children spent their time at the far end of the back yard around a campfire, roasting marshmallows and wieners. Nel and Marie peered into the dark through the back window, trying to spy a bit, laughing at their teens. Nel had produced the binoculars, peering at their oldest boy and girl to see more of what they were doing out there. It seemed to them that Gerald and Elly were attracted to each other. Whether or not it was just wishful thinking was beside the point. The two women would have been delighted if, somewhere in the future, their families would come to be connected.

When Joh and Jan came home with the rental car, The teenagers were delighted with the Volkswagen Beetle that stood in front of the house. A very small convoy consisting of station wagon and a Beetle full of teens, spent days exploring the Fraser Canyon and Seattle's World's Fair. Joh's first real vacation was, he felt, well spent.

That fall, as the first leaves were turning on the giant cherry tree, the announcer on the snowy black and white TV set made the dire warning: **Typhoon Freda is set to slam the west coast of British Columbia and the**

western states tomorrow! It was the evening of October 11, 1962. Nel and Jo looked at each other in alarm. They still remembered Hurricane Hazel and the devastation it caused. Hurriedly the next morning, they ran through the property to make sure everything that was loose was put away or tied down.

"The announcer did say that they didn't expect it to be as strong, once it gets here," Joh said optimistically. "By the time those storms get this far, a lot will have blown off steam." Hopefully, Joh and Nel both wished he'd be right. They'd said that of Hurricane Hazel too.

They were wrong again. Freda ripped through the Lower Mainland like a bull in a china shop; power lines festooned like garlands over top of cars, signage scattered over the roads, trees, splintered like matchsticks. Residents had seen nothing like it, except those that had already felt a hurricane's wrath.

Early in the evening, the power out, Nel sent the children to bed by candlelight. They listened nervously as overhead the roof shingles rattled and shook with the wind screaming.

"Mommy? Is the roof going to blow off?" Nancyann anxiously asked, her mother. "I think I'd rather be downstairs." Nel thought for a minute. "If it gets worse, I'll let you sleep on the couch," she promised.

Joh, ill-advisedly, but feeling somewhat responsible for his place of employment, went out, driving slowly to the bakery, picking and weaving his way through the branches strewn over the road. Phone lines were down as well, but he thought his boss would appreciate the check. The bakery looked fine, and he sat in the lee of the building, just watching for a while.

When it looked as if everything would hold, he returned home, much to Nel's relief. "That was a stupid thing to do," she scolded. "You could have had a tree fall on you!"

He'd faced far harder dangers, and, thinking of the war, he replied, "Ach, you worry too much!"

In the end 4,000 trees were gone, including some 3,000 in Vancouver's famed Stanley Park alone, and seven people were dead.

Two females came screaming out of the house through the front door, and Joh, pushing a lawn mower, looked up in shock. "What's happening? Why all the screaming?" Nel stood, shaking in front of him, Elly behind her, wide-eyed.

"Go look in the back porch!" She pointed at the house and described what she'd seen, shuddering. "There's something horrible covering the whole inside of the door frame and walls!" Mystified he went in through the kitchen and had a look at what sent his wife and daughter scrambling and spooked. There, three feet outward from the porch door, covering the doorframe, entire wall and ceiling, was a roiling mass of large carpenter ants, some with wings, resembling a massive, moving carpet. He had an infestation to deal with.

It wasn't the only time outdoor denizens had invaded their space. A snake had somehow found its way into the kitchen via a large head of cabbage brought home from Nel's sister-in-law's garden. It, likewise, had sent the same two screaming from the house. Joh had to laugh, *city women, what can you do with them?*

He called an exterminator for the ant problem, and after the work was completed, he inspected the walls, ceiling, and floor thoroughly to make sure there wasn't any structural damage. There was some, and he'd need to talk to the landlord about it. At the same time, Joh thought he'd try and bring up the subject that he and his wife had recently discussed. They were ready to buy, and they wanted to buy this house. The next day he paid a visit to his landlord.

"Well? What did he say? I hope he's willing to sell," Nel said, looking hopefully at her husband when he came home. She had her heart set on buying the home they were already living in. He slowly shook his head back and forth. "He doesn't want to sell."

Nel's face fell, as Joh explained, "I talked to him this morning, told him how much you loved the place, and me too, but he says it's a good source of income for him. He's not ready to sell yet."

"How long until he is?"

"I don't know. He didn't say if he even wanted to, in the near future."

Nel swallowed her disappointment. Joh said, to assuage her disappointment, "Let's do a little looking. It's my day off and we can check out some of the real estate listings." They spent the rest of the day, driving around looking at homes for sale. None suited. Weeks went by, Joh often investigating places he'd seen on his way to the bakery. Finally, one caught his eye. It was on a street not too far away from his work.

As he stood there looking at it, he wondered at the slope it stood on. Like a lot of things on the North Shore, it was built on what was, basically the side of the mountain. Not the actual mountain, perhaps, but on the lower slopes. The property was stepped in five sections at the front, and perhaps at the back as well, but he couldn't see from the road. The driveway had a steep grade that led up to a carport at the side of the house. He wondered what it would be like in the winter. There usually wasn't a lot of snow, but when it did, or if it froze while wet from the more usual winter rain, he'd have to make sure it was well salted and sanded. But he'd appreciate a real parking space with a cover, whereas the house they currently lived in only had street parking. This house even had a view overlooking the inlet and the city below, something his wife always looked for.

At home, he told Nel, then made a call to the real estate agency and made an appointment to view. "I think this is it," he told Nel. "This might be the place I can die in." She looked at him curiously. "Are you planning on dying soon?" He laughed, "Well, no, but once I buy a house, I don't ever intend on moving again. Ever."

They looked the house over thoroughly, noted things they liked and things they didn't. Joh could visualize a lot of improvements in the split-level, three-bedroom house, that would keep him busy for a long time to come, and his creative juices were already kicking into high gear. Back in the car, they looked at each other, trying to discern some sense in what the other was thinking.

"I think I could live in that house," Joh began.

At the same time Nel started, "It has a view! I think it's lovely."

They were agreed. They liked the house and would make an offer. After a few days of anxious waiting, the answer came back. Offer accepted. They could move in that summer, two month's away, upon the removal of subjects.

CHAPTER 22

1964 - 1966

There were so many things to do. Everywhere he looked, jobs he'd started lay unfinished. They were already a year into the house, and Joh, on his days off, spent his time working on all the improvements and changes he'd visualized when he bought the place. If he couldn't finish one task because he needed something that was missing and couldn't find it right away, he'd wasted no time idling, by starting on another job. Now there were so many things that were left undone, that Nel was beginning to look sideways at him.

"Why don't you *finish* that job?" she asked him, pointing at the half finished landscaping along the west side of the driveway. They were standing in the back yard, looking over what had already been done. "I want to build a rockery there, and I need more bushes and plants," he explained. "Besides, I'm busy with this right now, pointing at the rock wall he was building to create a retaining wall for the back half of the yard. He'd get back to the previous job, he reckoned, when he had time and materials. He'd already collected some small, potted trees to plant there later

Why couldn't she see that he was busy, working a full-time job? Sure, it was mostly at night, but getting some rest after he got home was important too. The job allowed him a lot more daytime hours to work on all the projects he's set for himself, but really, there was more to life than just work. She should be able to see that.

Over time, he was quite pleased with what he accomplished. Some of the wiring had been re-done, he'd eradicated the hated horsetails that choked the bank beside the driveway. Even though they kept growing back year after year, he was determined to get rid of them for good. There were flowers ringing round the property, he'd planted small shrubbery in amongst the rocks and boulders that made up the very rear retaining wall bordering the back alley, and built a fence at the top, to afford more privacy for the secluded back yard. A Maple tree had been planted in the front lawn for eventual shade, and the grass seed he'd thrown over everything was starting to come in thick. Only the potted tree he'd intended for the sloping side along the driveway still sat in their pots, or rather, what was left of them. The pots were now mostly disintegrated and the roots went down into the hard packed soil. Joh left them there permanently.

Inside was another matter. The hardwood floor needed refinishing, the living and dining areas could stand a fresh coat of paint, and the kitchen needed something. He was sure Nel would have plenty of suggestions.

His son's behaviour had, so far, been exemplary. Joh wondered if the church they'd become members of, had something to do with it. They had welcomed the family almost immediately into the fold, after arriving in British Columbia. From the church in Barrie, he'd obtained a name and contact number for the affiliate church in Vancouver, another Dutch Reformed Church, and he'd called the number when the family had moved to the North Shore from Langley.

Hope Reformed had a strong young people's group, something that the church in Barrie did not. His two older children eagerly joined, and quickly became an integral part of it. Joe had even become president of the Youth Group, something that filled Joh with pride. What didn't sit so well, was his son's decision later to quit school. After he'd finished Grade 10, Joe had given up, and instead, opted to get a job. Joh had done the same thing at about the same age so he couldn't say very much. In his heart he was disappointed, knowing that these days a high school diploma was far more important than it was in his day.

His oldest daughter graduated two years later, something he was proud of. He was pleased that she'd stayed in school, even though it was a struggle. He knew that, like him, she was creative, and had aspired to become an artist. Academics didn't seem to be her strong point, although he sometimes wondered. It had more to do with her interests, rather than her intelligence. But he thought that for girls, the academics weren't so important. They'd get married, have babies, and run a household. They didn't need academics for that. Still, it was an accomplishment to graduate.

They'd finally become Canadian citizens, something they'd never given much thought to. In truth, they'd just put it off because there were just too many other things that took precedence. It really didn't change his life that much, he thought, except that now, they could cross the border into the States, without having to make the claim of, yes, they were Canadians, to the border officers.

The whole process had been a bit of a nuisance, as far as he was concerned. They wanted him to know a lot of things about Canada, information he really had no use for. Things like: who was the first Prime Minister of Canada, *does it matter?* how many provinces there were, *more than I could ever see in my lifetime,* how many Territories, *Canada has territories?* What's the population of Canada, *how would I know, I've never counted them.* The list of questions was endless. It was like he was back in school, memorizing stuff.

He'd lived here so long, he felt he was Canadian enough already. They'd never really voted, because as far as he was concerned all campaigning politicians were the same, and would do the same kind of job as the incumbents, so it made no difference who was voted in. He wasn't interested in politics anyway. The current Prime Minister Pearson was doing a good enough job, in his opinion.

Joh didn't know at what point he made the determination, but, after seeing a small red Triumph sports car sitting on a car lot one day, he thought, *that would make a great first little car for my son. Something to make him feel proud of himself, an accomplishment of sorts.* Later, after the thought had gelled a bit in his mind, he approached Joe.

"I have a proposition for you, boy. Have you got a minute?"

"Sure Dad, what's up?"

Joh proceeded to tell him about the car he'd seen, offered to pay the down payment for it, a substantial amount, and buy it, if Joe would make the monthly payments after that. Joe was interested, and felt, with the job he had, he could make it work. After that the seventeen-year-old drove around in a sporty little car that everyone wanted a ride in, and Joh felt that his son was on his way to success.

Joh stood looking at what Elly had come home with from the Vancouver School of Art. It was her first oil painting. *That's not too bad,* he thought. At the urging of her school friend and fellow artist, Lynn, she'd joined a Saturday morning class and had been introduced to oil painting.

Joh had watched his daughter from the age of seven, blossom into a budding artist, coming home from school with sheet after sheet of pencil and crayon drawings. Now she'd graduated to oils. He was glad that years ago they'd stopped buying paint-by-number sets as gifts after someone had told them that these things could severely hamper a budding artist's abilities. He thought her work showed promise and to encourage her to continue he built a wooden case to carry her paint tubes and brushes, instead of using the bag she dragged to art school every Saturday.

Joh wondered if his youngest would also be artistic, but it was hard to tell. Nancyann seemed to emulate her big sister in copying whatever Elly did with paper and clay but showed her own creativity in the everyday crafts she worked on.

Joe too, showed promise in his creativity with a camera, so Joh built a darkroom in the basement and bought the equipment to let his son expand his knack for photography. It filled him with pride to see Joe develop the skills needed for such a profession and he hoped that he'd pursue it.

At the same time, the relationship still had its mountains to climb because Joe always had a mind of his own and took any advice from his father rather hesitantly, if at all. There were always little arguments that surfaced unexpectedly between them, over nothing, over some small point, over advice or instruction, and it set the quality of their relationship.

Elly's relationship with her mother fared a little better; the girl's confidence somehow creeping its way into their everyday lives. Nel still coloured her hair, denying the grey hair from its function of making her look older. It was near Christmas and Elly, in a flash of creativity, looked at her mother's salt and pepper hair and said, "Mum, you should colour your hair in time for Christmas! I think a coffee brown would look *so* good on you!"

"Fine, go out and get me the colour you think is best for me," Nel instructed her daughter. The girl bought what she thought was the appropriate colour of boxed hair dye and on Christmas Eve morning Nel sat and had her hair dyed by her daughter. When she was finished, and the towel whipped away for the reveal, Nel began to wail, "What haf you done to meeee!"

Her hair had turned jet-black. "I look like en *whoooorrre!!*" Nel continued to commiserate loudly. The coffee brown colour turned out to be black coffee, not cafe-au-lait, the only kind of coffee the girl had been used to seeing her parents drink.

As Joh waited for his wife to pick him up from work that afternoon, he was greeted by a very unhappy and almost unrecognizable wife, with very dark hair, who, instead of coming into the bakery, sat in the car waiting for him to come out. He got the full story on the way home. Joh kept staring at the black hair, wondering if he'd get used to it, shrugged his shoulders and figured, *I won't have any choice. Anyway, it's only hair,* and he left it at that.

At home, he went to bed, needing some sleep. A few hours later, he awoke and made his way to the living room looking for some coffee. He shook his head in disbelief. His wife now had another colour, orange. She'd made an emergency trip to the hairdresser to have her hair stripped, but she'd have to wait a week to have another more permanent colour safely applied. Wisely, he hid his smirk behind the newspaper.

The next day was Christmas and the entire family went to Christmas morning services, Nel with a hat jammed down on her head so nothing would show. Nel never wore hats and Joh wondered if it would garner just as much attention as the offending locks would have. One curious parishioner, who knew Nel very well, tried to pry the edge of the hat up, to see what was underneath. Nel jerked her head away, but not before the woman had caught a glimpse of what she was trying to hide. She started to hoot loudly, "What happened to your hair?!!" Everyone within earshot turned to drink in the details. The jig was up, and Nel reluctantly explained.

For the rest of the week there was a palpable level of anxiety in the house as she waited for her appointed time with the hairdresser. When she returned from the beauty salon later that day, her hair was now the shade it was going to be.

Forever after, Joh laughingly recounted the experience from his point of view. "I leave for work, her hair is grey. I get picked up, her hair is black. I wake up from sleep, her hair is orange! Now, it's a beautiful shade of coffee brown … with milk!"

CHAPTER 23

The Nest Empties

Just when he'd begun to hope that his relationship with Joe might improve, the bottom dropped out.

"I quit my job!" Joe came home and made his perplexing announcement. "You did what? Why? In heaven's name, why? A responsible person doesn't just quit his job." Both parents stared at him. "I got fed up with it. That's all. My decision," he stated flatly. Joh stared in disbelief, astounded that his son would make such a stupid mistake. "Why?" he asked again. The answer was the same. They argued over the whys, wherefores and consequences but Joe held fast, and walked away, angry that his father couldn't see reason.

It was all too much. All Joh had tried to do for him, to instill the importance of work, of a job to meet the responsibilities of a young adult, to stand on his own two feet and carry his own weight. None of it had done any good. For no good reason he could see the boy had just up and quit. He had a car to continue paying on, and now, no job to meet even that obligation. The agonizing thought that his son could be that unreliable sent him to the bedroom. He laid on the bed and wept, angry, and hurt, until Nel came in to comfort him. He shrugged her off and turned away. It was his failure, his burden to bear.

Someone else came into the darkened room, his older daughter, who laid a hand on his shoulder. "Dad," she hesitated, "I know it's hard … but you have to … to let Joe make his own mistakes. They're his to make. Maybe he'll learn, but it'll be the hard way," she said gently.

Joh began ignoring the young man, no longer willing to let himself be hurt. Nel, on the other hand kept nagging until an argument ensued. She couldn't help herself. She had to say something. It was not in her nature to ignore or keep her mouth shut. The tension in the air was thick enough to cut and it was only a matter of time before something gave way.

Joe's appearance began to look a little different, and his clothes took on an appearance that, to his mother, did not look quite normal anymore. Nel was infuriated that he no longer resembled the fine clean-cut young man she thought she'd raised. These new "hippies" that were springing up everywhere had far too much influence over her son. Arguments arose over clothes, hair, habits, and a steady job, and the tension ratcheted up even more. The two were like oil and water.

The little red sports car still sat in the driveway, beaten up, forlorn looking, and badly taken care of, a sad parody of the little beauty it had been. The bank had been looking for payment for some time now and were ready to repossess it. Joh remembered the words, *he'll have to learn the hard way*. He let the bank repossess the car.

Nel began hinting that her firstborn should find a place of his own but she was torn. Her hints countered her own desires. She wanted her children close, not gone away somewhere to do whatever, unbeknownst to her.

Joe finally moved out, helped by a tearful mother and pragmatic sister. On the way home, the car empty of the last of Joe's possessions, Nel wept openly. Elly looked over at her mother and remarked sharply, "What are you crying for? It's what you wanted, isn't it?" All Nel could come back with was, "Oh shut up."

Despite Nel's unhappiness that one of her children had flown the nest, there seemed to be a more peaceful atmosphere in the house. But, underneath, there were still currents of dissatisfaction and clamour; wishes and feelings, outed in passive aggressive behaviour and words. It was only a matter of time before the full force of Nel's negativity had the upper hand once again.

"They warned me about you, before we got married." Overwhelmed, he snarled at her one day, after another frustrating nag session. "Yes, they warned me about you, too," Nel snapped back. Her eyes dared him to continue with this conversation. Both stayed stubbornly at odds with one another, neither one giving in. The nagging continued; the driveway was too steep to climb in the winter, there was too much junk piled in the carport, the kitchen shelves needed something done to them, on and on.

Yet, somehow, there were tender moments too. A delighted thank you for a favourite bottle of cologne, the laughter at funny stories retold, fond shared memories together. During the bad moments, instead of focusing on the negativity of his wife's unhappiness that so easily surfaced, he remembered to weigh everything together, and found that a lot of it balanced out.

He couldn't sleep, tossing and turning. He'd finally gotten up and now sat in his recliner, his thoughts a jumble made up of his failures, disappointments and even the work around the house that still needed doing, looming over him like a pall. The demons plagued his mind over and over in the darkness. Try as he might, he couldn't find his way out of that black labyrinth. It ate at his soul. Frustrated, he got up and walked to the kitchen, looking for that bottle of wine his wife had brought home earlier in the week. *Maybe a glass of wine would help.* Filling a tumbler and taking a swallow, he walked back to the chair. It felt good on his tongue. If it helped him sleep, he'd do it again.

Finally, bed called again, and he settled in, hopeful that sleep would come. He had to get up early for work. The alarm woke him from a fitful dream much too soon, but he had that responsibility and dragged himself out of bed. *I need a cigarette and a cup of instant.* He stuck last night's butt between his lips, lit it, and fixed a cup of coffee in the kitchen. Fortified thus, he set off to work.

"Hey Joh, good to see you! How was your weekend?" The greeting upon his arrival at work grated a bit, but he presented himself as cheery and called back to his fellow employee, "Not too bad! And you?" The banter that followed seemed to lift his spirits and slowly the dark thoughts and feelings lifted. As Joh mulled this over, the ebbing and flowing of light and dark in his soul, he began to think of ways to stay on a more even keel. He didn't like falling into a funk so easily. It was not a good feeling.

His two oldest children at eighteen and twenty were approaching adulthood, if not already there. Where was the line between childhood and adulthood anyway? Nel, still looked at them as children, but he knew there was a vast difference between those young people today, from the children of yesterday, and certainly with one of the two that still lived under his roof. Only Nancyann, at thirteen, could still be considered a child, and that would change quickly as well.

He threw himself into his work, never stopping, except to take a nap after he came home from his job. The home and property became his lifeline and anchor, never without something to do, to keep his mind from dwelling on what he viewed as his profound failures. Church helped as well, and every Sunday he stood, smiling broadly at every friend and acquaintance. He'd accepted the position of usher and relished the responsibility. People remarked at the wide, friendly smile that greeted them at the door. It became his oasis when dark clouds threatened to overcome him.

Everyone did their best to make sure Nel was content. Elly had honed her skills enough at the easel to present, as a birthday gift, a pair of paintings, portraits of Nel's parents, taken from old photographs out of one of the family albums. Nel was impressed and pleased and Joh was stunned at the likenesses. This was far better than anything he had ever done. When Jan and Marie came calling for the birthday, Jan stood staring at the semblances of his parents now hanging over the mantelpiece, too moved to say a word.

None of it was enough, the problems between him and Nel persisting to the point where she finally insisted they get some marriage counselling. He half-heartedly agreed, if only to assuage her. Personally, he didn't see what they could say or do to fix things. But he'd try. At least he could say he tried. After several appointments, and even going from one unsatisfactory counsellor to another, Nel finally gave up on the idea. She angrily deplored that she could not get anyone to convince her husband he needed to change. *Funny,* he thought, *I had the same thought about you!*

By the time spring came, Joh's allergies were once again making his life miserable. On top of all the continual little dramas that usually pervaded the home, it did not help that Joh continued to suffer from constant sneezing and heavy congestion, to the point he could barely breathe. This spring was particularly bad, as things began to bloom and pollen was heavy in the air. Sneezing, congestion, sinus pain, more so than usual seemed to infuse his every waking hour.

Another visit to the doctor to find some relief, revealed a sinus infection that couldn't be cleared up with the usual antibiotics. He was made aware of another type of treatment . They could clear out his sinuses with an operation that might give him some relief from the ongoing allergy related infections. The downside was that he'd probably lose some sense of smell.

Joh didn't care, he wanted relief, so he agreed to the procedure. It was not a pretty sight that greeted his family when they came to visit afterwards. Joh lay in his bed, face purple and swollen, his nose and half his face swathed in bandages, and tubes siphoning something out that sent Nancyann running out of the room, gagging. Afterwards, when the bandages were removed, and his nose closer to its normal size, he was sent home to recuperate, his face still a little bruised and tender. Everyone hoped that Joh wouldn't suffer quite so much the following spring. The disadvantage the doctor had warned him about became a reality. He lost his sense of smell completely.

The dark clouds continued to rain on his life. Nel constantly worried obsessively. Little things. Everything, it seemed, was a disaster. Worry about finances, what to have for dinner, what would the mailman bring tomorrow, and most of all, worry about her children and their comings and goings. They were no longer small, he reminded her, needing to be home and under her watch. But curfew was a must for Nel. Eleven o'clock, twelve, if need be, but not much later than that, unless it was supervised by real adults like youth group leaders from church. If one of them was late, Nel would lie in bed with eyes wide open, waiting for the sound of the door, all the while imagining them somewhere, broken and bleeding.

On this night, Nel lay awake waiting. Elly should have been home from her shift at the restaurant that supposedly closed by midnight. Twelve thirty a.m. came and went. One a.m. Two a.m. At two thirty, both Elly and Joe came quietly through the door, surprised to find both parents sitting in the living room, the lights ablaze.

"What are you two still doing up?" and "Where have you *been?*" was mashed together at the same time from a dismayed daughter and an angry mother.

"What do you mean, where have I been? I've been at work, and after work I went with Joe to a friend's place for a quick visit," Elly replied, perturbed at her mother's anger. Nel glared at her daughter, "Who are these friends? Do I know them? Are they trustworthy people?"

"What? Yes! No! You don't know them, but I do. Besides, I was with Joe the whole time! Anyway, why on earth wouldn't I be able to visit people I know? I'm not exactly a child anymore!"

Nel was unrelenting in her position. "You need to always let me know where you are! I want to know where at all times, especially at night. I worry when…"

"You worry way too much, Mum, *way* too much! Besides, I wasn't alone out on the street, was I? Do you think I'm totally irresponsible? There was *no need* for you to worry!"

The interruption fell on deaf ears and the continuing argument escalated until angry tears sent the young woman out of the room. An stifling silence filled the house the next day. Neither side changed their stance. Elly disappeared for a while, taking the bus, presumably to work. She was home for supper, but silent through the meal. Joh began to breathe easier, hoping that maybe another family drama had run its course.

That evening Elly disappeared into her room and did not show her face for the rest of the evening. Her parents dared not disturb her for fear of dredging up the argument again. The next day, Nel found a letter in an envelope addressed to both of them and left on the coffee table at some point during the night. Elly had gone to work and had not returned before Joh came home from his job. She pushed it into his hand and told him to read.

It was a long letter, starting with an apology for the lateness of the other evening and went on to list the reason why she felt her parents still treated her as a child, writing,

".. *you don't trust yourselves that you did a good job, therefore you don't trust me.*
I have been thinking seriously of moving out because if I stay around here any longer, I'm sure things will get worse."

It ended with *"I wrote this because I can never seem to get anything through to you when I talk to you."*

Nel was beside herself. Her daughter could not leave her, could not go out on her own. "What does she know? Nothing! I'll never rest or sleep again! I can't stand not knowing what she's doing, and with whom, and where, and she'll never be able to make the right decisions..." on and on the wailing went.

Joh, in the process of trying to calm his wife, and his own heart, promised, "Don't worry, I'll talk to her! I'll try to change her mind. She's not gone yet."

When his daughter returned home, Joh carefully approached her with the letter in his hand. "Honey, you don't have to leave. It's not necessary..." he began.

"Then you have to start treating me like an adult," Elly cut in. "I'm not a child anymore, and I hate that you and Mum treat me like one! I don't want to leave, but I can't live like this anymore either. I need to be trusted."

Joh promised he and her mother would try to view her more as an adult, but there were limits. She was still under his roof, after all. Concessions had to be made on both sides. If she was going to be out late, he stressed, she had to call her mother. She was a worrier, and a leopard doesn't change its spots that easily.

To Nel's relief, Elly did not move out. But she had a hard time keeping her controlling habits at bay. For the most part, Elly seemed to come home most nights at a reasonable time. Nel even patted herself on the back for letting her daughter go on a vacation train trip alone back to Ontario for a few weeks. She'd only once given herself over to worry, before tamping it down.

Occasionally, Joe would come home for a visit. On one such an evening he came with a young man in tow, another Dutchman, fresh from the shores of the old country. They'd met at a church function and Joe began a friendship. Almost immediately sparks crackled between Elly and the young man, Roel Langen. Joh wondered about it. She hadn't had many boyfriends yet, just a few crushes that didn't seem to go very far and she didn't date much either. Joh sometimes wondered if they had been too strict with the girl. He knew very little about those things.

Joh didn't need to wonder much longer. Soon enough the romance was in full swing. It looked serious. Also soon enough, Nel realized the implications. The spectre arose of another child, no, not a child any longer, a young woman, that would eventually leave home. For Nel, that thought was still unbearable. Still, Elly showed no signs of packing up anytime soon, to follow her own path, as Joe had done, much to her mother's relief. But, as with all things, Joh knew it was just a matter of time.

Roel was a second time immigrant to Canada who came with his mother and sisters for another stab at immigration. An older brother and sister were already here. They'd stayed in Canada after their parents decided to return to the Netherlands. The Langens hadn't taken too well to life in Canada the first time around, but the two oldest, one of whom was married to a church deacon, had made the choice to stay. The parents and three younger children returned home. Eventually, Roel's father passed away and, Alida Langen, missing her older children, once again returned to Canada, her three younger ones in tow.

The whole story set Joh's head spinning, when he first heard it, but eventually he learned the ins and outs of the connections between Roel, the rest of the family, and who in church was the link. It turned out that at least one of the Langens was Deacon Vandyke's wife, and they knew Gerry very well.

Joh and Nel decided to become acquainted with the rest of the family, considering their children were becoming an item of sorts. In Joh's opinion it would help to solidify the underpinnings of the relationship. The sociability did not go very far. After six months, Alida Langen decided to once again return to the Netherlands for good, having come to the conclusion that Canada was not for her after all. Her two youngest daughters concurred but she would leave another son behind, Roel, who had found a very good reason for his decision. He'd found the woman he loved.

After his mother and sisters left, Roel came to lodge at the Grin residence for a time and paid for his room and board so he could work and save up his money to eventually set up housekeeping for himself. He helped Joh around the house as well, taking over some of the chores that needed doing. One of those jobs was digging the hardpan out of the back yard with a jackhammer, so Joh could put in some good soil and have a proper back lawn.

Unfortunately, as time went on, Nel, after getting to know the young man, had not taken a liking to Roel. She found him too arrogant for her taste. She considered him somewhat bossy over her daughter and didn't understand why Elly didn't stand up to him a little more. Joh didn't want to start another argument but he thought to himself, *yes, but we raised her that way, always obey, always acquiesce, try to please people before you please yourself. Listen and obey. This is probably the result.*

"We're going to have to let her make her own choices, aren't we? Didn't we do the same thing?" was all he dared to say, trying to stay pragmatic about it all.

"Doesn't she see it?" she countered, rounding on him, as if he would dare defy her opinion. "Don't you see it? Maybe we should encourage her to move somewhere, like, like … Vancouver Island! You know, to get her away from his influence. That's not so far away, and we could see her lots, make sure she's doing okay, I like Vancouver Island…" Nel ran out of words, knowing it would never happen.

He wondered if somewhere in the process they'd taken the spirit out of the girl. But he dared not say it out loud. He hoped he was wrong. There always seemed to be a stealthy power struggle of sorts going on between Nel and Roel, for control over his daughter. It was a subject he had no idea how to broach without bringing an insulted and enraged wife down on his own head. But it resulted in constant little battles of wills between two very opinionated and stubborn people.

He recalled the evening when Nel and Roel had finally had it out, over a request that Nel had made to him. She had asked with the idea that the request couldn't be refused; a mistake on her part, and Roel wasn't about to comply. "You don't get to command me," he haughtily told her.

Nel was furious that he had the audacity to say *no*, something her own children had never dared to do. Mother's requests were mother's orders. She was at once aghast and up in arms. Roel, not to be cowed by a controlling mother and armed with what he felt was his right to refuse, held fast. Before Joh could blink, the shouting match was full blown and nasty. Elly sat silently in the middle, not looking at anyone, then, abruptly, she got up and walked out the door, slamming it behind her. The two continued to argue, but before long it petered out, with the realization that Elly had not returned.

"Maybe she's only outside," Joh offered, hoping he'd be right. There was something about his wife's fear for her children out in the dark. He went to look, but she was nowhere in sight. Where could she have gone? She had no car, couldn't even drive. *Another thing I've neglected*, he thought. Nel and Roel both came out to see if Elly was there. When the realization hit them that she'd fled into the dark, Joh started the car, everyone piled in and began a search. It didn't take long to find her on the road leading up to the shopping centre.

She got in silently, and then announced vehemently, "I hate the arguing, always the arguing. I *hate* it! Stop! Just stop!" It was all she wanted to say, and folding her arms tightly across her chest, stayed silent and withdrawn the rest of the way home. Roel held his tongue as well and Elly went straight to her room. Roel followed, only to emerge a short while later and left. Whatever it was that accounted for his daughter falling for someone like Roel Langen, it was too late to change it, barring some epiphany of her own, and on her own terms.

Eventually, Roel rented an apartment with Joe as a roommate.

They were not exactly compatible, Roel being fastidious to a fault, and Joe not exactly blessed with the tidy gene. But, Joh concluded, it was none of his business. They could sort that out for themselves.

When Roel had enough of Joe's sloppy habits, he found another apartment that he could rent on his own, a downstairs suite in an older home in Vancouver, very near Stanley Park. The stocky Russian landlord, Kolesnikov, who lived upstairs, was only too pleased to have a fine, clean-cut young man as a tenant, and went out of his way to ensure he'd take the suite. The young girlfriend, who'd accompanied this nice young man, also impressed him. To everyone's satisfaction, first and last month's rent was paid.

Kolesnikov proudly showed them his stacks of printing equipment and finished material stashed in the basement of the old house. The Russian was pleased to be able to spread his tracts, in Russian and English, containing messages he believed in, to the good people in Canada, land of the free. The young couple nodded politely. It was all things they had no understanding of, had no idea of what it was about, and really none of their business. Roel just wanted a place to live.

A week later, as they sat at the dining room table together: Joh, Nel, Nancyann, Elly and Roel, were having their usual Sunday dinner, and the story was coming out in fits and starts.

Roel, wide-eyed and dead serious, looked at Nel as he spoke. "I had those bed sheets you gave me, in a bag, and I was being *followed*! I didn't know why, or *who* was in the car!" The fear radiated off him as he recounted the experience.

Him, walking down Oak Street, on his way home, the car, driving slowly behind him. He'd noticed it earlier, on another street and thought it strange at first, but chalked it up to someone looking for an address. But on Oak, the long main thoroughfare through the heart of the Vancouver suburbs, there was no mistaking it. The same car, and it was *following* him! He'd run to his brother's house in a panic with the wild story. He was being followed! His brother wouldn't let him in the house. Then, he found a pay telephone and called the police.

"They were there within minutes," he exclaimed. "Like they were right there around the corner, and the car following me, those guys pulled up behind and got out of the car too."

Roel was still spooked by the entire incident. "Then they put me in the police car and started questioning *me*! Like I was some kind of criminal! They asked me about the bed sheets I had in the bag, the bed sheets of all things. They wanted to know where I'd gotten them, where I was coming from. What did they think I was, some escaped lunatic from the insane asylum?" He shook his head.

Finally, from the conversation between the men in the car and the police, it became apparent that these mysterious men were government agents, conducting surveillance on something Russian or other. He'd immediately thought of Kolesnikov, his Russian landlord. As Roel related this realization to the family, Elly burst out laughing, *"The Russians are coming! The Russians are coming!"*

The whole table joined in, the entire episode taking on a hilarity that Roel did not find remotely funny. He'd seen the movie currently showing at the theatres, carrying the same title as Elly's outburst. The movie had been funny. This was not. He'd been badly frightened.

Joh couldn't help but laugh at the young man. "Boy, you got yourself mixed up in something you know nothing about." Still laughing, he continued, "I know you're innocent, but something is going on with that Russian guy, that the government is keeping an eye on, and because you live there as well, they have to check you out too."

Then Joh thought back a minute, and he realized something else. "I remember not too long ago, I was sitting in my chair one night, I couldn't sleep, and I saw a car sitting there, in the lane behind us," Joh pointed out the back dining room window. "Just sitting there, two guys in it." He shrugged, "They were there again the next night, and the night after that, I think for about a week. After that I never saw them again."

Joh's house had been under surveillance as well. He had no qualms about it. He was an upstanding citizen, after all, and he had no problem with the government doing its job. But it did address some curiosity he had over the whole incident. Roel sat at the table, unable and unwilling to see the humorous side of it. At the end of that month, still spooked and frightened by the entire episode he, stealthily moved all of his things out of the suite, and into Joh's borrowed car. But it wasn't quite the end of it.

Kolesnikov knew where Elly worked, and he showed up one day demanding to know why her boyfriend had moved out. He looked more than just a little upset. By this time, she'd grasped the fact that the Russian was probably a shadier character than they first realized. The government wouldn't be tailing just anybody for no reason. Elly didn't trust the man anymore and was a little nervous of his true intentions towards them.

Joh got a call later that evening. Would he please come and pick her up from work that night. Joh complied, knowing that there might be some danger for his daughter, and neither of them had an appetite for a young girl waiting at a lonely bus stop in the dark, not knowing if someone was out there with ill intentions.

One day a short time later, Roel and Elly came through the front door, looking for all the world to Joh like proud peacocks. *What now?* Joh thought, *something's going on, but what?* The answer hit him full in the face.

"Dad! Mum! We're engaged!" Elly stood in front of him, grinning from ear to ear, while she showed off the ring on her finger. He was stunned, as was Nel. The four of them, stared at each other. The smile on Roel's face slipped a bit, "Aren't you going to congratulate us?" he asked.

"You never asked me for permission," Joh stated, his disappointment clear on his face. Elly started to laugh. "Dad, who does that anymore?" Joh shot back, "I did, before I asked your mother to marry me, I went to her father to ask permission!"

"Dad!" Elly looked wounded, "I really don't think it's done anymore."

Roel added, "If you like, I can ask you now. Mr. Grin, do I have permission to marry your daughter?" Joh looked sideways at him and had to laugh a little, edging past his disappointment. "Well, it's a little late, but yes."

The excitement of the engagement never quite materialized. Nel struggled with her daughter's choice of husband, and Joh's disappointment at the hippie generation's penchant for arbitrarily flinging norms and traditions on the burn pile guaranteed that the evening fell flat. He was only thankful that Elly had never been tempted to 'turn on and tune out' by this new age arising out of the sixties.

Some months later, both parents thought that perhaps the epiphany they'd so desired had finally materialized, when Elly came storming into the house on an evening, slamming the door behind her and heading straight into her room. Roel followed behind a moment later. They heard voices from behind her closed door, raised and angry, a word here and there; *engagement... ring ... back ... enough .... can't ... done ...* Was she breaking up with him? Joh held his breath, hoping his spunky little girl still had some of that spunk left in her. Then he could only hear Roel talking, and talking, and talking some more. The man could do that. He was good at it. In the end, the ring stayed on Elly's finger, and somehow Joh and Nel, especially Nel, had to come to terms with their daughter's choice. They married a year later, two weeks after another very special occasion, Joh and Nel's Silver Wedding Anniversary.

CHAPTER 24

Silver and Bells
1968

There had been a lot of changes in Joh and Nel's life in the years between 1961 and 1968. In a small way they'd become more political. Thanks to someone name P. E. Trudeau, who was elected Prime Minister, Nel finally took voting seriously. She couldn't stand him. "Just the look of him makes me sick to my stomach!" she'd say with a sour expression on her face. Thanks to the likes of Trudeau she'd become more aware of the voting responsibilities of ordinary citizens. Joh followed suit. Both voted Conservative down the line. He didn't care about parties, just the man in the lead; what was he like? What were his principals, his character? That was what mattered. He demanded that of himself and of those in power as well. It would be years before they'd consider the Liberal Party.

Joh stood looking in the mirror at the man reflected back at him. Twenty-five years. It had been a long twenty-five years from the time he'd promised to love and cherish. There had been questionable and tumultuous love and cherish moments and he was pleased with himself that, so far, he'd still managed to hang in there.

Tonight, the house would be filled with guests and caterers. The living and dining rooms had been cleared out and a line of long, covered tables in an L-shape followed its way from one area to the other. They'd cleared enough room for fifty guests. Nel had baked two large slabs for a two layered cake and Joh had decorated it with a delectable combination of vanilla and mocha butter cream icing swirls, and added fruits and flourishes of chocolate. It stood now on the kitchen table, being eyed with mouth-watering anticipation by all who passed.

It would be hectic in a while, and Joh stood in the bathroom in front of the mirror, enjoying the calm before the storm. "Joh? Where are you?"

A voice was calling, and his reverie was over. "In the bathroom," he replied, "I'm coming!"

"When are the caterers coming to set the tables? I have to go out and I need somebody to be here when they come." Nel looked at him expectantly. He knew what she meant. *I have to go out and you need to be home.* "I'll be here, don't worry. Go out and do what you need to do." He smiled and went to the basement, intending to work on a few things in the interim. Balloons needed inflating; the rest of the decorations had to be put in place. He had Nancyann and Elly to help. The caterers arrived on schedule with all they needed for the celebration, dishes, cutlery, and most important, the food.

That evening, as Joh surveyed the crowd that had assembled, he felt a moment's satisfaction that tonight, at least, all was well. There hadn't been any major row, or unresolved argument hanging between them this week. There had been no bickering between mother and soon-to-be-married daughter, no son coming home with news he wouldn't be able to digest without his stomach knotting up again. Joe actually looked half decent with freshly trimmed hair and a neat jacket. It almost felt like everything would smooth out to normal for real this time.

Dinner was served, toasts were made, the cake brought out to oohs and aahhs and eagerly eaten with relish and raves over the taste. The evening ended with an aura of success he hoped would carry on for a while.

The entire exercise became a dress rehearsal for the wedding the following month. In the interim, Elly was hard at work, finishing her wedding dress on the old Singer treadle sewing machine that Nel still used for her sewing. Joh planned on giving his wife a new Pfaff sewing machine for her birthday in November, one he'd had his eye on for weeks already. He retreated to the basement while the women sewed or prepared other items that were needed.

Nel watched her daughter carefully sewing the veil, stitch after stitch. Each stab of the needle felt like a stab to the heart. She felt like she was bursting with unidentifiable irritations that scrabbled at her insides to get out. After a little grumbling at her daughter, over nothing really, Nel finally blurted out what really bothered her. "I wish you weren't getting married!" Elly stopped sewing and looked up angrily. "I suppose you want me to stay at home with mommy for the rest of my life," she snapped back. "Is that what you want?"

It was exactly what Nel's heart of hearts wanted, but knowing she had no right to expect or demand it, she said nothing, and walked out of the room before it escalated to a point she wouldn't be able come back from. Elly was already in tears. It was no use. Nel would never be able to fully accept that her daughter was marrying a man who would not hold his future mother-in-law in high esteem, who dared talk back, who outright defied her at times. Worse, it was he who would be the boss in their lives together. It was a hard pill to swallow but swallow she must.

In the middle of all this upheaval and change that Nel really didn't want in her life, an aggravation from long ago walked in. Joe decided it was time to go back to his original name. "My name is Jacob," he announced emphatically to his mother and father one day. "It's not Joe. It's not Jopie. It's Jacob. I'd appreciate it if you addressed me by my real name!"

By now, his hair had gotten longer than Nel liked, another irritant that she couldn't see past. He'd also rejected the suits and ties of his father's generation, preferring the long, sloppy shirts and jeans of the day. Nel's hatred of jeans was another of her opinions she stubbornly insisted on holding on to. "Jeans are for workmen on the job, dirty jobs, not for nice," she'd say in awkward English. Her children knew what she meant but they also understood the fast-paced changes in fashion that prevailed and were all too willing to espouse the more relaxed standards.

But the name 'Jacob' tipped the scales. "I will never call you Jacob!" she hissed at him, a fire in her eyes that meant business. "I never liked it, it was not my decision to name you that, and I will never use it!"

Jacob insisted, and another long-running fight, this time with someone else, was on. Joh was almost a little relieved that Nel's critical spotlight was off him for a while. He wondered, however, how long that would last, as he didn't know if she could carry more than one long-running conflict at a time.

It rained heavily on Elly and Roel's wedding day. Joh had heard it said that *rain on a wedding day means good luck* and he hoped it was true. Bride, bridesmaid and matron of honour sat in the back seat of the Pontiac, Nel up front and Joh driving. They were lost. Elly had indicated the wrong turnoff, confused by the unfamiliar route to the church in Surrey, in which she was set to be married. They were now somewhere on a back road, parked at a gas station, while Joh went in, asking for directions.

They finally arrived, forty-five minutes late. Joh had to laugh privately. Maybe it was an indication that this wedding shouldn't happen at all. But it did. He walked his oldest daughter down the aisle and handed her over to a beaming young man who'd waited patiently, knowing she'd come.

And, as he stood with his wife, watching his daughter in place beside the man of her choice, he remembered, in another church far away and long ago, beside a woman he loved, making those same vows. Was she making the right choice, now? Did he make the right choice, then? He didn't know the answer to either question, but he hoped both were, *yes*. Only time itself would answer it.

After a reception in the church hall, a select number of invited guests made their appearance at Joh and Nel's home for another small reception, using the template of the first catered event a month ago. It worked perfectly. Instead of a slab cake, a beautiful three-tiered affair, with swans separating and supporting each tier, posed in all its glory on the table. The top held a small arrangement of flowers, designed by the bride. It was Joh's signature rum-laced fruitcake wedding confection that he'd made for every wedding he'd ever done.

Afterwards, Joh drove them to the bus station to embark on a honeymoon to Victoria on, Vancouver Island. It was the last time she would call her father's house, 'home'. The nest was a little emptier. He wondered how the newlyweds would do, worried that neither of them even had a driver's license. Never mind, he shook his head. They'd have to figure it out for themselves. They were adults now.

The nest may have emptied out a little more that summer, but late in the fall, news came that the family would be getting another addition. Roel and Elly came by one day with the news. Elly was expecting her first child.

Nel flew at the girl with a loud cry of elation and clung fiercely to her. "A baby! I'm going to have a grandchild!" she cried.

"*I'm* having the baby, Mum," she gently reminded her mother, pushing her back, "and please go easy, I'm not feeling that great." "Oh! Sorry, sorry, I didn't mean to be so rough." she replied laughing, and letting go. "I'm so excited! When is it due?"

"Probably June, we figure. I haven't gotten a date from the doctor yet, but I'll let you know."

Nel immediately began making plans for knitted layettes, blankets, hats, and booties. She wondered what patterns she still had stashed away. After the couple left, she began to dig through what she had. Tomorrow she would go to the wool shop and find the right kind of soft baby wool.

Three months later, more news, tearfully delivered this time. Whatever had been there, was now no more, and Nel silently put away whatever she'd been knitting, the enthusiasm gone. Life went on.

There were plans to go to the Netherlands the following year, the first time Joh would be going back. This time he looked forward to returning with something to show for his hard work. Perhaps he'd never made it with his own business, but he was still a baker, with some measure of success to show for his hard work. He owned his own home, something that many in the Netherlands still couldn't boast of. Successful man or not, homes to buy were a hard thing to find in that tiny, overcrowded country and many were rented from the municipality.

The three of them, Joh, Nel and sixteen-year-old Nancyann finally made the trip the following year. Before they left, they learned that Elly was expecting again. The trio was gone for six weeks, and Roel and Elly house sat and took care of the dog. Nel waffled over taking her abandoned knitting with her, but opted not to, thinking, I'll be much too busy visiting and touring to sit knitting.

The six weeks flew by, Joh felt overwhelmed by the changes he saw in his old country. The crowding was far more apparent from when they'd last lived there. Cars, bikes, people all clamoured for space. Joh considered the materialism he saw around him a little too pervasive, and it made him realize he'd much rather live where he was.

He remarked that he didn't think he'd ever be able to go back permanently. Nel thought of the moment ten years ago, when she herself, had almost made the decision to stay, something she'd never revealed to him. At that moment, she still didn't know if she'd want to stay in Holland or not and it surprised her. Her life was certainly a far cry from what it was, when she'd cried on her sisters' shoulders. But still, she thought she could easily live in her native country, even now.

The reconnections with his brothers and sisters were wonderful. Acquaintances were renewed and stories shared over coffee, a glass of wine or cognac, and *gebak*. Joh thoroughly enjoyed himself.

The arrival home was not as joyful as the arrival in the Netherlands had been. Roel and Elly had picked them up from the airport. Elly looked thin and pale. She'd had another miscarriage; this time, threatening her life. After the miscarriage, she'd developed sepsis and came precariously close to needing a complete blood transfusion. She might not have made it. The two weeks in hospital had left her wan and listless but game to carry on. They were both young. Babies would come.

His life returned to what it had been; a mixture of some joy and satisfaction, tempered by a plethora of little things resembling a few drops of ink in a glass of water, not enough to do him in, but enough to make it somewhat unpleasant to drink. Joh put his head down, bottled it all up, and carried on.

The endless nagging and small, veiled complaints were almost a constant given, cropping up like weeds in his beautiful lawn. He'd barely taken care of one when another would take its place, over and over, punctuating his orderly world with little bits of aggravation.

Despite the thanks and appreciation she showed him for a job well executed, Nel would soon find another little something that didn't meet her expectations and the ritual would start over. This needed doing. Why didn't he try this or that? Hadn't he started on it yet?

His stomach hurt. For years already, he'd suffered from ulcers, and it was getting no better. He drank copious amounts of milk per day, trying to quell the stabbing in his gut. *Maybe I ought to pay another visit to the doctor.* Nothing else seemed to work, and he needed to do something, anything. It was keeping him up at night and he found himself sitting in his chair in the dark much too often.

Desperate, he sat on the other side of the doctor's desk, describing the symptoms, the pain, the sleeplessness. The doctor looked at Joh after he'd been examined, and shook his head,

"I don't know, my friend. I may have to operate. I'll need to do some tests first, put a scope down to see how it looks in there, but I'm not hopeful that we'll avoid surgery of some kind." Joh didn't care. He wanted to be free of the pain, once and for all. "Do what you have to do," he said.

Late that fall, he'd entered the hospital for some exploratory surgery. By the time he came home again, he'd lost forty pounds, thin and haggard. In his hand was a list of what he could and couldn't eat. He'd also left three quarters of his stomach behind in the operating room. The surgeons had found a massive, ulcerated stomach that they could do nothing with, except remove what was not salvageable and reconstruct it with whatever was left over.

As a bonus, he dumped his entire stash of cigarettes, tobacco and rolling papers unceremoniously into the hospital room waste basket before he left for home. He'd found the perfect opportunity to quit his lifelong smoking habit for good.

Nel nursed him solicitously and slowly back to health, realizing perhaps that she'd had a hand in his condition. It wasn't lost on her that ulcers were known to be an indirect result of stress. She worked hard to make it up to him and to appease her own sense of guilt.

Joh had enough time off work with sick leave and had his vacation time tacked onto the end of it. When he felt well enough, he and Nel decided to get away.

Years earlier, Joh had purchased a used tent trailer. In it they'd toured the British Columbia interior, Washington State, Oregon, even going so far as Arizona. The tent trailer gave way to a motor home, a step up from the nuisance of the tent portion of the trailer. They spent this vacation travelling to Arizona to visit some friends who had moved there.

On his first trip through Arizona, in the sixties, Joh had become fascinated with cacti. Driving through the desert he could see hundreds, no, millions of cacti of all kinds: Barrel, Saguaro, Santa Cruz, Cholla.

On this second trip, he again stared at all those beautiful plants. He pictured them in his front yard. So, before they left, he dug up a good dozen and stashed them carefully in the motor home, to take back with him. He had no clue that this was illegal without a permit, but Nel had an inkling that, at the border at least, they'd be in some kind of trouble.

"Joh, you can't take those with you. If the border people see that, they'll never let you take them into Canada, I'm sure of it. And you might get a fine!" Joh, after years of Nel telling him what he could and couldn't do, was no longer listening or taking advice from her.

"Don't be ridiculous! They're just a few plants. There are millions of them out there. Who's going to miss a few? Besides, they'll never see them. I've got them well stashed."

Joh was right, and lucky. They were never found. The very small Saguaro he'd dug up might have been worth some time in jail.

The cacti were installed lovingly in the flower beds along the front of the house and glassed in during the winter months. More stood in the yet-to-be-finished recreation room in the basement. Somehow, most of them survived. After running into the indoor cacti and tweezing the sharp needles out of her skin one time too many, Nel wasn't particularly enamoured with them.

CHAPTER 25

Separation 1970 - 1975

The kind of parting Nel had dreaded all her life lay before her. Roel and Elly had decided to return to the Netherlands for a period of six months. A working holiday they'd called it. Nel was devastated and Joh could not understand why. It was only six months, not a lifetime. He thought her reaction was highly over dramatized and he let her know.

"For heaven's sake, why are you carrying on like this? They're adults! We did the same thing, didn't we. Only we left family for good," he reasoned.

"If my mother had been alive, I would never have left," Nel declared. "Anyway, I'm her mother," she moaned. "It's different!"

Joh was incredulous. "Different? Different, how? How is it that you can't stand to have that girl out of your reach? What is wrong with you?" Nel tried to find the words to answer him. She couldn't even describe to herself why she couldn't find the resolve to let her daughters become independent adults. Finally, Nel blurted out, "If they leave me, I'll never see them again!" Her worst fears, unrealistic or not, were out in the open.

Joh threw up his hands and walked away. "This is not going to do your relationship with her any good, you realize that don't you?" he bunted back as he walked away. Nel did on some level, but she couldn't help herself. For whatever reason, the thought of Elly so far out of reach tore at some inner demon she couldn't control.

The timing of the couple's departure and the rental they'd have to move out of did not jive, so for the last week before departure, Roel and Elly stayed with her parents. The few things they owned could be stored in Joh's basement. A large stereo-record player console had to be moved in his station wagon, as the couple's small car was already filled with boxed up items ready for storage. As Joh and Roel lifted the heavy stereo out of the back, Joh in his haste, knocked it up against the side of the tailgate opening.

Roel, already over-particular about his things and finicky about everything, cautioned Joh, "Easy, easy, let me guide it out to make sure it doesn't scratch." Joh thought he could easily slide it out without too much contact with the door but Roel was far more cautious and stopped him from continuing. Joh, already on edge over Nel's adverse reaction to her daughter leaving, grew a little impatient with his son-in-law's exacting manner and he bulled his way through. Again, Roel protested that the console would get damaged. Joh thought about the incident later and wondered why he didn't just let the man lead in easing the piece of furniture out of the station wagon. But instead, without thinking, he carried on pulling at the console with, "I've got it, I've got it."

Finally Roel, a little exasperated that the man just wouldn't stop and think about what he was doing, physically put a hand on Joh's chest, to get him to cease, saying, "wait a minute ..." It was as far as he got.

Nel, standing by watching, abruptly and furiously lit into Roel, slamming her fists on his chest, and driving him backwards. *"You don't talk to my husband like that!!"* She screamed in his face. It was apparent to all three shocked onlookers, that Nel was deeply and emotionally overwrought. Joh calmed his wife down and got her to step aside. "You need to calm down," he told her. "Your behaviour is out of control. I can handle it."

The atmosphere was uncomfortable for the rest of the day and not much better for the remainder of the week. In the meantime, Roel and his father-in-law, took his car to a dealer to be sold, another small loose end tied up. Roel's brother, Filip would handle the sale and wire the money to his brother overseas when it sold.

For the last evening before the flight out, Nel had arranged for a small get together at home with some mutual friends. But for the whole evening, Nel sat aside in her chair and, speaking very little, put on a grieving face, as if she was in mourning. Joh noticed and ignored it. He was familiar with his wife's tactics by now and so was her daughter. The guests were not. They'd never before seen Nel's, *I'll look this way until I get what I want* face, a look reserved only for her immediate family. But this time, she couldn't help herself.

Joh determined he'd have a word with her afterwards; now was not the time. It was embarrassing enough without bringing it out into the open in front of guests. At three o'clock the next afternoon, Nel, having been spoken to by her husband about her over-exaggerated and very bad behaviour of the entire week, comported herself admirably at the airport, despite the tears that ran in rivulets down her cheeks. *Six months,* she kept telling herself, *six months. It wasn't like it would be years.*

They'd picked up where they left off in their lives. And time proceeded at its own pace, much too slowly for Nel. Six months did not pass quickly enough and her patience was taxed to the limit. Peering at the calendar did not help.

The old dog, Lassie, that they had since Ontario, was old now and showing signs of ill health. Joh watched her carefully over the next months. He patiently dealt with her limited movement and made sure she could go outside for her business without having to wait too long. Soon enough though, she couldn't wait at all, and left stinking, sloppy messes all over the house. Finally, after another runny bowel movement and falling down on top of it, Joh made the decision to have the old dog put down. But as he led her into the vet's clinic and gave over the leash, Lassie turned her head and gave Joh a mournful look.

Joh choked back the strange lump in his throat as he left. *It looked as if she was saying, 'what are you doing to me?'* He resolved never again to take a dog to the vet to be put down. The house seemed empty without her but he kept himself busy with his hobbies and his new job.

He'd recently been hired as head baker at another bakery. He had to admit to himself, that he was just a little jealous of the man, for actually being able to put together a successful one like that. Joh didn't know what his secret was, but some people just seemed to have it. He had to accept the fact that he did not "have it", or, at the very least, that the stars had never aligned to grant him that kind of success. It didn't matter, he had to look at what he had attained.

The letters flew back and forth those six months, Nel busy writing every day, ready with a letter by the time another one appeared in the mail. She'd simply have to add whatever responses she needed from the new letter and drop it in the mail. One morning the news came a different way.

The telephone rang. Picking up, Nel was surprised to hear Elly's voice on the other end. Overjoyed to be hearing her voice, she began to talk. "Oh honey, it's so good to hear your voice. I've been sitting here hoping there was a letter …"

Elly cut her off. "Mom! I'm calling because I have something urgent. Roel's mother has been diagnosed with cancer. It's terminal and there are things I need to tell you."

"Oh! Cancer! That's awful. I'm so sorry to hear that." Nel was sincere, but she had the premonition that whatever it was that she would hear next, she wouldn't like. She was silent as Elly continued.

"Mama has been given anywhere from six weeks to six months to live. She needs care at home and Corry and Janny are not able to handle it alone. We're going to stay longer."

Nel closed her eyes, unable to protest, for very good reasons. She had no right to protest. Roel's mother had been given a death sentence. Of course, they should stay and help. She tried to give as much sympathy for the family as she could but it worked its way around a growing disappointment that felt like a giant barrier to her proffered compassion. *Was this what it felt like to have mixed feelings?* she thought.

Meantime, she heard her daughter's voice on the line saying goodbye. "I've got to go. I'll write when I can and give you updates. I love you." "I love you too." and the line went dead. Nel hung on to the handset a few minutes longer, the connection to her daughter still tangible.

It would be another two years before she saw her daughter again, but it wouldn't be the last time she heard her voice. In March of 1972, another phone call came with devastating news, Roel this time, choking back tears. "Elly lost the baby! It was born too soon," he gasped through his grief.

Nel couldn't believe it. Another one. How many had it been, five? Five losses in total so far. How many more would there be before she was finally able to finish the layette she'd started knitting so long ago?

"Give me the name of the hospital and phone number, Roel. I want to talk to her," Nel asked. Roel looked it up quickly and gave the information, adding which floor and station she was on. "Don't do it right away, please, Mum. Give me a chance to give them a head's up that you're going to call from Canada. They'll make sure to have the line handy in the room, so she can talk to you. Tomorrow would be good." The call ended and she was left to give the bad news to Joh. They'd been so hopeful this time. Elly had even had a special procedure done to enable her to carry the baby to term. What had gone wrong?

The next day, both sat with the telephone between them. With trembling fingers Nel dialed the long overseas number. It rang, and Nel, in English, requested the floor and station connection. At first there was confusion as the switchboard tried to parse out the English, then momentarily, another operator, in a heavy accent, asked, "You vant vich pay-shent, please?"

Again, Nel made her request, floor and station, a little exasperated that she was having trouble making herself understood. Finally, there was a hissing in the line as the connection was made, and a voice, crisp and efficient answering in Dutch, *nurse's station, maternity.* Nel identified herself, and a delighted laugh came back, "*Mevrouw* Grin! We've been expecting your call. Hold on. I'll bring the telephone to *Mevrouw* Langen now!"

A moment's fumbling, voices and footsteps in her ear, and then a soft, "Mum?" Her anxiety still at the forefront of her mind, the first thing Nel could think to say was, "Hardly anyone could speak English when I called!"

She could hear Elly chuckling at her over the phone. "Mum. Think about it. Why didn't you just speak Dutch? That would have made it a little easier for you."

In her jitters, she'd forgotten that she was calling to the country and language she'd been born to. Joh, who'd been listening in, could only shake his head, and laugh. *Typical Nel. When she's all befuddled, she'll forget she's got a brain.*

They learned that the baby had been lost at six and a half months, due to 'placenta previa', an anomaly in nature usually causing a premature birth. The baby, a girl, had fought to live, but succumbed. Too small, too weak. The timing of this secondary abnormality was particularly heartbreaking, and there were tears at both ends of the line.

Joh sighed; the bitter disappointment still conspicuous in his heart. Another blow, with no explanations, no reason for it to be so. He turned his mind heavenward and asked, but the only answer he could get was, *timing*.

Eventually Elly and Roel came home. Alida Langen had passed away after a hard fought two-year battle and there were no more reasons to stay in the Netherlands.

It was eight months on from the hospital phone call, eight months since she'd heard her daughter's voice, and now Nel stood with her husband, who'd taken early vacation time to enjoy their homecoming, and youngest daughter. They watched as people filed out of the arrivals gate, looking for that familiar face. She felt jubilant that finally her whole family would be safe within her reach again.

The young couple finally materialized in the crowd, and Nel cried out in joy, "There she is, there she is!" There were hugs, kisses and more hugs. As they drove home to the North Shore, the newly arrived couple remarked, laughing, "look at the size of the cars!" They'd forgotten how much larger everything was here, how much more spacious. Two and a half years was enough time to become used to tiny houses, smaller furniture and much smaller cars.

Elly had returned home, once again expecting a baby. Again, she'd had a Shirodkar suture put in place to ensure the pregnancy didn't terminate early. She had to be watchful, rest, no excessive physical activities, the list went on and on. Everyone, especially the parents-to-be, were overly protective and nervous.

Shortly after arriving home, while Roel was out looking for a place to rent and check on some leads for work, Joh took his daughter, accompanied by Nel, to his work. He needed to take care of some business for his boss and make sure a few complicated orders had been followed properly. He'd invited Elly to go with him, so he could show off the place. Her mother, clinging to her daughter, was not far behind.

They toured the bakery, Joh pointing out some interesting things, when suddenly Elly gasped weakly, *"Oh! Dad ..."* and grasped his arm. To his consternation, she stumbled forward, still clutching his arm, sinking towards the floor. Nel began making loud unintelligible sounds. Joh supported his daughter, guiding her to a stack of flour sacks, to lie prone, while someone else ran for a glass of water. Nel bent over her, crowding, still babbling, frightened for her daughter.

"Give her room, give her some air!" Joh pulled her aside and offered the water. Elly drank, her hand trembling.

"What happened? Are you all right?" Joh wanted to know, as she revived a bit.

"I ... I don't know. I just got a little ... faint." She laughed, embarrassed at the incident in full view of strangers. "I guess I better make that doctor's appointment sooner rather than later."

She would come under the care of an obstetrician, a dour Scot, who guided her through what would be her first successful pregnancy. Names were picked, Dwight for a boy, Katherine for a girl. Nel scoffed and critiqued the boy's name they'd chosen.

"Dwight? What an odd name. I'm sure your father would be pleased to have a child named after him. Why wouldn't you name it after their grandfather or grandmother?" Nel asked.

Elly thought about it for a moment, not really wanting to start an argument. "We like that name, and besides, I think it's time to throw some fresh ones into the family tree, don't you? Besides Johannes is actually the Dutch version of John, a very common name, and your name...," she looked at her mother, "Neeltje is unpronounceable in English. And besides, you hate that name yourself," Elly countered.

Nel belaboured the point, "Yes, but you don't have to use the actual name, or make it a second name, or one that sort of sounds like ours, or..."

Elly interrupted the flow of words; reasons looking for a problem. "There's a thousand Michaels, Christophers and Jasons, another thousand Jennifers, Amys and Melissas. I don't want a name that a thousand other children have, and *not* ..." she emphasized, "... something *so* different, that the poor kid is going to get picked on."

In good time, seven weeks early, Dwight Andrew arrived to a jubilant couple and an equally jubilant set of grandparents. The baby, after spending two weeks in an incubator, was pronounced fit to go home.

A year later, the young family, crowded in their tiny apartment, started looking at homes, found one, and Joh co-signed for them, because they didn't have enough assets to fully qualify for the mortgage. Roel had come back from the Netherlands, fully trained as a carpenter. His perfectionist personality made him a perfect finishing carpenter and the small business he'd started with a partner, was generating a good income. Joh sat back, content that one daughter, at least, was secure.

Joh found himself standing at Elly's door, an unhappy man. Another argument had raged between himself and his wife over yet one more contested point that morning, and in the aftermath he'd found himself driving around aimlessly.

"Dad? Hey, it's nice to see you!" Elly greeted him, pleased, and then looked past him, "Where's Mum?"

He sighed, "I had to get out of there for a while. She's so difficult and I don't know what to do." Elly seemed to understand. She knew what her mother was like. "Gosh Dad. Yes, it's a hard thing. Have you tried counselling?" He shook his head. "We've tried that before; nothing seems to help."

"I don't know what to tell you," she told him quietly. "I'm not a marriage counsellor. I know Mum's difficult, but you have to try and take each situation on its own merits. Feel your way through and take a common sense approach." She lifted her shoulders apologetically. "I know that's not much help, but ..." then petering out and shrugging again. "Come on, let's have a cup of coffee, and talk about happier things."

The visit seemed to perk his spirits up a bit, and by the time he got home, he'd thought carefully about what she'd said. *Take each situation on its own merits.* Each time an argument surfaced it did seem to come from a different direction. He never knew when one would unexpectedly arise. Maybe he could do something with that.

Joh's relationship with his youngest, Nancyann was not at its best these days either. Like Nel, this daughter had a certain personality that sometimes clashed with his own. She had finally found another boyfriend after one broken relationship that had left her moping around the house. Doug, the boy Nancyann had been dating was well-like by Nel. He came from good Dutch stock. The mother opined that this young man showed her proper respect and deference, a quality that she prized. When the couple broke up Nel was heart-broken.

Nancyann eventually got back into the social scene and she'd met Ross. They'd been at a roller rink where regular monthly church young people's events were being held. The two seemed to gravitate to one another. After several more of those events, they finally began to date. Eventually, they'd become a steady couple.

By the spring of that year, Nel somehow got wind of a doctor's appointment the girl had made, without her knowledge. She was suspicious. Not having a hand in every aspect of her daughter's life, she seemed to gravitate to the worst possible circumstances she could imagine, when she didn't know what was going on. Then she discovered that Nancyann was pregnant and had made the appointment to discuss her options. Nel interpreted that as "discussing an abortion".

She surprised her daughter on the afternoon of her appointment by appearing at the doctor's office at the same moment Nancyann was waiting to go in. Mother was adamant that she was going in with her daughter to make sure an abortion was not going to happen and Nancyann was furious that her mother had the gall to think she could interfere in her private business.

It did not end well, but Nel did not give an inch. No daughter of hers was going to commit the sin of an abortion. She would raise the child herself if need be. Nancyann scoffed at that idea. She was already twenty, an adult, and if she was going to birth a baby she could and would look after it herself. She just wasn't ready for that baby quite yet.

A wedding took place after the fracas over the surprise pregnancy had died down. Jacob and his girlfriend, Janet set the date for their nuptials and were duly married. He had become a skilled painter by trade and Joh was glad of that, although it surprised him that photography only served as Jacob's hobby. No matter, it looked as if his son was beginning to take on the responsibilities of adulthood, although the long hair still irked Nel to no end and she made her displeasure known whenever she found an opportunity.

A week after his son's wedding, Joh walked his second daughter down the aisle to marry Ross Lawton. They'd decided to be a respectable married couple and raise a family. Neither of them relished the idea of Nancyann as a single mother. Nel's attitude at the wedding was unequivocally clear; she was not happy with a shotgun wedding. Not that she didn't want the wedding, she was just angry that it wasn't the way she'd envisioned it.

There was nothing Joh could do to change his wife's disapproving countenance. Ross's mother certainly noticed it, and it didn't impress her one bit. She loved Nancyann. She had no daughters, Ross being her only child, and she delighted in finally having one.

The dust never completely settled between Nel and her youngest and newest daughter/husband combination. Ross was not Doug - was nothing like Doug in Nel's eyes. Ross was a dyed-in-the-wool Canadian, with Canadian ways, and not quite compatible to Nel's particular rationale. He felt and acted uncomfortable around his new in-laws, sensing their underlying disapproval of his Canadian-ness, which he couldn't do much about, and his sin of getting their daughter pregnant, which he could have. It was awkward all around. Even their honeymoon was fraught with protesting mother, angry and insulted that their honeymoon location was kept secret. Nel's great need to know everything was obliged by no one this time around.

Another grandson, Lorne Ross was born in November of that year, and around the same time Joh and Nel learned that Elly was pregnant with her second child. Earlier in that year, she'd had one more miscarriage, at which point Nel as good as ordered her daughter not to have another baby. She was too afraid that it would kill her, and she would not be able to weather that kind of loss.

But Elly was well past taking her mother's suggestions as edicts, as she'd done in a younger life. And so, just to prove that there was really no danger to worry about, the following year their third grandson, Owen Daniel, was born by caesarian section.

CHAPTER 26

Family Growth 1976 - 1980

Joh considered himself a blessed man, as he bounced his fourth grandson on his knee. The little boy sat happily as Joh contentedly drank his coffee, looking through the paper, reading an article on travelling overseas. While he absently read, not really absorbing the words on the paper, his mind wandered over whatever waited in the future now.

In early 1976, Peter Jonathan had been added to the family, his fourth grandson, born to Jacob and Janet. It almost looked as if all three of his children had planned to collectively have one a year. But that wasn't the reality and he knew better. It was just the way it happened. It overwhelmed him to think of it. From nothing to four in the space of three years.

All four were his pride and joy. There were so many plans. He'd bought a small boat to take them fishing. There was dirt galore in the garden to root around in. A box of toys stood on the floor of the hall closet that each child eagerly dug into when they arrived.

Nel had taken on the role of a strict Dutch *Oma*, but she was in her glory, Joh could tell, and she loved every minute. The boys all learned very quickly that Oma was not to be trifled with, but they could also easily wrap her around each and every one of their small fingers.

There was a lot of laughter in the home when grandsons were over. But Nel still tended to quibble with him over things. They never crossed swords on anything major, Joh realized, but for minor things, his wife's go-to mode of contentiousness had become second nature. *If that was the way she wanted to be*, he thought, *he'd give as good as he got.*

Oma - grandmother

That evening Elly brought young Dwight over to enjoy a day of fishing the next day with his grandfather. She visited for a while, and they watched a documentary on television, the volume turned up to 'ear shattering'. The subject was *the tombs of Egypt*, and they were looking at the grave of some unknown mummified and partially unwrapped corpse. Nel pointed at the television screen.

"See? Hair does not disintegrate in a grave!" Now emphatically pointing her finger at him, decisive in her conviction.

He couldn't remember how the subject originally came up, but suddenly that evening, that familiar argument reared its head again. He couldn't help himself. "Hair *does* disintegrate!"

"No, it *doesn't!*"

"It does, I've seen lots of pictures of skeletons and never seen any evidence of hair around the skull!"

"And I've seen lot of pictures with hair *STILL ATTACHED* to the skull!" Nel countered, her voice rising, determined to be right.

"Who the hell *cares*?" Elly barked at them, from the couch, listening to their utterly ridiculous argument. She'd heard exactly the same one multiple times in her life, and had become accustomed to their bickering. However, she'd been gone from the parental home long enough that she saw the pointlessness of it, and was sick of the years-long running argument to boot.

Later, she made moves to go home, leaving Dwight to spend the weekend. "Be sure you dress him warmly," she instructed Joh as she left, "and for heaven's sake, don't let him get pulled out of the boat by any big fish!" She smiled as she said it. "You have high hopes!" Joh laughed.

The next morning, Joh sat in the early hours, watching eagerly for the weather report on TV. Dwight was still asleep, and he needed to know what the day would bring him. He'd promised to take the boy fishing and he was anxious to keep his promise. A half hour later, he shook the boy awake.

"Time to get up boy. We gotta go fishing!" Dwight opened his sleepy seven-year-old eyes, and smiled. He'd waited excitedly for this day and had talked to his Opa many times about going fishing with him out on his boat. Opa had promised. He was ready to go.

They spent the day off Robert's Bank. From the muddy bottom, they pulled flounder after flounder until Joh had something much bigger on the line. Dwight watched, excited as Opa pulled in something *really big*. When it landed in the boat with a wet smack, thumping wildly as it did, Dwight stared in amazement. He'd never seen anything like that! It almost looked like a very small shark! "Yup," Joh confirmed that it was. "They call it a dog fish." "It's ugly, Opa!" the boy declared, "Kill it!"

"No," said Joh, "we're going to put it back very gently. Even dogfish deserve to live." He did, and later, grandfather and grandson returned home with a pail full of flounder for Oma to clean, and some amazing details to hear about as she did.

Nel had the impression that their day had been engaging, and then, she had another thought. "You should teach me how to drive while towing the boat," she told him. "Do you realize if I ever had to, I wouldn't know how to do it, especially backing it up?" Joh promised that, someday, he would. Later, he bought another boat, a Bayliner, sleek and newer, that the boys would spend hours in. Still, Nel had yet to learn to drive with, and back up a car and trailer.

Wintertime, and as usual, it was wet, cold and a light layer of snow had fallen, melted and froze again. Joh was indoors, monkey-wrenching in the basement on another nameless little job that had niggled at his mind and needed to be done. He'd just come upstairs to get a drink when he heard a noise. Puzzled, he couldn't identify it.

As he stood there, the thought crossed his mind to ask Nel if she heard it, but then realized that she wasn't home yet from a shopping trip. *And even if she were,* he thought, *being so deaf, she probably wouldn't hear it at all.* The sound came again. *An animal?* The new dog, Teddy, a small

Pomeranian, should be with Nel since it went everywhere with her, sitting in the car to wait patiently as she shopped.

He was about to return to the basement, when he heard it a third time, louder now, but not by much. Curious, he stepped outside to look and listen some more, but saw nothing, except the car, back in the driveway. *Oh, Nel's home.* Teddy was out, running back and forth. He could hear the mewling clearer now. Where was she? Joh walked over to the car, and then to his shock, saw his wife halfway down the steep driveway, crawling slowly on her belly towards him. The sound came from her, as she cried out in pain. One look at her ankle told him it was broken.

With difficulty, he helped her to stand on one foot, and supporting her, got her into the house. There was no way he'd get Nel to climb the three steps up into the living room to sit down, so he brought a chair down for her. Then he called for an ambulance. Incredibly, she wanted to put on some clean underwear, but he couldn't see how either of them would accomplish that, considering how much pain she was in.

An X-ray at the hospital showed a bone, broken in three places. It was set with a series of pins to hold it all together. Eventually, the doctor told her, they'd be removed. But it would be a while. Nel hobbled on crutches and it was Joh's turn to nurse Nel back to health.

It didn't take long for her to point the accusing finger at him. "You didn't believe me, did you, when I warned you years ago! Someone was going to slip and break a leg on that icy slope! *Now* will you build a set of steps down the side, like I suggested, so people can walk up and down safely in the wintertime?"

Joh had to admit to himself, this time, she had a very legitimate reason to nag at him. He'd also admitted to himself that day, that sometimes she had very good reasons for her badgering. As he looked around, he could see all the things that had been left half done. His conscience played devil's advocate. *But I hate being in the middle of a job, and running out of material, or time, or some other little glitch that stops me from carrying on. What am I supposed to do, sit there idle, twiddling my thumbs?* He'd rather use the time to get a few other things done. Rock and a hard place; it was always rock and a hard place..

An uneasy truce prevailed as Nel hobbled around on crutches. In the spring, Joh duly put the cement steps in place down the drive, but by the time he was six or seven feet shy of the bottom of the driveway, he ran out of cement. *That's probably far enough,* he thought. *The drive levels off mostly here, there's little chance of slipping at this spot.*

Nel later looked at it and shook her head. *Half a job. Always, he does half a job.*

"Your wife is such a delightful lady," a congregation member gushed at him, as he sat in the church basement drinking coffee after the service. He smiled indulgently, *yes, to those on the outside, she's lovely, but don't get too close.*

He wondered then, *why was she like that?* Why was she so nice to everyone else, but not to her family, her husband, her children? The difference was striking. The persona she projected to others was agreeable, easygoing, feisty. But, alone with one of her immediate family, a different side of her appeared; critical, negative, and up in arms with another bone of contention in her teeth, unable to let go. It made for a roller coaster relationship.

In spite of their constant bickering, somehow, they still seemed to appear as a couple with common interests and goals, coexisting as a loving pair for a time. They often went fishing together, enjoying each other's company out on the water. That camaraderie was shattered one day, as Joh, Nel and young Dwight busied themselves with end-of trip details after just such a fishing trip.

All the fishing gear was emptied out of the boat and sat on the wooden pier. Nel, standing on the grassy bank above the wooden dock, was dealing with the stern line, winding it on her hand as she walked forward, ready to hand it to Joh, already in the boat. It needed to be moved over to the ramp, to be hauled out of the water.

Joh reached over to untie the bow line, forgetting that the stern line was not yet in the boat, and gunned it towards the end of the pier. He heard a screaming behind him and turned around to look, bringing the boat to a sudden stop. Dwight was shrieking and waving his arms. He wondered what was happening that had upset the boy so much, and then, to his shock, saw the stern line played out behind the boat still attached to his wife lying face first on the dock. He'd yanked her violently forward from the top of the embankment onto the wooden pier below, the line wound around her hand.

Wide-eyed, Dwight was terrified that his Oma was dead. Instead, she was bruised and livid. "Are you trying to kill me?" she shouted at him, after she recovered her breath sufficiently. "Didn't you *look*, before you took off like that?"

"I-I thought you'd finished," he stuttered, "and besides, you should *never* wind a boat line around your hand like that!" He tried to justify his own cause for the accident a little, but he felt guilty just the same, for his carelessness. Dwight was only relieved that his Oma was okay, he didn't care who did what. It was a subdued trio, one of them hurting badly, that returned home that afternoon.

Joh, at times, played fast and loose with safety. He'd seen and done so much, perhaps he began to feel invincible, that he could do anything, and not kill himself in the process. Or so it seemed to those around him anyway.

In small matters, he'd simply lose sight of what most people considered safe. The first double-hulled boat he'd bought was designed as a lake boat, but he took it out on the ocean, inside water to be sure, and mostly calm. In the beginning, having the double hull was a feature Joh was sure would prevent the boat from overturning. Later, he discovered that in rough ocean water, under windy conditions it was no more safe than a single-hulled boat; that on the ocean it could just as easily be swamped in rough water. After that his rule was straightforward; when the weather was calm, he'd go out. When it wasn't, he'd stay home. To him it was the simplest solution.

He'd disappointed his grandsons more than once with that rule. After they'd spent the night, ready to go fishing in the morning, they'd woken up to the news, "we can't go fishing today". It always ended in a few tears. What could he do? Putting them in danger because of his own carelessness, was unthinkable. The same proved true of the second boat he had.

But happy memories of fishing with Opa were still plentiful. Recollections of Oma's apple sauce, served with every meal so the boiled potatoes and mushy vegetables would go down a little easier, and platters of sweet smelling *Boterkoek,* were also in good supply. *Boterkoek* was the one treat she always baked to have on hand and the boys demanded that their own mothers also have the recipe.

Despite living in Canada now for thirty plus years, small European customs were still sprinkled throughout their daily lives, customs that many Canadians, far removed from their own Old World ancestors, had long since abandoned. Part of that was: wives served their men cups of coffee, made their lunches, in general, obedient service to their husbands, one of the many practices that still prevailed in the Grin household.

Nel had long since gotten her own small car and coming home one day she saw, to her surprise, Joh's car sitting in the driveway. She didn't expect he'd be home so early from his fishing trip. It was four o'clock, time enough to cook dinner for him when he'd get home at six or so, but there he was, sitting in his chair, scowling at her as she came through the door.

"Where have you been?"

"What do you mean, where have I been? I've been visiting my brother. I never expected you to be here already. Why are you home so early?"

He continued to scowl at her. "I couldn't fish, the wind came up and it was too rough to continue, so I came home." Then accusingly, he added, "You weren't here to make me my lunch and coffee. I've been sitting here since one o'clock waiting for you to come home!" His anger came up a notch at the thought of the wasted day.

Nel's jaw dropped. "What's the matter with you? Couldn't you even make your *own lunch?*" she pointed out incredulously.

Then she had another thought. "If I'd known that you would be home a lot earlier today, you could have spent the time teaching me how to tow the boat and trailer. I really need to learn this, just in case." Joh again agreed, but as the days passed, the lessons never materialized.

Both of them had their feet planted firmly in both worlds, old and new, hanging onto customs that had long been discarded. Such were the old ways ingrained in him. Change was hard, it made him feel unstable. Uprooting his life so many times the way he'd had, he needed something constant and familiar to make him feel secure. Old customs, old habits made him feel connected to his roots.

He went back to those roots in 1988, the first time since 1969. Nineteen years was a long time to be away, and again he saw many changes he was uncomfortable with. What made it all worthwhile was a reunion with all the living members of his family, all his siblings, and spouses, even his sister from Australia. Looking around, Joh was acutely aware that he might not ever see some of them again, should he make another trip.

Joh and Nel loved children. They'd become Oma and Opa, surrogate grandparents to the little sisters that lived on the same street a few houses up. Nel also cared for two young brothers in her home, the older first and, the younger brother after his birth. The boys lovingly called her "Nelly", and Joh as "*Oom* Joh" - Uncle Joh. Having young children in their lives seemed, more than anything else, to bring the bickering to a temporary halt.

Playing *Sint Nikolaas* every December became one more way for him to maintain harmony with his wife. They had a standing invitation to perform for a class of children in a private Christian school affiliated with their church. Every year, Joh would get a list from the teacher of the class he'd be entertaining. He'd get reports consisting of what the children had done, how they'd behaved, their strong points and exemplary deeds. The teacher's list told him everything he needed to know, so he could talk to them on a very personal level.

Sint Nikolaas - *Saint Nicolas, or Santa Claus*

On the fifth of December - *Sint Nikolaas* Day, Joh, as *Sint Nikolaas*, Nel, in Dutch costume, and someone from the school, dressed as *Sint Nikolaas's* aide, *Zwarte Piet*, arrived with great fanfare and the children were delighted.

"And who do we have here?" boomed Joh, as each child was called up to meet and receive his gift and treat from the good Saint. He looked in his Book of Good Children and read aloud the name of the child standing before him.

"Joel! I see you've had a very good report card, and I know you've worked very hard," The 'Saint' then looked at him with a frown.

"But you talk too much in class, don't you?" Joel looked down at the floor. In a very small voice, he replied, "Yes."

"This is something you better work on. You shouldn't be disrupting the class and your teacher like that, don't you agree?" Joel did.

"Amanda. Please, come up here." Amanda came up and stood, trembling just a little. "Amanda, you have very beautiful handwriting and you do very good work, but I find you are a little slow in your work. Maybe you are trying to make every single letter too perfect? What do you think?" Amanda replied that she liked her letters to be perfect.

Sint Nikolaas advised her, "Not everything needs to be absolutely perfect. Things like that can slow you down and make other problems for you. I'm going to suggest that you try not to erase too much. Put your eraser in a jar in front of you, so you won't use it so much. Maybe that will help."

By turn, every child in class stood before Sint Nikolaas and had strengths praised and weaknesses revealed, along with some sage advice to help them along. Then they'd get their present and treats.

Afterwards the couple drove home to the North Shore, pleased with another successful Sint Nikolaas day performance, knowing that those

---

Zwarte Piet - Black Peter - Traditionally someone of Moorish descent that acted as St. Nicolas' helper and Aide children had a positive experience they could use to further their development. Joh often thought, *why couldn't I have played Sint Nikolaas every day for my own children?* He'd been too busy, too occupied, too exhausted. He regretted it now.

So, as many times as they could, visits were made to their married children and the boys that now occupied their lives. Roel and Elly's two boys were always delighted to have Opa visit, and Oma too, but Opa was special. He listened; he didn't talk at them.

"Opa? Did you see my new dump truck?"

"No! Show it to me!" The boy led Joh out to the back yard, where a large, dirt filled area had been set aside just for a little boy's need to get dirty. There, sitting on a mound of soil, half filled with sand, stood a yellow dump truck.

"That's a wonderful dump truck! Does it really dump dirt?" The dump truck's capabilities were proudly demonstrated by a delighted grandson. "See it dumps and everything!"

"That's the best dump truck I've ever seen!"

Another little voice called to him, "Opa! Come sit with me in the swing chair!"

Later, he stood watching, as his daughter expertly piped out the dough for cream puffs onto the baking tray. *How did she know that?* He thought. *Did I teach it to her?* He couldn't remember doing it, but she'd picked it up somewhere, as she'd watched while he himself stood in his own kitchen, working, or maybe in the bakery long ago, doing the same thing. He remembered she'd always watched him, so interested in how he created his confections, asking questions. He smiled to himself.

Later, when he tasted the finished product, filled with sweet, whipped cream and covered in a chocolate glaze, he remarked, "You know, there are a lot of bakers out there, who can't make a cream puff like this. They'd love to know how you do it." She grinned back at him, "I learned from the best, Dad."

On the way home, Joh thinking how lucky he was. Nel sat beside him, talking, but his mind was on the visit, reflecting how much he'd learned on what not to do in dealing with children. He'd made so many mistakes with his son; not listening enough, always ready with a correction, telling him how he himself would do such and such, instead of listening to the boy's ideas. But sometimes late at night the old guilt rose up in his mind and tormented him, and he wished that he'd be free of it.

He was in the left lane, and a car raced by on his right, much too fast. "That driver is going to have accident, if he speeds like that," Nel remarked.

Five minutes later, they watched horrified, as the speeding car tried passing again on the shoulder of the highway and collided at full speed into the rear of a parked vehicle. Joh pulled the car to the side and got out, Nel behind him. He raced ahead, hoping against hope that the driver was still alive. But when he got to the crumpled wreck, there was no one behind the wheel. The windshield was completely smashed out, and Joh expecting and fearing it, looked for a body on the road somewhere ahead. He didn't have far to look. Whoever it had been, now laid broken and headless on the pavement. He didn't want to look any farther, knowing what he'd find if he did.

Nel hadn't quite reached the wreck, and he ordered her back, "You don't want to see this," he told her. "Go back to the car." Others had stopped by now, and he was afraid that in the dark, someone else would get hurt in the traffic, piling up behind the accident.

The accident, and sight of the headless corpse, stayed with him for a long time. *If I was a worry wart like Nel,* he thought, *I'd have visions of kids and grandkids in just this kind of accident.* He was grateful that Nel hadn't seen the body.

Young children continued to be the important ingredient in the elder Grin household, spending happy hours playing with Opa, Oma and the dog. Teddy was an equally important element to the two children of

Roel and Elly. They had no dog of their own, their father was far too finicky of his indoor surroundings to tolerate an animal in the house. So when they visited, Teddy became their dog too. For both grandsons, 'Teddy' became their first real spoken word.

When the first Teddy died suddenly of old age, Nel got another Pomeranian that she also named Teddy. Somehow it seem fitting; this Pom as well, had the appearance of a fluffy little teddy bear. When that Teddy passed a scant seven years later of heart failure, Nel was again bereft, and there were little boy tears of grief shed for the loss of a great playmate.

Another dog made its appearance in the grandparent's home some time after, a small puppy that delighted the boys to no end. Kaya became the focus of Joh and Nel's disciplinary skills. The dog was smart, smarter than any they'd ever had, and they were able to teach her many things.

During the process they learned that Kaya had some funny quirks. She'd sit every evening for a half hour outside at the east corner of the front yard, overlooking the lower neighbouring properties, and just stare out at nothing. Neither Joh nor Nel ever knew why. When the couple were having their meal Kaya refused to enter the dining room, and sat watching them from the kitchen doorway.

The couple discovered she could sing. Joh would say, "Sing, Kaya sing!" And she would. She'd lift up her muzzle to the sky and *'aarrroooo'* to her heart's content. Joh and Nel often delighted an audience of oldsters in long-term care homes, when they came with Kaya to entertain them with her singing.

Above all she loved the grandchildren, even when they'd run her ragged until she had no strength left to continue with the chase through the house.

CHAPTER 27

Breaking Down
1980

Joh stood in the centre of his front yard. Standing where he did, he could look down at the road below, as well as down on his neighbour's lower set property. He still thought it was strange how the entire neighbourhood had been tiered and stepped, so that each house on the street was above their neighbour on one side, and below on the other. He also noted with satisfaction that the maple he'd planted in the middle of the yard had grown significantly. It threw some wonderful shade now in the warm summer months. Nel came out to join him.

"Where would you like me to put this?" Joh pointed to the new rose bush he'd bought.

Nel stood thinking, looking around the front yard. Flower beds had been put in along two sides of the grassed area and she considered which spot would work best. Finally, not able to make up her mind, she threw up a hand and said, "I don't know, any place along those two sides looks good to me."

Joh insisted, fearing that if he planted the bush in one spot, she'd find a reason to be unhappy with it and insist he'd planted it in the wrong spot. "Come on, just name a spot you like, I don't care where."

"Okay. There," she said, pointing to the far corner where the border made its turn around the yard. Nel made her way back into the house, as Joh carried the bush over to the designated corner. As he dug the hole, he thought, *it might get a little windy here.* He was afraid it might suffer a little from the elements in this spot, being so high and unprotected in the colder months. He filled in the hole and moved over closer to the house. For good measure he intended to put in some other shrubs beside it, just to give it a little more shelter.

Later, he noticed Nel giving him the stink eye. *Now what?* He thought but didn't want to ask. *It was probably the rose bush, and I'm tired of always having to explain myself.*

He could hear her rattling around in the kitchen as he came in for a drink of water. She'd been bending over to peer into the cupboard below the counter, muttering. Straightening up, she looked at him, "When are you going to take all that arborite you dragged home ten years ago and line these cupboard shelves, like you promised me?"

Another chore to do that will not be simple, he thought. It was tricky to take the hard-to-work-with material and fit it neatly into an enclosed space. Sometimes he wished he'd never found the stuff and given her the idea of what to do with it. "Yeah, yeah, I'll get around to it sometime."

"When?"

"I don't know. When I have time. I've got to get the planting done first. Otherwise, the beans won't grow right." The answer was short, his mind on the broad beans, his favourite, needing planting in the tiers between his front yard and the boulevard below.

"For ten years I've been scrubbing the black marks from the pans off the shelves! I'm sick and tired of the dirty marks and I want the arborite in place. I want clean cupboards!" Nel slapped her hand on the counter for emphasis. "You've been promising me for ten years!"

To that, the only thing he could think to say was, "Oh, you've got no patience!" But the moment it was out of his mouth, he knew it had been the wrong thing to say. It was true, the woman had very little patience, and his mind had been stuck on the 'right now'. Then he remembered it *had* been ten years, and she'd spoken from that perspective. There'd been patience enough in this particular case.

He escaped to the safety of the basement, as she sputtered angrily at his misplaced critique. There, he pulled out the bottle of wine he'd put in to cool. Instead of taking it back upstairs to offer his wife a drink, as he intended to, a peace offering of sorts, he carried it outside, using the back basement stairs. Staring absently at something in the carport, he uncapped the bottle and took a drink, still deep in thought on how to gracefully get out of the fresh trouble he knew he was in.

"*What are you doing drinking?*" A sharp voice directly behind him shattered his reverie. He spun around, startled. Nel stood there, accusations smouldering in her eyes.

"Nothing! I'm not … *aahggrr!*" Growling in frustration, he couldn't explain himself, and walked away. He'd absent-mindedly taken a swallow. Would she accuse him of being an alcoholic now? It went from bad to worse. Now she'd think he had a drinking problem. What next?

Unsure of what to do, but knowing he needed to do something, he walked back into the house, still holding the bottle. "I wasn't drinking," he pointed out angrily to his wife. "I just had one swallow. I was trying to figure out how to put in the arborite." Then he added solicitously, holding out the bottle of wine, "Do you want a drink before dinner?"

Nel looked at him, "Yes, thanks, but I better not find you drinking secretly behind my back! That's a sure sign of alcoholism!" Inwardly, his eyes rolled. *Sure,* he thought, *everything done, that you don't know about is wrong somehow.*

For the next week, in his spare time, he took measurements, spreading the arborite out on his workbench downstairs, then measuring, cutting, and fitting, until Nel finally had her cupboards lined with free arborite that Joh had pulled out of a dumpster.

Over the years he'd discovered that Zellers had the policy of throwing out anything brought back as a return, relegating it to the dumpster at the back of the building. He'd found such treasures there; brand new microwave ovens, floor lamps, building materials, tools, shelving units. Everyone benefited from these finds that were first thoroughly checked over, cleaned, and/or refurbished or repaired. Four floor lamps became three, as the worst one was used to replace parts for the other three.

All three families ended up with the same model floor lamp and on visiting each other would remark, "Ah, I know where you got that lamp!"

Everyone got a microwave.

A shelving unit only had a small metal part missing. Joh wrote to the manufacturer, requesting the missing part, which he got, then gifted it to Elly. The tools came in handy for his own use. It was a nice hobby, this finding of treasures in the dumpster. *It was incredible how wasteful people were,* he mused, *but maybe that's a bonus for me.*

His hands had begun to feel irritated again. Coming home from work this day, he'd found himself scratching at his hands constantly. They were so itchy! At home, he'd eaten, and then applied eczema cream before going to bed for a while. The chores he set for himself went by the wayside as his hands got worse by the hour. By now they were red and raw, despite the cream he'd applied.

Sighing, he called the medical centre to make an appointment. A week later he found himself once again, sitting across from the doctor as he described what was happening. "It looks to me like you have a severe allergy to something. I'm going to send you to an allergist."

He wondered, "I've never had this reaction to anything before. I don't understand." Dr. Hassan explained, "It's not unusual for people to develop allergies later in life, especially if they're allergy prone, like you are. Let's not get ahead of ourselves though. First, we find out what it is you're allergic to."

In the weeks following he finally learned what had been causing the rash on his hands. Cinnamon was the culprit, something he'd handled all his life. It was devastating news, and he didn't know how it would affect his job. Cinnamon was used in so many bakery recipes. He didn't know how his boss would take it, being told his head baker couldn't work with anything containing cinnamon. In the meantime, he bought a box of surgical gloves from the pharmacy, after getting his prescription filled for the new eczema cream the doctor had prescribed.

The next day he came to work, wearing his surgical gloves, and the boss questioned him on it, smiling, "What's this Joh, afraid to get your hands dirty?"

"I got a real problem," explained Joh. "You'll never believe what I got an allergy to. Cinnamon! That's why I've been getting eczema on my hands!" The boss was surprised and remarked on the same thing Joe had to his doctor, "You've worked with that spice for years! How is that possible?"

Joh recounted what the doctor had told him. The boss shook his head. "Shit! Let's hope you don't get an allergy to flour, then. You'd have to wear a gas mask as well!" Both of them laughed, but Joh worried he might have to take an early retirement. He had plans for his retirement. He wanted to travel, fish, and he needed a full pension, working to the age of sixty-five to get it. He was three years short.

He tried valiantly for a time, wearing the surgical gloves, but it didn't fully help. The eczema returned, time and time again, his hands were raw and bleeding, and he'd have to take time off work to let them heal. Finally, his boss suggested kindly that Joh retire. He needed a full-time baker.

Joh did some calculations and thought, maybe just maybe he could pull it off; take the lesser pension, still follow his plans for retirement, just maybe scaled down a bit.

After Joh officially retired, his thoughts turned to fishing again, and he had listened just last week as his twin nephews talked about crossing the strait to Port Renfrew on Vancouver Island to spend a weekend fishing. He'd heard that Port Renfrew was a hot spot for salmon fishing. Suddenly Joh had a brilliant idea. He could launch the boat at Tsawwassen the next day, and motor over to the Island to join them. He turned to Nel in his excitement. "I want to go over to Port Renfrew and spend the weekend fishing with Pete and Bill!"

"That sounds like fun, but it will cost quite a bit to take car and boat over on the ferry!"

"No, no, I want to launch from Tsawwassen and go from there with the boat!"

"I see. What do I do with no car then?"

"Well, you'll come with me, and when the boat is off the trailer, just take it empty back home. You'll just have to come on Monday and pick me up again. That way, you've got the car for the entire weekend."

"You want me to drive the car and trailer home? Now, when you've never ever taught me how to drive with it attached? I have no idea how to back it up, never mind how to hitch and unhitch the thing!"

"Ah, it's easy..." he began, but Nel cut him off abruptly. "There's no way I'm driving that car and trailer all the way to Tsawwassen and back at this point, without having some lessons and a lot of practice beforehand."

"I'm sure you could do it, it's so easy!" he argued. "I really want to go fishing with Pete and Bill!"

"No way. I'm not doing it. It's your own fault for never taking the time to let me practice. We've had plenty of opportunity to do it, and you were never willing to let me take the wheel."

They argued for the rest of the afternoon, to no avail. Joh had put off teaching her the skill of towing a trailer and she wasn't at all comfortable trying it now. So, unless he wanted to pay the big bucks for the ferry, he could stay home. "That's what you get for never teaching me to drive the car with a trailer!" she chided him, thinking of the lessons she'd constantly asked for.

It was around the same time that Roel and Elly came by with some plans of their own. It was more Roel's plans. He'd already talked endlessly about it, how he wanted to build expensive homes; fancy homes, homes for rich people that still had money. He had no desire to build ordinary homes, and his own finishing carpentry business was, for some inexplicable reason, not enough for him. It seemed to be slowing, and he wanted to try something else, certain he'd be successful at it. The man was ambitious, that was for sure.

Roel talked about how he wanted to sell the house, the house Joh had co-signed for, to finance his new plans. He needed a builder's mortgage, to build two homes, fancy ones, on side by side lots. If he sold the house, he still wouldn't have quite enough other equity to cover the new mortgage, could Joh co-sign again for him? It all sounded like a fair plan, and he could.

Joh was curious, "Where would you live if you sold the house?"

"I know of a place near the lots I have in mind, a townhouse. The rent is pretty decent considering the booming real estate market and it would be close to the job. I'd function more as the contractor, sub-contract out to the trades, and do the finishing myself. Once I sell one house, we would have enough money left over to cover the down payment and carry the mortgage. Then, I just carry on building more houses!" He had it all figured out.

That week, Joh co-signed for the loan, and then wondered about it. He had heard rumblings about the market that sounded as if things might not go as Roel expected them to. But he didn't know enough to be able to make a prediction.

There was a lot he didn't understand these days. Everybody seemed to be mumbling. "I'm not mumbling," Nel would tell him, "you're deaf." She claimed to hear him ask far too often, *"What? Speak up, you're mumbling."* Too many times. Nonsense, he wasn't old enough yet, only mid-sixties. *My father was the same age as I am now when he died, and he hadn't been the least bit deaf.*

But the requests to repeat things continued, and Nel, true to form kept insisting he was going deaf. Before he'd had a chance to even consider whether or not to get a hearing test, Nel presented problems of her own. She now sat on the couch, white faced and looking extremely distressed. "What's the matter. Why are you looking so uncomfortable?" Joh peered closely at her, "Are you feeling all right?"

"I-I'm not ... sure ... my heart is-is.." She seemed to find it hard to explain. "It doesn't beat right."

Joh jumped from his chair "I'm taking you to the hospital, right now!" And he ran to get his keys.

"All right, just-just let me change my ... clothes."

"The hell with your clothes!" He spun on his heel and looked at her, almost shouting. "If you're having a heart attack, a change of clothes won't help you!"

He rushed Nel to the hospital, breaking every speed record there was. In Emergency, the cuff was put on and monitored, a saline IV started for good measure, and a doctor put a stethoscope to her chest, listening carefully.

"Mrs. Grin, you're not having a heart attack," the doctor began, "but I detect an abnormal heartbeat. I suspect you have a heart arrhythmia."

"What's that?" Nel looked up curiously at the doctor. "Will I die? Will my heart stop all of a sudden?" The doctor laughed, "No nothing like that."

He left briefly, then re-entered the room with a sheet of paper, and explained. "This is an order for an echocardiogram. They're going to look at your heartbeat, and if it's warranted, an electrocardiogram and perhaps a stress test to determine if it's severe enough for medication."

Nel had an appointment at Vancouver General Hospital for tests within a few days. Her 'heart attack' turned out to be atrial fibrillation, an irregular heartbeat. With medication, the disorder would be under control. Joh wondered if he could use this new wrinkle when she got angry with him. *Calm down, dear, think of your heart.* Maybe. Maybe not.

He hadn't been paying much attention to his own health these days and considering the turn of events with Nel's heart problems some time ago, he thought he better have another medical done soon. There were some odd things lately that had caught his attention, trouble urinating for one, and he'd found blood in his urine one morning. Nel made an appointment for him.

Sitting in the doctor's office again a few days later, the doctor looked grave. "Your prostate seems very large Joh, and the indication of blood is not a good sign," the doctor said solicitously. "I'm going to refer you to a urologist. They'll take good care of you." There, tests were ordered, blood samples, a biopsy. Everything came back and the news was not good: early-stage prostate cancer.

Cancer. The word itself scared him. So many people he knew had died of it; his sister-in-law, Leny, Alida, Jacqueline, so many people he'd known in the past, all gone due to that dreaded disease. The urologist looked at him and shook his head at the look of dread on Joh's face. "Mr. Grin, you have no reason to fear, it's very slow growing cancer. At your age, you'll sooner die with it, than of it."

Still, he needed to do everything in his power to fight it. He wasn't ready to give up yet. The urologist had suggested an operation removing the testes; that the cancer was feeding on the testosterone, as he put it. Joh balked at that, and he walked out of the office, indecisive, unsure if he wanted to have part of his manhood removed. At home that night, he had the strangest dream, something he rarely did.

In the mist, a large ship was leaving harbour, bound for the open sea. Joh stood on the bank watching it go, but the ship had a massive hole in its side, and it was clear that it would sink. He called out, but the vessel kept moving forward to its doom. Over and over he called, screamed, anything to get its attention. Finally, spent, breathless, and exhausted, he watched as it sailed over the horizon, knowing it would inevitably go down.

Joh woke up in a sweat. *What was that?* In the morning, after lying awake for the rest of the night, he recounted the dream to Nel. "What could it mean?" he asked. "It was so vivid, and there seemed to be such an ominous feel about it."

Nel looked at him. "Joh," she said, "that ship is you. You have a great injury, like that hole, and if you don't do anything about it, you too will sink." He thought hard about that.

It was true. Cancer could go in many directions; he was in his mid-sixties. If the cancer could be fixed, that great hole plugged, he might live to a ripe old age, *dying with cancer, not of cancer*. He had his answer. He would opt for the surgery.

It seemed that when it rained it poured. Roel had defaulted on his builder's mortgage. The market had inflated to the point where, when he'd attempted to purchase the second fancy home he'd built, he couldn't even qualify for the home mortgage, even with the successful sale of the first house. He'd tried to sell the second house then, but inflation, an overall buildup of private debt, greed, high interest rates, and high unemployment, had all come together to bring the real estate world crashing. Trying to sell the house, he'd chased the market down, until it finally sold at a price that wouldn't pay off the builder's loan.

The Royal Bank of Canada finally called Joh regarding the loan payments, and he set an appointment with the manager, Mr. Trask, to find out how the whole fiasco could be resolved. They had no idea what to expect when they walked in, but sitting in the office, facing the man behind the desk, he heard the worst possible news he could have imagined.

"You know that, seeing as you co-signed the loan," Trask coldly pointed out, "you're just as liable. We could easily look to you to pay the entire loan out, by foreclosing on your house. We could take everything you've got, to satisfy the loan."

"Nel gasped, "WHAT?" She began to sputter in fury, "You, you … *horrible* …" enraged, she couldn't continue, lost for words.

Joh was stunned and shocked. He could lose his house? Something dropped out from under him and, for a moment, he drifted in a helpless empty space. Then anger set in. "No! That's not going to happen! The loan will be paid!" The house was his. No one was going to take that away from him.

He called Roel, sick at heart, angry, worried. "You have to find some way to pay this. They'll take my house! Do you realize that?"

Roel went on about how he was a victim of bad circumstances, things beyond his control. He'd had no idea it would come to this. It wasn't deliberate. Joh realized, after the fact, that the man had ploughed ahead, despite advice from others to hold off on his grand plans. He'd learned from nephews, Pete and Bill, who were long-time builders themselves, and well versed in the trends of the real estate market, that they'd advised Roel not to go ahead with his new plans, that the timing was all wrong. Roel hadn't listened, so sure of his own abilities and potential success.

His son-in-law promised he'd try to take care of it, and Joh hoped he would. The calls from the bank continued each month, another payment had to be made, and each month Joh would plead, beg, warn Roel that he'd start talking to lawyers soon. The interest payments were inflating the loan and there was no way anyone could keep up with the now staggering payments. He couldn't continue to carry this debt. There was no action from Roel in return, only more excuses, and the same old sob story of how he'd been a victim of circumstance.

There looked to be nothing further forthcoming from his son-in-law. Joh would have to go back to work, never mind the severe allergy. His retirement plans were washed away in a rolling sea of misery and uncertainty. A lawyer advised him to send monthly bills to his son-in-law, and perhaps consider a lawsuit as a last resort.

Roel continued to insist on being his own boss. He'd reinvented himself, creating a title, business card, and letterhead for a company with no assets, no customer base, no seed money, and no training for himself, to start another type of business. Elly begged him to just get a job, any job, but he refused to 'abandon my dream' as he put it. He'd rounded on her at the suggestion he get a job, saying that she was supposed to support him, not tear him down, quoting from his Bible that God had given her to him as a "helpmeet". It was her duty to be supportive of him in all things.

She went to work herself, to cover her family's bills, and help her father carry the debt load. She'd been a stay at home mother and had no real job skills. She took on two jobs, that of a waitress, to pay for their own food, rent and necessities, the other, delivering early morning papers to help her father. There was even a third job, cleaning a house once a week. Roel took it all. Joh was still holding the bag.

Finally, Joh's younger brother Wim, came up with a plan. Wim, or Bill, as he was now called, was a successful man with his own business. Bill's company took on the role of mortgager and created a reverse mortgage. With that, the Royal Bank debt could be met every month, and hopefully, somewhere in the future, he'd be reimbursed by Roel. Not a perfect answer, but a better option than what he had now. His retirement plans were still in pieces, however, and Joh was left with a bitterness that was hard to look away from.

The relationship between Roel and his in-laws was shattered beyond repair, but the disintegration was far from over. It took another seven years, Roel, unbending, not listening to his wife, arrogant in his conceit, hadn't even noticed that his wife's life had turned into a drudgery-filled existence, that he'd used her simply to fulfil his own pipe dreams. Joh thought, *he probably sees her as a commodity or chattel, rather than as a partner.*

1961
While travelling to BC, the family ate most meals in this manner, picnicking at the side of the road.

(Below)
Setting up the tents

Joh & Nel's home
(Photo taken approx. 1996)

1965 - Joh, at home on a Sunday

The first grandchild
Dwight Andrew
July, 1973

(Right) Joh, delighting in his third grandson, Lorne. Jan. 1975

(Left)
(L to R) Grandsons, Peter, Owen, Dwight, Lorne
1978

**Visit to the Netherlands
1988**

Joh, proving he's still got the skill playing hoops from his childhood

Punting along the canal in Krabbendam like the old days
Accompanied by Nel, Brother, Jaap and his wife Rien

Showing off his grandsons
(Right) - L to R - Owen, Lorne, Opa, Dwight

(Left) Clockwise from top left, Peter, Lorne, Owen, Dwight

Cates Park - first launch of his Bayliner. 1993

Showing off a catch of crab 1995

Nel, Joh and unidentified school worker as Sint Nikolaas & Zwarte Piet. (Dutch Santa Clause & his aide) (student unknown)

THE FINAL CAKE

Joh, a guest on board, relaxing on the hatch of the commercial salmon troller, *Blue Eagle* as she motors home from Prince Rupert to Chemainus, BC.

CHAPTER 28

Going Forward - Looking Back

Joh didn't want a hearing aid. He'd never wanted a hearing aid. They bothered his ear, it was a nuisance, uncomfortable, and he was always forgetting it. The silence around him was heavenly when he didn't have it in. Most days he'd be found in his garden, like now, happily puttering, and mumbling to himself, intent on his work. The dog, Kaya was always beside him. She followed him everywhere, and stayed close, except when he climbed the ladder. She'd done it only once, a long time ago, before *the great fall*. After that, when Joh brought the ladder out, Kaya made sure to stay well away.

The great fall was Kaya's watershed moment. Joh had climbed the ladder to do some pruning in the front yard Maple tree, while Kaya sat directly below the ladder, supervising. Joh had just about finished cutting one limb, when he over-reached himself and lost his balance. The ladder, and Joh with it, came crashing down, almost on top of the dog, who managed within a hair's breadth, to escape being crushed. She never sat by the ladder again, opting to sit at the other end of the yard if Joh occupied it.

He smiled at the image in his head, his thoughts flitting randomly like an insect from hummock to hummock. So many memories. So many milestones and experiences. *Peter, with his dreadlocks ... Dwight shaving his head, leaving only a long greasy ponytail at the top* His thoughts took more twisting turns as he worked *... fall was coming, he needed to cover the cacti soon ... shovelling snow from the steep driveway ... did he have enough salt? ...the last New Year's Eve they'd had ... when was that again? ... such a long time ago...*

He went to the house, a little thirsty. A cup of tea would fix that. Nel sat in her chair, peering through the magnifying glass, frowning at the embroidery she was working on. He didn't want to disturb her, he could make the tea it himself, couldn't he? Sitting down, he reached for his hearing aid on the side table where he left it, only to grasp at empty space. Where was it?

"Nel? Have you seen my hearing aid?" Joh shouted, puzzled at its absence. "No," she said, "didn't you leave it on your table? I thought I saw it there earlier."

Nel got up, looking around the floor, under the side table, checking under the book stand. Nothing. "Maybe I moved it somewhere else," he said, more to himself. He walked to the bedroom to check his desk. Maybe he'd left it there. It wasn't, and as he returned to the upper level of the house, he heard Nel call out, "I found it."

He was about to say, "Oh good", but was stopped short when he saw what she held; mangled pieces of plastic that resembled a hearing aid, chewed and spit out by the looks of it. "That's not going to fit in my ear anymore," he remarked dryly, and looked over to Kaya, lying innocently beside his chair.

"Did you eat my hearing aid?" Joh held the pieces in his hand and bent down to present the evidence to the dog. Kaya looked away, her eyes rolling over to the side as if to say, *I'm not seeing that. It's not there.* Guilt was written on her face, the teeth marks, like a signature, showed plainly on the plastic bits.

"Bad dog!" "Bad, bad Kaya!" A chorus of recriminations rolled over the dog's head, and she cowered in shame.

Joh sighed. Maybe his insurance would cover it. "By the way ..." a previous thought struck him, "... can you remember the last time we had a New Year's Eve at our house?"

Nel looked at him a little annoyed, "Please don't shout."

"I'm not shouting," he shouted, then lowered his voice. "I'm not shouting." Nel laughed, "Don't forget, you can't hear your own voice right now, you're deaf, remember?"

"What did you ask me again?" she continued. Joh thought a minute. "Oh yes, I was wondering, when was the last time we had New Year's Eve here?"

"I don't know," Nel thought a minute, and then, "it's been a while. We always seem to be getting invited out somewhere. Are you planning on having one now, in the middle of summer? Why are you asking about New Year's Eve parties? The last one we had, years ago here, wasn't so great, if you remember."

Joh smiled, a little sheepishly, remembering it. It was all his doing.

≈≈≈≈≈≈

It was almost 1974. "Happy New Year Mum, Dad," a pair of cheerful voices wafted through the door with a cold draft, "We're here, the party's on!" Elly and Roel climbed the steps into the living room, baby in his bassinet, and looked around. "Hey, Kiddo. Hi Ross! Great to see you again!" It was their first New Year's celebration at home, after returning from overseas.

Nancyann and Ross sat on the couch, side by side. Body language did not project 'comfortable', and Elly wondered what had been going on. Her mother came from the kitchen, all smiles, "Wonderful! You're here!"

Wine glasses, teacups and saucers, plates of home baked sweets, bowls of chips, nuts and pretzels covered the coffee table in a haphazard arrangement. Nel waved to the goodies on the table, "Help yourself! Joh, could you pour some wine? Or do you want something else? Ross, some Pepsi?" Nel peppered her guests with questions, and Joh got up without a word to go retrieve the wine bottle from the basement. Nel pulled out wine glasses. "Who wants wine?"

"I'll have some. We'll stay for a while, but we're going out again at nine," Nancyann eyed her mother nervously, as her father came back from the basement, bottle in hand. The mood seemed to shift suddenly. "I told you! You're not going out!" he barked at her. "You are staying here! You belong home on New Year's Eve!"

Nancyann, at twenty years old, still lived at home, under her parents' roof and the rule 'under my roof' was still very much in evidence. She would be twenty-one in a few months, legal age, and until then, if she lived at home, she was still under the law of her father. That was Joh's opinion. And in his opinion children stayed home with mother and father to celebrate the incoming year.

Nancyann argued, while Ross, as usual, sat mute and uncomfortable. The back and forth raged on for a short while, but Dad's rule prevailed, with a compromise. She could leave after midnight. They had to see the clock turning twelve midnight together with her parents. Nancyann and Ross were not happy. Everyone else looked ill at ease.

The evening devolved into an awkward, stilted affair, with stunted conversations, a few half-hearted attempts at frivolity, hours dragging by, until finally, midnight crawled on all fours across the floor. Happy new year wishes were passed from person to person, and Nancyann and Ross left, relieved to be free. Elly and Roel, gathering up their sleeping infant, said their goodbyes a short time later.

≈≈≈≈≈≈

"I seem to remember that the last party we had here wasn't too cheerful," Nel mused. "I remember ..."

Joh cut her off, "I remember too." He sighed. "I may have been to blame for that." Huffing out a breath of air, he reflected. "I should have let her go out. There was no good reason to demand that she stay home, except, *I* wanted it" Sometimes he wished he could turn back the clock, just a little.

The doorbell rang at that moment. "Who can that be? Are you expecting someone?" Nel looked at her husband, eyebrows raised, as she got up. "Not me," he shook his head. She went to answer the door and opened it to someone who normally walked in without ringing. He did not look happy.

"Mum, hi. Can I come in?" Roel stood looking at her, with sorrowful eyes. *What now,* she thought, as she let him in.

Roel made his way into the living room and Joh's face darkened considerably. "Something terrible's happened!" he blurted out. "Something awful. Elly left me!!" Both parents stared at the man, waiting for him to continue, not wanting to believe it at first. *Good for her,* Joh thought, and he wasn't sure if he should act shocked or elated.

"Isn't that awful?! Isn't it terrible?!" Roel kept up the lament, "What am I going to do now? How could she do this to me! She needs to come home! The boys …. Owen is so upset!" Nel's heart skipped a beat and something stabbed at her heart, thinking about those boys. But they'd get through this. She and Joh would help where they could.

"You've got to tell her to come home! She has to come home! You tell her!" he cried, his face in his hands. "She just left, took all her clothes and left! She's staying with those … those … theatre people …" He made a face, "that gay guy … perverts … I can't believe she'd mix herself up with people like that."

"Look Roel," Joh stabbed his finger at him, "First of all, I can't tell her anything, she's an adult! I can't just command her to do something and she'll obey. It doesn't work that way." He sat back in his chair again, "Second, consider yourself lucky she only took her clothes. In Holland, if a wife leaves, she takes everything, furniture, dishes, everything, with her."

Roel stared at his father-in-law. "What am I going to do?" Joh looked at him sharply, taking a measure of the man. "If you're smart, you'll figure it out, and you *might* … just might … get her back … but I have the feeling it's not going to be an easy job."

Joh pictured his spunky girl with her back up. He hadn't seen *that* girl in a very long time, but she'd finally resurfaced. He was rooting for her.

A very unhappy man left the Grin residence, and husband and wife looked at each other. "So, what do we do now?" Nel wondered. "I think we let things play out as they will," Joh advised. "There's no sense interfering at this point. It wouldn't do any good. Whatever she decides, we accept it."

He went to get another cup of tea. "I've got to get back to what I was doing." As he walked to the kitchen, he said over his shoulder, "She's grown up enough to make up her own mind, and she's smart enough to do it right."

He stirred the cup. "God knows she's been stuck with doing it his way for years and she's probably sick of it, and ready to get her life back." He shook his head as he sipped the drink, thinking of all the crap that woman had experienced; *struggling to find enough money for a few groceries, creditors hounding them, on welfare, moving from place to place, the car constantly breaking down, or not enough gas, Roel begging people for loans, all because of his grandiose plans.*

Joh snorted at the thought. *He's got a 'business' because there's a letterhead and business card in his hand. Imagine, refusing to just get a job to pay some bills. He'd let her do the dirty work, so he could play 'businessman'.* The thought still made him angry. *There's nothing wrong with plain, honest work, that has an actual paycheck attached to it.*

Kaya followed him back outside. Joh turned and called back into the house as he dug the keys out of his pocket. "I'm going to run up to the shopping centre for a while. I have to get some fertilizer for the roses. Kaya's coming with me!" Nel answered something back, but he had no idea what. The acknowledgment was enough to let him know she'd heard him.

"Come on Kaya," Joh called the dog as he opened the back door. Kaya hopped up onto the back seat and sat in her three-sided box. In the driver's seat, he backed carefully down the steep driveway and made his way towards the small, local centre and Home Hardware. His mind wandered again as he drove.

≈≈≈≈≈≈≈

On a trip, they'd stopped somewhere for something. He didn't even remember what anymore, but they stopped, briefly and then drove on again. A few kilometres down the road, Nel turned casually back, to look at Kaya on the back seat. The dog had been unusually quiet. Nel gave a shriek.

"She's not in the car! Joh! Kaya's gone!!" He brought the car to a stop and turned around to look for himself. "She must have gotten out of the car, when we stopped!"

"She never does that!"

"I never noticed she even got out, did you?"

"No, not me. I thought she stayed in the car!" They looked at each other in horror, thinking of Kaya wandering around on the road somewhere back there. "We have to go back."

As Joh raced back he asked, "Do you still know the spot?" Nel thought a minute, getting the mental picture of where they'd been in her head. "I think so."

They raced back to where they thought they'd stopped but saw no sign of the small Spitz cross. The car parked off the road now, they wandered up and down calling, but no excited little dog came running. Over and over, they called, crying the name, Kaya! *KAYA!!*

"Are you sure this is the spot?"

"As sure as I can be, there's the field of flowers where you took a picture. She's got to be here somewhere."

"What if someone already picked her up? She could be anywhere by now." Twenty minutes had gone by, but it seemed like ages. They thought they'd have to head for the nearest population centre and leave a report; approach the SPCA too, or a local animal shelter. In their temporary confusion and befuddlement, they weren't certain what to do first, loath to even leave this spot, the last place they'd seen their pet.

Nel, desperate now, got out and called one more time, "KAYA! *KAY-YAH!*" as loud as she could. There in the distance, a small blonde lump of fur finally came flying out of the bush and scrambled into the seat, almost bowling Nel over in her hurry. She was trembling.

"Oh Kaya, where have you been!" The couple were besides themselves. Relieved and happy they drove on.

≈≈≈≈≈≈≈

Joh reached the hardware store, got out, and locked the car. Kaya sat obediently in her box. Joh smiled and recalled the aftermath of the disappearing dog.

≈≈≈≈≈≈

When they'd all returned home, a special cut away box had been placed on the back seat and Kaya had been told to sit in it when she travelled. Kaya was determined never to get lost again. Once in the box, she refused to come out, until she was told to. They'd discovered that quirk one day when they'd again asked each other, "Where's Kaya?" The couple had just come home a half hour before. Puzzled, they'd gone back outside, and found the dog, still sitting obediently in her box. No one had told her to get out. They'd tested it out on several occasions. The dog would only get out of the car if she was told to - by the driver. Kaya would never be wandering away unnoticed again.

≈≈≈≈≈≈

The fertilizer purchased, Joh hurried home, thinking about his daughter again, her situation; *I should get Nel to talk to her, see if she's alright ... she hasn't even called us yet ... what if she's afraid ... we were always so strict about things like divorce ... Christians don't divorce ... told her, anybody who divorces is wicked ... goes to Hell.* He was on the fence with that particular dogma now. He didn't know anymore, but God was understanding, wasn't He? He'd always thought so, church dogma or not. Otherwise, they were *all* doomed.

As he worked the fertilizer into the soil around the rose bushes, his mind played on all the things that had so recently occurred. He worried about his two grandsons, now that a mother was no longer in the home. Where were they? With her? With him? The more he thought about it, the more he needed to know. Someone else's personal problems weren't any of his business, even his own daughter's, but even so, he'd feel a lot better if he knew. Was he getting to be like his wife, needing to know everything?

When he looked down, he saw he'd been working the same spot under the rose bush, over and over, his mind far away on other things. Patting the soil down now, he couldn't put his mind to the gardening any longer. In the house, he looked at Nel and cleared his throat. "I think you should try and call Elly, find out what's going on. Do you know where she'd be right now?" Nel frowned and thought a minute. "Roel said something about those theatre people, didn't he? I can look up the number for that theatre in Cloverdale." She dug out the telephone book and started riffling through the pages.

"Here ... I'll call and see if anyone is there." Nel dialed and waited. Someone answered, and she asked if her daughter was there. She wasn't. "When you see her, can you please tell her to call her mother?" Nel asked hopefully.

She turned to Joh after hanging up. "That's all we can do. We'll have to wait and let her call us."

Elly called the next day, while Joh was at work. "Hi Mum."

Nel took a deep breath. "Roel was here. He says you left him. Why didn't you tell us?" She tried not to make it sound like an accusation. "Were you afraid to?"

She heard a sigh from the other end. "I don't know. I wasn't ready to talk to anyone yet."

"I need to talk to you. Not on the telephone. Please come home, so we can talk."

A short pause, and then, "Okay ...." another short pause, then emphatically, "I'll come over, but if you start preaching to me, I'm out the door, I'm gone. Understand?" Nel understood. "I won't preach, I promise."

Joh came home shortly after and Nel told him she'd called. "She's coming over this afternoon. Maybe it's better if you're not here, better if I just talk alone with her for now." Joh agreed. Mother/daughter conversations like this might be easier in private. He'd find something to do somewhere else.

Nel waited, impatiently pacing the floor, going over in her mind what she should say to her daughter. She, along with Joh, knew what the message had always been regarding marriage breakup and divorce. There had always been a rigid ruling on that taboo. It wasn't done. It was against God's will. She still remembered her own decision from long ago, threatening to leave and finally going back, the warnings of her sisters still echoing in her head. Things like breaking vows were simply not done. She'd raised her daughter the same way. 'til death do you part. 'til *death*! But now, it all looked so very different.

Elly walked in and stood at the bottom of the steps looking warily up at her mother. *I suppose she's wondering how I'm going to react.*

"Hi Mum."

"What took you so long?"

"Uh … what?" Elly looked at her mother with her mouth open. "What … took … uh, what do you mean? To get here?" She looked confused.

"No. What took you so long to leave him?"

Afterwards, with Elly gone, and her husband waiting to hear how it went, Nel told him. The boys were fine. Elly had had a long conversation with both of them, giving them options and stressing to them that they were not to take sides. She had found another job. She was staying with friends, saving up money to pay first and last month's rent for an apartment. Owen would stay where he was, he wanted to finish high school and graduate. Dwight would live with her, after she'd found a place, and since he'd quit school last year, find a job himself. They'd all be fine.

Joh breathed easier. The next time he'd see her, at least he wouldn't have to ask so many personal questions, and maybe make himself look like an interfering fool.

A few weeks later they'd had one more announcement from Roel that finally convinced Joh to never pay heed to him again. It was the strangest disclosure he'd heard yet.

"Elly is at the casino in Surrey with those awful theatre people and she's *gambling!* It's terrible what she's gotten into. Terrible!" He'd sounded shocked, outraged, and self-righteous. They looked at each other, should they be concerned? Too bizarre to ignore, they decided to at least find out if it was all gross exaggeration or should they really be concerned for her. To be on the safe side, they decided to visit the casino to see what all the fuss was about.

There, they saw no daughter sitting at one of the slots, nor playing a table. Asking one of the floor people, they learned that she was working in the cashier booth and asked if they could speak with her. A few minutes later Elly came out, bewildered at their presence. "What are you doing here?" she asked. Nel told her how they'd gotten a call from Roel, telling them she was gambling at a casino.

"Gambling? I'm not gambling, and so what if I am? Anyway, it's not true and beside the point as well! Does he still think I need his permission for everything? The idiot!"

Joh knew there was more to it than what he'd been told, and asked, "What's going on then, what are you doing here?"

Angry now, Elly explained, "The theatre is having a fundraiser. We're a Community Theatre and we need money to run it. The government has a program that community groups like us can benefit from. One of them is having a "Casino Night", like we're doing right now, and all proceeds go to us. I'm functioning as one of the cashiers. That's all."

Nel and Joh were at once relieved and angry. They'd once again been taken in by a melodramatic and distorted piece of information from an equally histrionic bonehead. He wasn't going to fall for that again.

Joh was disgusted. He was supposed to have been working 'under the table' for his old North Shore boss from years ago. He'd made a deal with Ari that he'd work for him, and it wouldn't show on the books. Any money he'd make, would be free and clear to apply to Roel's debt. Even with the reverse mortgage helping, he'd had to do it that way. Anything he earned would reflect in his monthly pension the following year, and he really couldn't afford a cut in his income. That debt still hung over his head, and it was a hard payment to make every month.

Now he was staring at a T4 slip. Ari had put his earnings on the books and disclosed the expense on his income tax declaration. He would now have to declare the income and take the hit next year. Angry, Joh called his boss, "I thought we had a deal?" "Sorry, Joh," Ari answered, "my accountant said I can't do that. I'm afraid I'm stuck with the rules."

Joh thought a moment. There was an amount still owing that he could deal with. He could manage for a little while longer on his own. "That's too bad, Ari. You've caused me a hardship too. I'm afraid I have to quit. Working on the books isn't helping me at all."

He was now, at seventy-three, an officially retired man, free to do with his time as he thought best. He still felt like he had at age forty, full of plans, some ambition, needing to do things, go places. Then he'd look in the mirror and think to himself, *who's this old guy staring at me?*

Now his time was also free to travel, helping his daughter move her things back down from Prince George when the time came. He'd been glad to see her move completely away from everything, including Roel's constant interfering, trying to persuade her to resume her marriage. Come fall she'd be moving back to the Lower Mainland somewhere. The winter had proved to be too much.

CHAPTER 29

Letting Go Again
1990 - 1992

Joh and Elly drove through the sleet on British Columbia's highway 96, a trailer full of her things behind them. They were coming back to the Mainland from Prince George, and she was grateful to be closer to all she knew. It had been an experience, but the minus forty below last winter had convinced her that she was truly averse to cold and snow. She wanted to get out before this next winter truly settled in.

They chatted amiably as she drove and Joh mused on the time they'd had visiting her this past summer, how much she'd changed from the doormat persona she seemed to portray during her marriage. She was so different now. Decisive, sure of herself, taking responsibility for her own life, instead of letting someone else determine it. He was happy for that.

"I've still got those letters Roel sent you," Joh began a different thread to the conversation. "Why don't you just burn them, Dad," Elly suggested. "They're just a whole lot of nasty accusations along with a lot of ranting and preaching. It's just a lot of verbal diarrhoea!" She made a face. "I stopped reading them long ago."

"One of them sounded like real threats, and your mother and I took them to the police station." Joh looked over at her, "I hope you don't mind. We did read them and they sounded almost like threats. We didn't trust it anymore."

"What did the cops say?" She was curious now.

"They put them on file and said, if it gets worse or if he really does try anything, call us. We'll deal with it."

Elly shook her head, then laughed a little, nervously. "Well, thanks for that, but I seriously doubt he'd really try anything stupid. He's really not the kind to get physically dangerous." She thought a minute further, "But he did scare me at least one time, so, I suppose … you never know." Her voice saddened at the thought of her ex-husband and the way he'd been at the end. "He was always such a … such a …." She searched for a word. "He was always so extreme, obsessive … with everything, and so controlling. It's why he wouldn't get a job. He couldn't work for a boss, couldn't take someone else telling him what to do."

Once the decision was made to leave Prince George, Elly had decided to move to Vancouver Island, something that years ago her mother had wanted for her. Ironic that she'd wanted it to get her daughter away from a controlling individual. Was she moving there now to get away from another controlling person, her mother, perhaps? It was feasible. Nel had tried often enough in the past to get her daughter to dance to her tune. Joh didn't know for sure but suspected as much. Else, why not just move back to the Vancouver area somewhere?

They reached home late, weary, and stopped for the night. The next day, all of them crossed the Strait of Georgia to Victoria and to the apartment she'd rented with her roommate, a good friend from her theatre days.

Content that his girl was still secure, they left. Nel seemed less sure. "You think she'll be all right? I hope so." He hoped so too. She'd already found a job, and with a job, she would be. He knew she had more plans but said nothing to Nel. That news would not go over well if he knew his wife as well as he did.

"She's given up her apartment, and she's going to *travel all alone, by herself, across Canada!*"

This pronouncement greeted him at the door as he came in, articulated by an agitated wife, waving her hands in the air, her voice rising a few decibels with the last few words. A year had passed, and Nel, after a phone call from Elly, announcing her new plan for the summer, met him at the door with the exact reaction he'd expected.

"Relax, relax, think of your heart." He tried to soothe her, but she wasn't having any of it. "She's going to be on the road in that little car of hers, camping, painting, just ... bumping about on lonely roads only God knows where, anywhere ..." He could see that the woman already had her daughter dead in a ditch somewhere, where they'd never find her body, murdered by a crazy axe murderer.

How could he get her to calm down? Nel really was going to give herself a heart attack if she didn't. He recalled when they'd put her on the bus to Prince George a few years ago. She'd bawled her eyes out as the bus pulled away. Why did she have so much trouble letting go?

"Look, you can't stop her from going, She's an adult. She's made up her mind. She wants to do this, so, here's what you do." Joh thought he had the answer that would let everything transpire as it should. "You tell her you want a phone call from her every Saturday at seven o'clock, our time. She can call collect; we'll pick up the charges."

Nel considered it, still averse to having her daughter, adult or not, on the road somewhere, far away, putting herself in danger, in her mind at least. "Let me think about that," she said.

The same evening, as they sat to dinner, Nel spoke up, "I've been thinking about what you said. It would be good that she calls but what if she doesn't, what if she can't, what if she forgets? I'll start worrying all over again, not knowing when or if she'll call." She sighed, wondering why her daughter would put her through something like this. Didn't she appreciate how much her mother worried about her?

"What about if we tell her, if she doesn't call, we'll know there's something wrong, and we'll alert the police!" Nel perked up at the thought. "That would make her remember to call if she knows we'll call the police. She wouldn't want that to happen." Nel calmed down a little at that.

All that summer, they waited by the phone, Nel anxious, chewing on her nails, waiting for seven o'clock. The phone would ring and one more week would go by with calmer nerves, until the following Saturday.

While Elly was gone her divorce papers were mailed to their address from the courthouse in Victoria. Nel, nosy as ever, opened the envelope and took a peek at the outcome. Joh could only shake his head at the insatiable urge of the woman to pry into their daughter's life like that. "I just want to see if the divorce went through." she justified. "I want to know now, not a month from now." Joh was pretty sure what that outcome was, without having to open her private mail.

It was the end of summer when his girl finally drove up the driveway again, a rack in the back of her car, filled with the beautiful paintings she'd done and hoped to sell. A happy and relieved Nel sat at the dinner table that night. Nel had handed her the envelope containing her divorce papers with the comment, "I opened them. I couldn't wait, I was too curious to see if you got the divorce or not. I hope you don't mind." Elly had learned long ago to pick her battles wisely, and said nothing.

Life returned to normal, Elly once again, safely in Victoria. With the winter approaching there was more news. His daughter had met someone, a man named Bill. Joh was curious what this new fellow was like. Elly planned to come over for their birthdays in November so they'd probably hear all about him then. Maybe they'd meet him. In the meantime, he hoped fervently that this time, she'd chosen someone they could all approve of and get along with, who wouldn't look down on them, or use them, the way his former son-in-law had. *An ordinary guy, that's all I want for a son-in-law, just an honest, ordinary guy.* And then he laughed at himself. An ordinary son-in-law indeed. She'd just met him. They were a long way from marriage, if at all. *I should stop thinking ahead like that, it might be embarrassing, if I say anything accidentally.* He smiled to himself, curious about the "new guy".

Jacob had long ago gone through his own divorce but Janet was still a part of her ex-husband's life, for which Joh was grateful. They loved Janet, a sweet and down-to-earth woman who'd won their hearts. She'd kept in touch with her in-laws, raising Peter on her own with support from Jacob. She'd also given Joh one more chance to be *Opa*, with the birth of another boy, Danny, whose father had abandoned the relationship when he found out that Janet was expecting a baby.

Since their birthdays were only thirteen days apart, Elly got away from work on the Saturday between, to celebrate both. She brought with her, an envelope of photographs belonging to Bill, to show them. Joh was instantly intrigued.

"Dad, he's a commercial fisherman," she told him enthusiastically, "You'll love him! Look at these huge fish! I bet you've never caught anything like that," she said, pointing to the fish in the photo. They showed a man on a boat, a commercial troller, his young daughter on board as deckhand and large fish in a chest of sorts on the deck. They were huge. Those fish! His eyes went wide, thinking of all the fishing advice he could get from a guy like that.

And a daughter. He'd never even thought of the guy having children of his own. Joh wondered if she would see him as grandfather. *She probably has her own and I wouldn't want to take the place of that ... but I don't have any granddaughters. It would be nice to have one, sort of.* Elly's voice cut in on his thoughts "... has three daughters, and two of them always go out with him to earn money for university," he heard her say. Three daughters? He potentially might have three granddaughters. Again, he laughed inwardly. *Slow down. Don't get ahead of yourself. It's too early in the game.*

He kept looking at the photos, wondering when they'd meet him, anxious now, to find out more of what this man was like. Elly described him as kind, soft hearted. He'd make up his own mind but the photos showed promise. Maybe it was all those big fish. They'd have a lot in common.

"I would have brought him over for Christmas, but he already has plane tickets to go see his family in Nova Scotia in December. He'll be gone for a month, so you won't see him until January." *January. I can wait 'til then.*

Joh was delighted with the discovery that Elly's new man, Bill, turned out to be a great guy. Early in the new year she'd finally brought him over and when she introduced him to her mother the first thing he did was to give her a big kiss on the cheek. Nel was instantly smitten. Joh wasn't far behind. He was an easy man to have a conversation with, easy-going in his manners. *Ordinary.* Joh appreciated ordinary. There were no mannerisms or affectations in the man. He seemed to be at ease at once, sitting on the couch, smiling, tea in a cup and saucer in his hand. He loved Nel's *boterkoek*.

They'd discussed fishing in general, the way Bill fished commercially, which was interesting to hear, and Joh wondered if some day he'd be able to go out on that boat.

They would be staying overnight, and tired, Elly had gone to bed, but the three of them sat up until late, talking. About her life with Roel, the way he'd treated her, what he'd done to them, Bill's marriage and divorce. To Joh, the conversation had the quality of honesty. There was no boasting of accomplishments from the man, no pretense or long stories of great and wonderful plans for the future. He was simply Bill, fisherman, living his life honestly, the best he knew how.

They'd retired for the night, and in the morning, all four of them had gone to church. Joh found they had one more thing in common. Neither he nor Bill could hold a tune in a bucket.

He didn't know how he felt about it. Sitting across from him was his oldest daughter and she had given him her latest piece of news. "Bill is moving up to Courtenay soon. The place he bought is ready to be occupied," she started. "And I've decided to move up there as well."

Joh raised his eyebrows, "Can you find an apartment yourself in Courtenay?" Elly smiled, and said quietly, "No Dad, I'm moving in with him." His face fell at that, *living in sin!*

She carried on, "Dad ..." now she looked at him earnestly, "I'm an adult, I make my own decisions, I don't need or want to live according to someone else's rules. I've done enough of that. This is my decision to make."

She was right. He knew she was right, but his own sense of propriety and morals stood in the way. *A man and woman should be married before living together.* Over and over he repeated to his inner voice, *it's a different world out there now, acceptable, no longer viewed as "living in sin", or immoral.*

But was that the way God viewed it? He didn't know, couldn't make that judgement. He did know this; they wouldn't be sleeping in the same room under his roof if they stayed overnight. He planned to play it safe.

A week later a young man, bedraggled and looking abashed, stood at the bottom of the steps leading to the living room. "Dwight! So nice to see you again, son!" Joh greeted his grandson happily but he wondered at the boy's appearance. "Hi Opa." Dwight came up the stairs and looked at his grandparents with a question in his eyes, "Opa … Oma? … can I stay with you awhile?"

"Sure, boy, sure you can! Is everything alright?"

"My dad kicked me out. I've been on the street for a couple of days." His voice petered out. He added quietly, "I'm pretty hungry."

They knew Dwight had been living with his dad again and that his mother had told him, "Get a job or go live with your dad. You need to act like a responsible adult. I can't have you just bumming around like some kid on a holiday."

Nel got up quickly from her chair. "I'll fix you a quick snack and get supper going. There's enough for all of us."

Dwight sat and related his story of the past few days. Joh knew, Dwight and his father had not seen eye to eye for a very long time. "My dad and me had another argument about me gettin' a job, and my hair and stuff … he's such a … he nags and preaches at me all the time, he just drives me crazy, and I don't have much patience for it."

Joh nodded sympathetically. He knew what that was like. Dwight continued, "So, I got kicked out, and I've been on the street … I haven't had anything to eat, hardly …" He looked at the sandwiches and *boterkoek* that his grandmother walked into the room with, and his mouth started to salivate. "Thanks, Oma!"

The sandwich was in his hand as soon as she set it down and by the time she returned with something to drink, it was gone, replaced by the *boterkoek*. Joh laughed, "Did you chew, or just inhale?" Dwight smiled and took a bite of the almond flavoured square.

At dinner, the boy ate like the starved, gnawing his chicken pieces to the bone and beyond. After a bed was made up in the guest room, they sat down and Dwight's options were discussed. At eighteen, he needed to find work. His grandfather made it perfectly clear that it was high time. What Joh determined he would not do, however, was lose his patience, and just dictate, as he had done so many times with his own son. This was his chance for redemption, and he grabbed at it with both hands.

Dwight finally managed to come under the tutelage of an older gentleman who ran a concrete restoration business. John was willing to teach Dwight everything he knew. Before long the boy had not only settled into a good job, but he'd found an apartment not too far up the road from his grandparents. His mother had encouraged him to take it, feeling that it would be good for him to find out what it was like to finally stand on his own two feet.

His grandparents were nearby for support should he need it. Joh knew the boy had begun to display a great deal of creativity in what he'd make or do for himself, which left his grandfather impressed. There was something there, and he looked forward to how that creative instinct would develop. Joh was happy he'd been there to help.

CHAPTER 30

Fifty Years
1993

There was a flurry of activity happening in several households, Joh knew, but not in his. Here it was calm and under control. They had nothing to do and nowhere to be until the big day. All the planning, the arranging had been done for them and he almost felt useless. But not quite. He sat back in his chair and thought about it.

He'd been married fifty years. He played the memories back in his mind; all the things they'd gone through, even contemplating divorce, briefly at times, not wanting to go down that road. It wouldn't be right. Not for him. It had been turbulent, and funny, and heartbreaking, and hard, very hard, to keep going, to find solutions. He didn't know if he'd ever found any big ones, but somehow it had always worked out, most of it anyway.

The announcement came from the pulpit. Joh and Nel were celebrating their fiftieth wedding anniversary. Most of the congregation already knew of it. They'd been to the big celebration the evening before at the Legion Hall that Ross had arranged through his father's membership. So many people had been there, a lot of them relatives.

Nel's brother, Jan, had passed away the year prior, and Marie two years before that. They were deeply missed. Ten of their nieces and nephews were there. Two of them had passed years ago. Family, friends, they were all there.

They'd sat at a long table, their children, spouses and grandchildren on either side of them. Gold balloons, and streamers all white and yellow, festooned everything. There were flowers, food, done by Elly, Bill, Nancyann and Ross, and a cake that, for once, he didn't have to make himself. Gifts had come in the form of money for a grand round-the-world adventure the two of them had wanted to do for a long time. It hadn't been counted yet, but from some of the cheques he'd already seen, there would be plenty to help cover the journey.

Now he stood in his pew, giving thanks to God for his long marriage, grateful to Him that they'd made it fifty years. "It was hard," he said stumbling through his words, searching for the right ones. He wasn't a public speaker, far from it, and he had a mild stutter that came out in times of stress. He stuttered now. "I-I-I'm so grateful to God for giving me so many years. It was so hard, but he saw me through it."

He suddenly thought, *I should stop talking now,* that he should sit down, but he didn't know how to end the speech gracefully, so he kept stumbling through the same words again. "I-I-I'm so grateful that God has been with me, because it was so hard." He sat down finally; glad he'd given thanks to God.

He deliberated in his head what he'd said and suddenly realized what it had sounded like, what words he'd used, ... *it was hard.* He knew he'd be in trouble for that, from the way Nel sat rigid beside him, and he suddenly knew, today of all days, he'd have to experience another blow-up.

After the service, they all trooped down to the basement for the usual coffee, cookies, and chatter. He managed to avoid Nel by walking around, taking more congratulations from church members, and general chitchat. Nel sat at a table talking with the ladies. Finally, it was time to go home, and he couldn't avoid any longer the confrontation he knew would come. He hoped that in the interim she'd have cooled down.

"How *dare* you?" she rounded on him in the car. *"It was hard?* You made me feel like a fool, like I was some kind of difficult woman you could barely live with! I was so embarrassed!"

"I didn't mean it that way. I have a hard time with words, and I said it wrong," he offered lamely. But really, that was the way it had been. She *was* difficult. She just didn't see herself that way. But there had been enough confirmations over the years from other family members that he knew it was true. Nel was silent the rest of the way home, another thing added to her list of things that could be thrown at his head from time to time, at a moment of her choosing.

Somehow, as before, Nel's anger seemed to dissipate enough to make the atmosphere in the house feel normal, whatever 'normal' was. He carried on. Dwight had found a small apartment up the road from them and now worked for a kindly man who was training him in the concrete restoration business.

They attended, very happily, the graduation of his grandson, Lorne, and then Owen's, so proud of the young men they'd all become.

Joh took up an old hobby he'd once dabbled in long ago when he'd taken a course in furniture making. He made small pieces, not furniture, but a pair of wooden lamp stands and tiny wooden cabinets to hold spices or other small items. He took great delight in presenting these homemade offerings to his children and grandchildren.

He continued to fish, using the little boat he so enjoyed taking out to Robert's Bank, his "happy place". This was 'normal' life for him, proud of his family, delighting in the hobby that took him to a peaceful place, far from all concerns.

That year, Joh had been following whatever newspaper articles he could find on the Federal Liberal leader Jean Chrétien. For some reason Joh liked the guy, something about his feistiness that he admired. He'd been getting a little tired of Mulroney, and what he perceived as the Conservatives' increasing authoritarian tendencies. In June Mulroney did him a favour and resigned, putting a woman in the Prime Minister's seat. He thought maybe, just maybe Chrétien would make a more balanced leader. He didn't like politicians getting too controlling in their interpretation of government. He'd seen first-hand what that did. In October he'd be voting Liberal for the first time ever.

CHAPTER 31

Incredible Journey
1994

The "Incredible Journey of 1994" as Nel had so aptly named it, materialized a year later. It was a trip they'd long been dreaming of. Excited and nervous, they were taken to the airport by Nel's nephew and wife, who wished them, "good travels, and come home in one piece to tell us about it!"

After a forty-five-minute delay taking off from Vancouver International Airport, and with another plane in the way on the runway, another fifteen minutes delay landing, they arrived in the Netherlands at Amsterdam's Schiphol Airport. In the baggage claim area, they watched as the carousel went around, the bags on it parading past, waiting to be reunited with their owners. At long last, they had three at their feet, but the one lone bag still going past time and again, wasn't theirs.

Concerned, they stepped up to the baggage claim window to let them know a bag was missing. "Excuse me. We are looking for one more bag that should have been on our flight." The attendant looked concerned, but efficient, and pulled out a sheet to itemize what the bag looked like and what was in it. They listed everything they could remember and then Joh said, "I'll show you what the bag looks like, the one still there looks about the same."

The attendant stepped out of the office following them back to the carousel. There, the one bag still made its lone way around and around. Joh picked it up and pointed to the sticker on it. "See? I did not put that sticker there, it's not my bag, but it looks a little the same. Someone else must have picked up mine by mistake!"

The agent turned the tag over, that was attached to the handle, and read the name on it, "It says, Joh Grin." All of them began laughing, relieved, and the newly arrived travelers slightly embarrassed. They must have been more tired than they thought; not even recognizing their own bag, and not thinking to check the tag for the name, before hurrying off to the wicket to make the report.

Thus began the most incredible journey of their lives. From a dream to reality, the two of them traveled, literally around the world; from Vancouver, British Columbia, Canada to the Netherlands, Israel, South Africa, on to Australia, and finally, home again. It took three months.

Nel started a diary. She wanted to re-live the experience anytime she wanted, and faithfully, almost every day, kept a journal of what they'd seen and experienced.

When the two came home in mid-November, relaxed, happy to be back, and skin browned, their family wanted to know everything. They gathered for Nel's seventy-seventh birthday, and began listening to all the gory details, peppering the pair with their questions. Joh and Nel hardly knew where to begin.

"The salmon came over beautifully," Joh told Bill. "They loved the fish!" Joh had transported a box of frozen salmon, a delicacy in the Netherlands using a few pointers from Bill; pack thickly in newspapers and old towels.

"I ended up with an ear infection in Holland," interjected Nel. I had to go to the hospital and get my ear cleaned out and then medication for it."

"I don't understand why didn't you have that done before we left? You might have prevented that happening in the middle of our trip," Joh pointed out.

Nel sighed, "I never thought of it. There were so many other things to think about."

Nancyann remarked, "At least it happened in Holland!" She knew her mother well enough to know that Nel could very possibly view any other doctor, not of her heritage or nationality, Dutch or Canadian, with some amount of suspicion.

"How did you like Israel?" Elly was curious about what they'd seen and done, considering the Middle East was the setting for all things biblical and such an important part of who her parents were.

"That was a really interesting experience," Joh began. "We landed in Tel Aviv and found a taxi. This lady we met on the plane says to us, 'I'll make sure you don't get cheated. They'll do that you know.' Then she went and found a driver and made sure he charged a fair price to Jerusalem. I think she knew her way around."

"And the taxi guy was crazy!" Nel's hands flapped in the air. "He was grinning, and saying, "Sure, sure, I take you!"

Joh picked up the story. "He raced away from the airport like a crazy guy!"

"I hung on for dear life!" Nel's eyes were wide, and Joh grinned, "You just kept looking at the speedometer!"

"I was nervous," she defended herself. "I don't like going 120 or 130 kilometers an hour!"

"What was Jerusalem like?"

"Well," Nel began, "the first time we walked around looking at the old section, I think it was the Jewish Orthodox quarter, we got lost a little."

"A little? How can you be lost a *little*."

"Oh, you know what I mean! We didn't stay lost for long, but it made me nervous, just a little bit, because we're in a strange place," Nel laughed self-consciously. "We were on the wrong bus."

"But we finally did find our way back to the hotel!"

Joh began to laugh in earnest. "Remember that one guide?" he asked Nel. "You mean the one who I thought sounded like an archaeologist?" She looked at Joh, daring him to say she'd made a mistake. "He really sounded like he knew what he was talking about! You thought so too!"

A questionable tour guide had crossed their path. "Where are you going? If you like, I can show you!" From the information he conveyed on the surrounding architecture of the city, he sounded educated.

He guided them through the Church of the Redeemer, climbing the stairway that wound its way up through the church, passing a huge set of bells, as they did. "I hope they don't start ringing those right now!" Nel remarked as they puffed their way past. The laughter echoed down the stairs. One hundred steps later they stood at the top, looking out over Jerusalem. Down again was easier, and Nel gave the bells another wary glance as they passed.

At the Church of the Nations, the guide suddenly began to act a little differently, and growing suspicious of the change in demeanour, Joh, tried to unburden himself of their escort.

Abruptly the man stopped and held his hand out. "You need to pay me 100 shekels." Joh's mouth dropped open. "Don't you think it would have been a good idea, if you'd told us that beforehand?!" The man was adamant, he wanted 100 shekels.

"No, you're not getting 100 shekels from me. You should have told us before you started showing us around." Joh was angry now. "I'll pay you fifty shekels, take it or leave it!" The man took it.

"We were sure more careful after that!" Joh told them. "There are a lot of those kind of guides walking around, trying to fool people into thinking they're trying to help, but in the end, they want money, and as much as you're willing to pay."

"But we took good tours too, to Masada, and to where they found the Dead Sea Scrolls, and the *Knesset*!"

"We walked around on our own a lot, to the Wailing Wall and to different markets."

Joh and Nel, in turn, began telling them of the visit to the Memorial of the Children, at the Holocaust Memorial. It contained five candles, re-

---

Knesset - Israeli parliament

flected in mirrors lining the walls and ceiling, giving the impression of being surrounded with a million twinkling stars. Within the enclosure, a recorded voice intoned the names of one and a half million children, all under the age of eighteen, who were murdered in the Nazi death camps. Nel had wept as she heard the names, and where they'd come from, all of them read out, continuously day and night. The reading would take six and a half months to finish, before starting over again.

"We read on the plaque that it was the wish of Abraham and Edita Spiegel, who had the memorial built in memory of their only son, who died in Auschwitz."

"And," Joh continued, "we actually saw Jericho … and Bethlehem, and Nazareth. And swimming in the Dead Sea is so strange. You really do float, you can't make yourself sink!" he proclaimed, still amazed by the experience.

"I had so much trouble keeping my feet under me," Nel recalled, "I lost my balance, and had trouble getting back to shore. Someone came to help me finally." Her profound fear of having her head submerged under water was evident in her eyes. The absence of her inner ear, and the stern instructions of the surgeon so many years ago, were still fresh in her memory. "Don't *ever* get your head under water, or get water in your ear," he'd told her. "The resulting infection could go to your brain and kill you!"

"You could have worn an ear plug and not have to worry so much," Elly advised. "I'm never taking any chances with that." Nel shuddered at the thought of it.

"I have to tell them about the camel!" Joh said chuckling, catching all of their attention. Nel began to laugh. "I need some more wine first!"

Giggling as she poured, she told them of being on a tour that day, and coming from a lunch break, Simon, their guide had put his arms around Nel and bantered, "Oh Nelly, you are my girlfriend!" They'd been teasing each other constantly, when out of nowhere they'd encountered a man with a camel.

The camel owner heard the comment, and exclaimed to Simon, "If she is your girlfriend, she must ride the camel."

"Yes! Yes, you must ride the camel!" Simon laughed.

Nel was less than enthusiastic about the idea, as she watched the camel kneel in front of her but let herself be persuaded. There was some difficulty getting on the beast, not able to swing her leg over, but finally she sat, straddling the hump, and clutching the pommel. The camel rose, Nel swaying side to side, shrieking, as the animal got all its legs under itself. The owner led the beast around the square, as Nel, in between squeals and giggles, hung on for dear life.

Joh was challenged to try it next, this time the camel owner insisted that Joh wear a *keffiyeh* before climbing on. "You must look like a real Arab if you ride my camel," reasoned the owner. Around the square they went again, Joh, grinning from ear to ear at the experience. Simon had wandered off dealing with another tour member.

Joh, finished with his ride, suddenly looked at a hand held out for money. "I want fifty shekels please."

Bargaining ensued. "Okay," said the camel owner, "Give me twenty shekels!" Joh offered him ten and turned to Nel who had the only cash they had left. "Give him ten shekels."

Nel dug into her change purse but could only come up with a fifty-shekel piece, which she held out. The man snatched it out of her hand.

"No, that is fifty shekels! Give it back, I need to make some change first!" Nel tried to take the coin back, but the man was loath to return the coin and stuffed it into his pocket.

Someone alerted Simon over the growing argument between his "girlfriend" and the camel owner, so he quickly returned from his other business. The man, seeing Simon approach, quickly dug into his pocket and handed Nel the coin.

Joh had been ready to pay fifteen shekels for the camel ride, but Simon told him ten shekels was fair and more than enough.

keffiyeh - Arab head gear

Their experiences continued, dancing through their memories and were related to the guests, delightedly listening to it all.

"But I got such a bad cold, I felt really awful near the end!" Nel informed them.

In South Africa, they'd connected with old friends and former neighbours Gaye and Don. They visited Pretoria and the Union Building where Nelson Mandela was inaugurated. The signs they saw flying by on the road all had names that were more than familiar to them; Middleburg, Alkmaar, Schagen; all names of Dutch towns, now also in South Africa

With Don and Gaye, they spent two days in Kruger National Park. During the day they'd toured the park, watching for animals they'd never seen in real life before. Nel and Joh recognized many of them from the many wildlife shows they'd seen on TV, but now they saw them in the flesh, excitedly pointing out the giraffes, kudu and wildebeest they spotted as they drove around.

"We even had a huge elephant walk right in front of the Land Rover!" Nel exclaimed, still seeing the beast in her mind's eye.

"Did you know there's a curfew in the park?" Joh asked them. "We stayed at a campsite that's all enclosed, inside the park, and if you're not back there by six p.m., you get a huge fine." They'd carried on with their sightseeing and the day had gotten late. "We had to drive like crazy to get back!" Nel laughed. They'd been enjoying the day's jaunt so much that time had been forgotten.

"We have to get back!" This from Don, who'd suddenly looked at his watch. "We'll end up with a 2000 rand fine if we're not back by six o'clock!" The clock was ticking.

Incredulously, Joh asked, "Why such a huge fine?"

"For safety's sake," Don told them. "Animals come out to hunt at night and if someone gets lost in the dark, they could die!" All park visitors had to be back in the camp as per the park's rules, no excuses. They were back at camp at 5:59 p.m.

"We visited another Holocaust Memorial in Johannesburg." Nel's face darkened at the memory. Gaye had suggested going to the travelling Anne Frank Exposition, considering that Nel and Joh had been fellow *Nederlanders*.

"I'm not sure I want to go," she'd told Joh. "I couldn't even watch that movie they made about it years ago."

"We really should go though. Gaye is expecting us to. You'll be fine, don't you think? It was a long time ago," Joh reasoned. She decided to try, but, remembering her tears at the Children's Memorial in Israel, she wasn't so sure of being okay.

Nel hadn't been okay, seeing the old World War Two photographs on the walls, crying through the half hour film, recounting the terror of the Frank family, the tattered diary, the images that showed a war ravaged city, and people being rounded up like cattle. It was too much and too devastating to have to relive it.

"I will never go visit a Holocaust memorial again," Nel told her visitors. She suddenly looked bereft, stricken. She shook her head, angry that she'd had to taste the nightmare one more time. "I just can't handle that kind of thing. It is too much, too upsetting for me." Joh agreed, they didn't want to re-live that time ever again. Remembering was enough.

The group took a break from the retelling of experiences, while Nel set a new pot of tea to steep. Joh brought out more wine, and a birthday cake. All the while, photos were handed around to look at and laugh over, especially the ones with their mother on the camel.

Sitting now, with a glass of wine in his hand, and Nel a little calmer, he began to tell his guests, laughing as he did so, about the incident at the hotel in Durban. In their room after dinner, they were in the middle of planning the next day's activities, when they both realized someone was rattling the doorknob. "Who can that be?" Nel asked, baffled at the odd interruption.

Joh went to look, only to open the door to a stranger, a very drunk stranger. "You have the wrong room!" Joh told him and tried to close the door. The very inebriated fellow put his foot in the door and mumbled something unintelligible.

Joh stomped hard on the drunk's foot, hoping the guy would pull back so he could close the door. He'd had to stomp on the foot twice to get the drunk to pull it away, but his shoe fell off and stuck in the door. Joh pulled it out and slammed the door.

Now he had a shoe in his hand, and a drunk on the other side of the door. In the meantime, shaking, Nel called security. They found a man lying in the hall outside their room, missing a shoe. The shoe was tossed out into the hall and the evening returned to its usual quiet state, even though Nel took a little while to calm down.

As Joh recalled the visit to a Zulu *kraal*, and told them about their dancers, the listeners began to laugh and tease, "Oh Dad, we saw the bare boobs in the photos! We're sure you enjoyed that show!" Joh grinned, but said nothing, throwing a sideways glance to his wife who assured them, "He didn't see anything he hasn't seen before."

"You know what?" Nel remarked suddenly, apropos of nothing, "Soweto is not all poor, like the media portrays it!"

"Did you visit Table Mountain in Cape Town?" Bill wanted to know. "I climbed it once. I've got a photo of me, looking like I'm hanging off the edge of the cliff!" Joh laughed, "We did, and the view was spectacular, but I'm not hanging off the end of anything!

The recollections and stories continued. They felt as if they'd packed a lifetime of wished-for trips, vacations, and getaways into a short three months of travel.

From South Africa they'd flown southeast to Australia, and, after a stopover in Perth, they landed in Sydney, where they switched planes to Canberra, and Joh's sister, Klasina, waiting for them. She was called Kathy now, having spent most of her adult life in Australia, but to Joh she was still his sister, Klasina, and always would be.

---

kraal - *a traditional African village of huts, typically enclosed by a fence*

By then, they didn't have any idea what time it was anymore. In Perth it had been eleven-thirty p.m. South Africa time. What time it was at that moment, was a mystery.

They'd gone on a tour to the Great Barrier Reef. "It's too bad the sun wasn't shining so brightly on the water at the Barrier Reef," Nel grumbled. "The photos didn't turn out at all." She'd taken them through the glass bottomed boat, and she'd wondered why the coral below them wasn't full of glorious colours like she'd seen in documentaries and magazines.

"What you see on those films is video or photography, taken underwater with very strong lights shining on the coral, to make the colours stand out," the guide explained. "It's not that sunny out today and the colours really depend on strong sunlight."

"We were trying to book the tour," Joh backtracked, thinking of the reef experience, "but my credit card wasn't working! I couldn't understand it at all!" He'd arranged for the bank to transfer money to his credit card and pay the monthly balance for him. The bank had neglected to follow through.

"I had to call the bank. With the time difference, they were closed, so I called the Canadian embassy and was given a fax number. They gave me a telephone number by mistake!"

"What a mess that was," Nel cut in.

"I finally got hold of somebody at the bank the next day, and got the whole thing straightened out!"

"We even got to feed some kangaroos on a sheep farm."

"And had a big barbecue at the place."

"Did they serve the sheep or the kangaroo?" someone asked.

Nel, with her mind still at the reef, continued, "Coming back from the reef, the wind came up so bad, the waves were crashing over the deck! I stayed outside to watch, and it got so rough, I couldn't walk to the stairs to go down, without getting soaked to the skin!"

"You would have gotten wet no matter what, if you stayed up top, Mum," Bill pointed out.

"Sure," she replied, "I got a little wet where I was, but not as bad as if I'd gone over the deck to get below!"

On a five-day tour they got out to explore a huge rock that had been hollowed out thousands of years ago. Joh had stood, looking at the primitive art, painted inside the hollow, and marveled at the old images made by human hands so many eons ago. Afterwards, Joh and Kathy made their way down the steep, rocky path, Nel following behind.

"Your mother needs some looking after on those steep trails," Joh chuckled as he looked over at his wife. She frowned back, "I do not!"

As Joh and his sister made their way back down the mountain, Nel, behind them, began windmilling her arms wildly in the air, shrieking, "Help! Help! *AH! Help!*" and then disappearing behind a rock.

"What is that woman doing now?" laughed Joh. Kathy wondered, "That was quite theatrical, but we better go check and see what she's gotten herself into." Back they'd gone, to find Nel on her knees on the gravel path. "What are you doing on your knees?" Joh and Kathy were laughing at the sight.

Remembering the incident, Nel retorted, "I lost my balance! I couldn't help it! I tore my favourite skirt, and my knees were scraped!"

But you sure looked funny, waving your arms in the air, and then disappearing like that!" Joh began laughing all over again at the memory. "Sure! Go ahead and laugh at me!" But Nel had to giggle as well.

The bus driver washed her scraped knees, someone produced a needle and thread from a travel sewing kit, and they continued on while Nel, still wearing the skirt, sewed the tear up.

"*OH! OH!* I have to tell you, Bill!" Nel abruptly sat up in her chair, grinning at him as she did. "Did you know there's a town in Australia that's named after you?" Bill looked at her. "I think I knew that. I discovered that when I was there in 1969."

Joh cut in, "You should have seen her! She was so excited, she stood up in the bus, yelling *STOP STOP!!* so she could take a picture of the sign!"

"Well, I was excited! And I had to get a photo, to prove to him that there was a town called Mossman."

"The whole bus was laughing." Joh told them, and Bill shook his head, laughing too. He knew Nel well enough now, to be able see the whole episode in his head.

There was far more they'd experienced; the historic Cairns-Kuranda Railway, a butterfly aviary, a marketplace in Kuranda, and bungee jumping, which all three passed on. At Henry Ross Lookout, the bus stopped and let them out to take in the view. From their vantage point, they could see Cairns, the airport, and Green Island, where they'd gone out to the reef.

After flying back to Kathy's home in Quean Beyan, they'd experienced some bad weather. It was already November, but spring hadn't arrived in Australia yet. Cold, rain, and a storm peppered the next few days. They'd spent the time with indoor excursions, including a gold mine tourist attraction in Gold Reef City, and the Questacon National Science and Technology Centre, which Nel wasn't particularly interested in, at least not the technology portion of it.

"But I liked the optical illusion room and the gift shop!" Nel assured them. "Is that why you got yourself lost, so you could spend time in the gift shop?" Joh wanted to know. "I wasn't lost! You were!" was her retort, and then turned to her listeners. "I couldn't find them anywhere, so I just started looking around by myself."

The rest of the bad weather days were spent shopping and buying gifts for home. "I hope you don't already have any of those little bottles we brought back for you, Ross." Nel pointed at the tiny liquor bottles that Ross regularly collected. "No, I don't have any of these, thanks Mum!" Ross answered, admiring them, as he spoke.

"I'm glad the weather got a bit better a few days later, so we could go to Sydney!"

They'd gone by train. "We finally saw some kangaroos in the wild, grey ones and red ones!" exclaimed Nel excitedly.

"And then I ended up with another cold *and* bronchitis," Nel groaned. She'd spent several days not well at all.

"Oh Mum, you got sick everywhere you went! You're just a walking disaster!" The remark came amid peals of laughter.

In Sydney, they booked a harbour tour, saw the Sydney Opera House, a replica of the Bounty, as well as the Sydney bridge. Nel started to laugh again. "Did you know that Australians call it "the Coathanger"?

"Yeah, that's going to be a tough one to put a coat on and hang in your closet!" laughed Jacob.

The remaining few days in Australia wound down, filled with souvenir shopping, buying gifts to take back, and a few excursions here and there. There was family to visit, a few more kangaroos to meet, and then it was over.

Now, they were home, reliving it all, happy with the memories and mementos they were left with.

CHAPTER 32

Beginnings and Endings
1995 - 1998

"I wonder if they're going to open their presents on Christmas Eve?" Nel turned to Joh with the question, as if he had the answer.

"I think they've been doing Canadian Christmas," Joh remarked. "I know Bill always talked about opening their presents Christmas morning, and how his girls always had him up so early, to get to the tree."

"I'm sure they won't be going to church then."

Joh looked at her sharply. "We're just going to celebrate the way they do it, without insisting on something they don't want."

Christmas was being celebrated at their daughter's home in Chemainus. Nel didn't have the energy to host the occasion, and they were gratified to be able to spend a restful day, free from the hectic activities of the season.

Owen had arrived, wanting to spend time with his mother and Bill. Nancyann and Ross had come as well, and now, Christmas mid-morning saw all of them ready for gift opening. Dwight would be here at some point during the day. Hot drinks and a table filled with the remnants of a late breakfast, and other extra goodies were there in the kitchen. Presents were handed out with exclamations and laughter. For Elly, there was a box the size of a very small loaf of bread, a gift from Bill.

Suspicious of the weight, she narrowed her eyes at Bill. "What's this? It's pretty heavy for something this size!" She tore the wrapping off, to reveal a fairly beat up box. She frowned at him, "Now, what have you got up your sleeve?" He was known for joke presents, and he now looked innocently at her and said, "Open it and find out." Inside was an old rusty faucet and a few odd pieces of plumbing. Joh suddenly had an idea of what the present might be.

Elly stared at Bill again, "What do you…" she started, then looked down at the plumbing again. A small, pink ring box nestled in between all the metal. Speechless, she pulled out the box and flipped the lid on it. It held an engagement ring.

Bill knelt beside her on one knee and asked, "Sweetheart, will you marry me?"

"YES!" Shouted Joh. "FINALLY!! They're making it legal!" The rest of the room erupted in shouts and congratulations. Everyone was jubilant, Owen excited, Nel laughing, and Elly still staring at the ring. "For heaven's sake, say yes!" Someone shouted at her. She did. Joh, in his heart, thanked his Lord for answering his prayer. He had another son-in-law.

"Nel! Nel!" Joh excitedly called out to his wife when he'd hung up the phone. "They want me to come down with them on the fishing boat from Prince Rupert, when they come home!"

She looked at him, questioningly. "Is the fishing season over?" Then, "Why don't you take the plane up to Prince Rupert and do it?"

"That's what they suggested, and yes, after the last delivery to the fish plant, the season is over and they're coming home!"

"Oh good! I always worry when they're out there, fishing, on that wild open water. I always pray that the Lord keeps them safe."

Joh laughed. "The way you fret over them, the Lord doesn't have to do anything. You're doing it all for Him!"

"Ha ha," was her only reply, as she turned to the pot on the stove. She gave it a stir, and then turned to her husband again, "You better call the travel agent then and book a ticket." She then added as an afterthought, "How did they do this season?"

Their daughter and fiancé had been gone all summer, he as captain of his fish boat and she as his deckhand, as she'd done for the last four years.

"Not well," Joh sighed. "Commercial fishing has changed so much, Bill said. Just being an ice boat, like his is, instead of one of those big freezer boats, and fishing for other types of fish like tuna, as well, is just not paying the bills anymore. I think he talked about giving it up and going into another business."

"What kind of other business?" Nel wanted to know. Joh shrugged, "I don't know. He might just get another job for now, until he finds something."

Nel began to worry over one more thing. They were getting married in September. What were they going to live on?

Joh made a phone call to his travel agent to book the short flight.

"*Dad!* Over here," a familiar voice called as he stepped off the shuttle bringing him from the tiny airport on Digby Island, in Prince Rupert's harbour. Through the crowd at the bus station, he saw two people he knew well, his daughter and Captain Bill, grinning at him from the sidelines. "Bill! Nice to see you again!" Then, a warm 'hi' and a hug for his daughter, along with a handshake for Bill.

"Come on, let's get out of here! We're ready to head out. Are you hungry?" Bill picked up the duffle bag and led them back to the harbour, where the *Blue Eagle* sat waiting for them. They chattered happily as they walked the short distance down to the docks.

On board, Bill stashed the duffle bag below in the fo'c's'le. Joh peered down, and saw his bunk already made up with a sleeping bag and pillow. *This is going to be interesting* he thought, as he pictured himself climbing up into the high bunk.

---

fo'c's'le - *the forward part of a ship or boat, traditionally used for crew's sleeping quarters. Original 15th century word: "forecastle". Today's spelling reflects sailors' pronunciation.*

On the way out of the harbour, Elly fixed something to eat, and some coffee. "This is to tide you over until the next meal," she told him. "It's a little early for supper, and I figured you might be hungry."

Later, he sat on deck, perching on the hatch to watch the remaining land slide by. Seagulls followed at a distance, then losing interest and disappearing when no fish offal from any gutting process came flying into the water for them to squawk over.

For the next few days, he did much of the same thing, sitting and enjoying the scenery as they motored along the coast and through the channels. Sometimes there would be a beer at hand as he watched the wilds parade past him. They played cards in the evenings after anchoring up for the night and eating supper. Bill talked about putting a line down so Joh could catch a fish.

"Oh yeah! I'd love to catch a really big one like I saw in those photos you had!" Joh suddenly realized he'd never have the chance again, if he didn't do it now.

Bill started to laugh. "They may not be as big as those!" he clarified, "Those pictures were taken a long time ago, and we were way up north in open water. We're going to fish inside waters now!" Then Bill assured him, "But don't worry, even if Coho don't get as big as Chinook salmon, the ones we get will be plenty big!"

As they neared Seaforth Channel, Bill announced that this might be a good spot to try for some fish. The two of them stood in the cockpit at the stern of the boat, and Bill threw a line out with a few leaders and lures snapped on, that he'd prepared early that morning. He turned to Joh, "Let's see how good a fisherman you are, Dad."

Bill grinned at him. Pointing up, he instructed the older man to watch the spring at the top of the line, where it attached to the trolling pole. "When you see that spring start to bounce, you know you've got something on the line." Joh kept an eagle eye out on the top of the pole.

Pretty soon a crick started in his neck and he had to look away and lower his chin a bit. "Keep watching!" Bill chided, "You never know when a fish is going to hit!"

They chatted as they paid attention to the line. "Boy," observed Joh, "that's all you do, stand here and watch lines? Pretty easy job I'd say." Elly started to laugh, "Easy job? You've never cleaned 60 to 700 fish in a day, have you?" "And iced!" Added Bill.

"And cleaned an entire gut and scale encrusted stern every eight days!"

"All on a couple of hours of sleep!"

"Okay, Okay, I get the picture!" Joh smirked, "But I do know about the couple hours sleep!"

Bill abruptly pointed his finger upwards. "We got a fish! Stand aside, I'm bringing it in! I'll show you how to work these gurdies!" He threw the gurdy in gear and started spooling the line back into the boat. "Watch how I do this. You can give it a try when the next one climbs on!"

Joh stood off to the side watching carefully, as Bill pulled the lever back to stop the spooling line, and then hooked a nice silver fish into the checkers with his gaff. "Nice one!"

There was no more to catch that day. The next day in Fitzhugh Sound, they tried again, and caught one more good-sized fish. Joh made an attempt to follow Bill's instruction but fumbled on the gurdies. For someone not really used to operating a piece of hydraulic equipment like that, one try didn't give him enough of a feel for the method. Bill, afraid of losing the fish, took over, and brought the line in. Under his supervision, Joh gaffed it in, and he proudly held the fish up for his daughter to take the picture. "These are going to taste so good!" he crowed, "Real good!"

Joh was sorry to see the five-day trip come to an end, but he was grateful he'd had the opportunity to fish from a real fish boat.

That September, in the large back yard of the home Bill and Elly shared, he watched as his daughter married the man who'd captured her heart and her adoration. Bill had secured theirs too. Joh and Nel's pastor had come from Vancouver to perform the ceremony, and all three now stood under the apple tree as the couple repeated their vows.

Lined up along the side of the patio, were three barbecues, emitting the mouth-watering aroma of cooking salmon, six or seven sides of fish under each lid, ready to attack with fork and knife when the time was right. Joh had brought enough cooked and shelled crab for fifty people. Balloons and streamers hung from the trees and buildings. There were even some antique cars parked around the property, something that Bill was an enthusiast of. He owned two of them, a red and white 1955 Plymouth Belvedere, and a black 1948 Hudson Commodore.

Joh thought back to the one thing that was missing …

≈≈≈≈≈≈≈

Elly wanted her father to make their wedding cake, and approached her father with the idea she had in mind, a simple slab cake covered in colourful sugar flowers over a basket weave design. She'd watched her father make them many times, and had no doubts he'd do a beautiful job.

Joh tossed the idea around, while Nel, baked two large slab cakes, to be layered together with a refreshing compote in the middle. When the cake had cooled sufficiently, he began the work, but he found his hands trembling as he worked at the design with the icing filled piping bag. In frustration, he wiped the mess off and started again.

Nel watched with a worried look on her face. She'd never seen him stumble like this at decorating a cake. He tried again, and again had to wipe it clean and begin afresh. Finally, after two more tries, he sadly admitted to Nel, he just couldn't do it anymore.

The old baker realized he'd come face to face with the unalterable loss of his abilities. He still felt the creative urge that had always driven him forward, but somehow, the impulses that ran from his mind to his hands had detoured to a place he could not name.

Nel suggested that maybe her niece's husband, a talented, and much younger baker, the one who'd done their Anniversary cake two years ago, could decorate the cake. Ever the pragmatist, Joh agreed. The baker from Krabbendam would never conjure up delectable pastries again. He closed his eyes, regret in every pore. A cake of his would not grace his daughter's wedding table this time. Joh reassured himself with the thoughts that he'd find other interests, different pastimes to keep himself busy. His garden needed tending. There were always things to do. Maybe he could still do a little fishing in his small boat.

≈≈≈≈≈≈

As his thoughts turned again to the ceremony in front of him, he marveled at the difference between the wedding of so many years ago, when he watched her get married for the first time, and now, this one. It felt right this time. He hoped that, at this late stage, Bill at fifty-five and his daughter at forty- eight, would still have a long life together, and that he'd be alive to see it.

"Nel, I lost my wedding ring."

The disappointment in Joh's voice was noticeable. Nel looked up from her crocheting, frowning at him. "Did you lose it in the garden? You've been doing a lot of digging around the cacti lately."

Joh thought a moment. "It's possible, but I'm not sure. I can't remember when I last noticed it on my finger."

His fingers had been getting thinner lately, he'd lost so much weight. Nel was annoyed. "I just bought you that to replace your old one."

"Maybe I can put the old one back on?" He suggested, wondering what she'd done with it. Nel frowned again. "Not a chance. It's so thin now, if you do anything heavy or rough while you're wearing it, it will break for sure. You'll have to do without, until you find it."

It crossed his mind to go out into the garden and dig around a bit, but the task seemed too overwhelming at the moment. How would he ever find such a small thing in all that dirt? It could have fallen off in the grass. Maybe he'd spend a few hours raking. He made himself a cup of coffee to think it through. Somehow, when he looked at his left hand now, the ring-less appendage stared back accusingly. *Losing your wedding ring. You idiot. You don't deserve to be married.* He didn't lose it on purpose. It had just gotten really loose all of a sudden and dropped off. His hand felt naked.

Nel's voice brought him out of his thoughts. "Elly's store certainly is shaping up, isn't it."

"Yes ... uh, yes," he switched to follow his wife's line of thought with difficulty. He had enjoyed the few days over at Bill and Elly's in Chemainus last week, and the puttering around that he'd done in the store, while she worked and attended to the customers. She'd opened the business in Chemainus shortly after coming back from their honeymoon, and he wondered how it would do, remember his own disastrous attempt at running one, so long ago. He'd have to ask her when they came for their birthdays next week. She'd been a year into it now and there should be some indication.

The birthdays, his first, then Nel's came faster than ever. Time seemed to fly by these days. For a long time, family had gotten into the custom of visiting on the Sunday between the dates, especially the out-of-towners. After retiring from fishing Bill had bought a boat transportation business and was doing well. Joh wondered if he'd have enough time to visit.

His unasked question was answered when Elly and husband arrived on the Sunday. She only had one day a week off, so they'd have to go back on the ferry the same night. Short but sweet. His daughter came up the steps, smiling, Bill behind her carrying flowers. "Happy Birthday, Dad, Happy birthday Mum." Then, "Hey Dad, I've got something for you."

"Oh, you didn't need to get me a birthday present. What does an old man like me need anymore?"

"Well, Dad, you still might find some use for this." Elly held her hand out, something glinting in her palm, a gold wedding ring. "Are you missing anything?"

Joh gave a cry of joy, "My ring! I thought I'd lost it in the garden. Where did you find it?" Elly laughed, "you'll never guess. It was sitting in the drain of the sink at the back of the store. I'm sure glad I finally noticed it. It was there for the last few weeks, and I could have missed it entirely."

It must have slipped off when he was washing up the coffee cups and he shook his head at the luck that she'd found it. As he slid it back on his finger, he realized how truly loose it was now. He took it off and laid it carefully in a small ornamental box sitting on the bookcase. He'd have to put some tape around it to make it fit or have it re-sized. But he had some visitors to look after now.

"Joh STOP! STOP!!" screamed Nel. She was staring in fright, as cars came towards them.

They were headed for the large shopping mall in Coquitlam and he'd turned left onto Lougheed, on the wrong side of the divider. Joh tramped on the brakes and turned to her, looking perplexed, as if he didn't quite know where he was. He stared at her in confusion. She stared back, in shock. "That's it," she announced. "From now on I'm driving!"

Luckily, the traffic wasn't too heavy yet, but cars swerving around, honked at them. Nel got out of the car and ran around to the driver's side, while Joh slowly struggled to get into the passenger seat. She shouted at angry faces as they drove by. "I'm going I'm going! Hold your horses!"

Nel slid into the driver's seat, threw the car into reverse and backed up around the barrier. She waited until there was room and then continued on to their destination. It was the last in a string of glaring mistakes Joh had made while driving, things he would never have dreamed of doing in an earlier time. Nel had seen enough.

At home later, she quietly took the keys off his side table and put them away. Joh did not make a fuss. The latest mistake, the ensuing confusion he'd felt, when he'd found himself in a bad spot and then forgot what to do, scared him. He knew his driving days were over. The past few months had been bad. He felt 'off', had lost his appetite, and he was losing weight – rapidly. Too rapidly. It was time to make another doctor's appointment. He wondered what waited for him around that corner.

The news wasn't good. The prostate cancer was spreading. There were some other treatments they could try, medications. Joh sighed, was this the beginning of more crap he'd have to endure? His eczema had subsided, and nothing else had surfaced that presented as an allergy. He got the usual heavy colds and sinus problems in the spring, but nothing new, or unexpected. *One day at a time, Joh, one day at a time.*

The pair sat looking at the doctor across the desk. Things had not been going well for Joh, the last number of years. His health was steadily declining, and more and more medications had been prescribed to keep symptoms from taking too much quality out of his life. It was apparent the prostate cancer was slowly making its way further.

Now there were more concerns. Nel was getting a little exasperated at the doctor's assurance that "it was just old age". Joh was seventy-nine. But the pain in his chest had continued, and he was having trouble breathing. She'd driven him back to the doctor and now sat listening at lame excuses. She grew angry, as the doctor droned on about 'maintenance' and 'nothing else we can do'.

"I don't believe that!" She raised her voice, "There has got to be a reason why his chest has so much pain!" She suddenly stood, and, slamming her fist down repeatedly on the doctor's desk, shouted at him, in sync with her fist, *"YOU .. DO .. SOMETHING!!"*

Shocked, the doctor reared back, and Joh, too exhausted from the pain, sat back and closed his eyes. *She's a fighter, I'll give her that, she's a fighter.*

"Very well, Mrs. Grin." Shocked, the doctor was suddenly a little leery of this feisty woman sitting in his office, "I'll order some X-rays and see if we can find out what's going on." He said it more to appease her but went ahead and ordered them.

They showed the cancer had spread to his lungs. The doctor looked embarrassed, as he made the results known. "Mr. Grin, Mrs. Grin, I owe you a huge apology."

Joh was determined to fight. *Die with the cancer, not of the cancer*, his doctor's word came back to him. He'd make it, with God's help, he'd make it. With more medication and radiation, the pain subsided, but he continued to lose weight, becoming more withdrawn and slowly felt himself slipping away from all of them. He sported black eyes or a bruised face more than once, getting up in the middle of the night, falling down on his face, and the next morning not even remembering.

Jacob came from McBride that Christmas, and stayed to help care for his father. There were many ways they interacted, that spoke about the love and forgiveness that arose in each of their hearts for all the sins of the past. Jacob gently guided his father's hand with fork or spoon, helped him to bed when he was too weak to walk, and did chores for his mother, who had begun to call him by his real name, Jacob, not that long ago.

The doctors had already confirmed that Joh's cancer was now terminal. Still he persisted. He was going to fight this tooth and nail, never considering his own death. One evening Nel sat by his side, listening to his willingness to keep going. Knowing he was too weak to even shuffle to his chair now to watch the news with her, she recognized that he didn't comprehend what was happening. She spoke as lovingly and carefully as possible, "Joh, don't you realize you're not going to come out of this?"

His eyes widened, knowing the truth of it. He called all his grandsons, one by one, to his side. As each of them in their turn came, he gave them some last words of advice; that he loved them, that he was so proud of them. His children came and sat by his side, holding his hand while he lay weak and spent, all of them with tears and forgiveness, letting him go.

He now invested his time in dying. He'd done all he could while living and done the best he knew how. He'd failed so many times, and so many people. He knew his efforts had been flawed, and sometimes not enough, and he hoped his God was gracious and forgiving.

Jacob sat at the table with the man, waiting for him to sign the papers to finalize the sale of his father's car. His mother had her own and she didn't need the second car. *This guy,* thought Jacob, *is one of the fussiest dingdongs I've ever seen! Dad would hate this guy!* The man had so many questions, even after the deal had been made, he'd called Jacob up, over and over, to ask about the oil, to query on the spark plugs, carping over the small dent in the back fender, over and over, more questions. He could have driven away with the car days ago, but here he sat, fussing over more trivialities.

"I'll let you read over the final paperwork, while I check on Dad." Jacob said now and got up from the table to see how his father was doing. The night nurse had left a while ago, and told him, it might be any time, that he should keep a close eye on his dad. Nel came and sat at the table making small talk, telling the buyer that her husband was very ill. The man nodded sympathetically, but kept his eyes on the paperwork, going over every small detail.

As he opened his mouth to ask yet another question, Jacob came hurrying back into the room. "Mum, I think he's going."

The man's eyes grew large, and he snatched the pen lying at his elbow, signing his name with a fast scribble. "There, done! Did I get all the keys?" And just like that he was gone.

Jacob started to laugh, despite the sadness waiting in the bedroom. Nel had already hurried ahead and gone in to her husband. As Jacob walked back to his father's side, he smiled and thought, *What a frustrating piece of work! Atta boy, Dad! Serves him right! You stuck it to the guy by dying on him while he's trying to buy your car."*

On April 28, 1998, the baker from Krabbendam died in his own bed, in the house he and his wife had proudly bought in 1964. He swore he'd die in it, and he did. He was eighty years old, at peace with meeting the God he'd tried so hard to serve, in spite of failing so many times. His son, Jacob and his wife of fifty-four years were by his side.

In his stead, his children carried onward the creative talents he'd been born with, in ways he never could have imagined himself doing. It was enough for him that his artistic and creative abilities were forwarded to his children and grandchildren, and who knows, perhaps even to the generation after, one that he would never meet. It was enough for him to know that, in a small way, he'd had a hand in it.

Janet's Danny, one more grandchild to be proud of

Working in his flower bed, covering the cacti for the winter

In the back seat of Bill's 1955 Plymouth Belvedere

50th Wedding Anniversary

Going in for the kiss

Youngsters from Nel and Joh's street, all grown up

The Incredible Journey - 1994

Swimming in the Dead Sea

Tourists in Israel

310

South Africa - decommissioned gold mine, tourist attraction, Gold Reef City.

Visiting a Zulu kraal

Australia - (above) on the tour bus, going to Woobadda River

(Right) at a termite mound

Christmas 1994

L to R - Nancyann, Ross, Nel, Joh

(Below) Newly engaged & delighted dad

1995 - Boat trip from Prince Rupert on board *Blue Eagle*

1997 - Sporting two black eyes from a fall he could not remember

Dec. 1997 - the last Christmas -

(Top) Joh and Owen

(Right) looking at a gift - a cartoon story, put together for Joh, from Elly, at the very beginnings of a career as cartoonist, illustrator, and author

Family Portraits

Pre-emigration - 1950

Barrie - 1959

Nel & Joh's Golden Wedding Anniversary - 1993

L to R - Owen, Elly, Bill, Dwight, Nancyann, Ross, Peter, Janet, Jacob, Lorne
Seated, Nel & Joh

GLOSSARY

anno - year

appelstroop - apple butter

banketbakker - pastry chef

bijzonder - unusual

boterkoek - butter cake

dijk - dike

Dominee - minister, pastor

draaiorgel - barrel organ

dupje - ten cents. (slang term for dime)

fatsoenlijk - proper, decent

gebak - pastry

gemeentehuis - a house owned by a township

gezellig - cozy ambiance

godverdomme - goddamn

goede morgen - good morning

griesmeel - seminola

hagelslag - chocolate sprinkles. Used as a sweet topping for children's sandwiches

havermout - oatmeal

hondelul - dog's penis

huisvrouw - house wife

kind - child

klaaverjassen - popular Dutch card game

kleuterschool - kindergarten

knecht - helper or aide

kreng - witch (used as a slur)

lieve Heer - dear Lord

meisje - little girl

Mevrouw - Mrs.

Mijnheer - Mister, sir

moeder - mother

moffen - plural of mof, a pejorative term for a German

GLOSSARY ....*continued*

muisjes - a sweet, crunchy, almond flavoured children's sandwich topping

nee - no

oma - grandmother

ondergoed - underwear

ontbijtkoek - a sweet breakfast bread/cake cross

oom - uncle

opa - grandfather

pakjes avond - literally, gifts evening

reetkever - beetle's anus (slang)

roepnaam - nick name (literally 'call name')

roepnaamen - plural of roepnaam - nicknames

roggebrood - heavy dark rye bread

schatje - literally, small treasure - a term of endearment

schijt - shit (slang)

slootwater - ditch water

stomme kind - stupid child

tante - aunt

trut - bitch (derogatory term)

tuinbouwer - horticultural farmer

vader - father

yongen - boy

Westfriesendijk - A dike, with a road built on top, situated close to Alkmaar and runs along the village of Krabbendam.

zuikerkoekjes - sugar cookies

RESOURCES:

Holland America Liners 1950-2015 - William H. Miller

Survival and Resistance. The Netherlands under Nazi Occupation - Linda M. Woolfe, Ph.D.
www.faculty.webster.edu/woolfem/netherlands.html

Dutch /review - Amsterdam liberated: The infamous shooting at Dam Square
www.dutchreview.com

www.historyextra.com
WW2 timeline - 20 important dates and milestones you need to know.

Food rationing & stamps:
The Milbank Memorial Fund Quarterly
Vol. 24, No. 4 (Oct., 1946), pp. 319-358

OPENARCHIVES - Search the genealogical data of Dutch and Belgian archives
https://www.openarch.nl/nha:6ABC1CEF-A29B-7FEA-E053-CA00A8C0CBDA

https://www.rijkswaterstaat.nl/en/water/water-safety/the-flood-of-1953

Population growth PDF -
https://www.buildingbarrie.ca/22277/widgets/90160/documents/56076

https://www.thepeoplehistory.com

https://littlethings.com/family-and-parenting/flour-sack-dresses

https://www.canadahistoryproject.ca/1949/1949-05-events-1950s.html

Hurricane Hazel -
Wikipedia - https://en.wikipedia.org/wiki/Hurricane_Hazel

https://www.thecanadianencyclopedia.ca/en/article/hurricane-hazel

https://www.ec.gc.ca/ouragans-hurricanes/default.asp?lang=en&n=255F2299-1#bar (Barrie)

https://www.hurricanehazel.ca/

The Big Bend Hwy-BC; https://en.wikipedia.org/wiki/Big_Bend_Highway

https://www.bcmag.ca/remembering-typhoon-freda/

https://www.readthepeak.com/blog/housing-market-crash-canada

ABOUT THE AUTHOR

Ms. Mossman was born in the Netherlands, and, at the age of three emigrated to Canada with her parents and brother in 1950.

She has worked in the past as an editorial cartoonist for several local papers in the Cowichan Valley, and has garnered two second place awards in the Canadian Community Newspaper Awards, and serving as judge for the 2022 CCNA awards - editorial cartoon - local humour.

Her work currently includes ..*Wait, WHAT?*, humorous autobiographical stories, a children's and young teens graphic novel series called *Grampa Was an Alien,* consisting so far of ten books, a poem and children's large print book, *Blue Eagle Bill,* and another graphic novel *Nmp-Chks & Numskuls*, first created as a gift for her father, at his last Christmas.

Other work includes illustrating for authors, Teresa Schapansky (*Along the Way series* and *One Little Coin),* and David Mossman (*Oh! The Wild Rascals)*

She lives in the Cowichan Valley, with her husband, Bill, writing and illustrating for herself and other authors. She paints, when there is time.

www.grampawasanalien.com

kribldor@gmail.com

Manufactured by Amazon.ca
Bolton, ON